The United Nations
and the maintenance
of international peace
and security

The Melland Schill Monographs
in International Law

General editor Gillian M. White

The United Nations and the maintenance of international peace and security

N.D. WHITE

Lecturer in Law,
University of Nottingham

MANCHESTER
UNIVERSITY PRESS
Manchester and New York

Distributed exclusively in the USA and Canada
by St. Martin's Press

Copyright © Melland Schill Fund 1990

Published by Manchester University Press
Oxford Road, Manchester M13 9PL, UK
and Room 400, 175 Fifth Avenue,
New York, NY 10010, USA

Distributed exclusively in the USA and Canada
by St. Martin's Press, Inc.,
175 Fifth Avenue, New York, NY 10010, USA

British Library cataloguing in publication data
White, N.D.
  The United Nations and the maintenance of international
peace and security. – (Melland Schill monographs in
international law).
  1. Peace keeping. Role of United Nations
  I. Title II. Series
  341.5′8

Library of Congress cataloging in publication data
White, N.D., 1961–
    The United Nations and the maintenance of international peace and
security / N.D. White.
      p. cm. – (The Melland Schill monographs in international
law)
    ISBN 0-7190-3227-X
  1. United Nations – Armed Forces. 2. United Nations. 3. Security.
International. I. Title. II. Series.
JX1981.P7W47 1990
341.5′8 – dc20   89-13354

ISBN 0 7190 3227 X *hardback*

Printed in Great Britain
by Biddles Ltd., Guildford and King's Lynn

CONTENTS

FOREWORD

This is the sixth volume in the present series of *Melland Schill Monographs in International Law*. The Melland Schill fund was established by the will of the late Miss Olive B. Schill in memory of her brother, Melland, who was killed in the war of 1914–18. Her bequest was motivated by a desire to contribute to scholarship and learning in international relations and, specifically, on the role of international law in the hope, we may surmise, of increasing that role and of decreasing the likelihood of further armed conflict.

Dr White's research which has resulted in this book was directed to an analysis and evaluation of the competence and functions of the United Nations in the maintenance of international peace and security. To those who say that this ground has been well tilled already in the literature of international law, he points to a gap in the existing reviews of the United Nations' role. Some studies take the form of an Article by Article analysis of the United Nations' competence and practice in this centrally important area of its work. Others have adopted a case study or chronological approach. Dr White undertook the task of combining both approaches to attempt a conceptually based juridical analysis of the United Nations' powers and a comprehensive review of its practice and the effectiveness of the exercise of these powers in the maintenance of international peace.

He takes first the Security Council, discussing its competence in terms of relevant Charter provisions, and its powers, practice and effectiveness. The vital significance of Article 40 is demonstrated, and he has some positive suggestions for improvement of the Council's practice and procedures, including a possible continuous and independent investigation process, using United Nations regional centres. The Security Council would then be obliged, in effect, to consider all conflicts and would be served with independently obtained factual reports. Any such proposals depend crucially on the degree of agreement and co-operation between the superpowers, and here we are in the presence of a rapidly shifting geopolitical context, in which the seemingly rigid East–West status quo is undergoing seismic strains. The potentialities of recent dramatic events in Europe are highlighted when we read phrases which for decades would have passed as commonplace in discussions of United States – Soviet relations such as 'the Soviet Union views "capitalism" as an attack on its block solidarity' (p. 11). Whatever future developments may bring, Dr White's study of the Security Council takes the story to the end of the 1980s and sets it in the historical context of the original Charter provisions and the evolving practice of the Council over the past four decades.

Part 2 treats the General Assembly's role and inevitably pays much attention to the division of competence between General Assembly and Security Council. The inherent weakness of recommendatory powers is inescapable. Dr White suggests that the members might do well to eschew paper 'demands' that States do or refrain from doing various things in relation to international conflicts or situations threatening the peace. The General Assembly should adopt a more balanced approach and concentrate on promoting peaceful settlement of disputes. But the Assembly has contributed valuably by its condemnations of States in breach of international law. This practice supplies clear evidence that the majority of nations support, at least publicly, the non-use of force and the promotion of peaceful settlement.

In Part 3 Dr White offers a comprehensive and up-to-date analysis and evaluation of United Nations peacekeeping in its two principal forms: observation teams and peacekeeping forces. The constitutional analysis precedes his review of the effectiveness of peacekeeping, each force and episode receiving separate treatment. Some of what he says in the geopolitical examination (Chapter 7) and in his *Concluding remarks* is controversial. I hope that it will provoke debate in diplomatic as well as academic circles. It is through increased understanding of past practice, achievements and failures that possible future improvements in the ways in which States use the Charter provisions and the powers of the United Nations may come about. Dr White's research falls squarely within the remit of the Schill Series and, surely, within the vision of those who, like Olive Schill, yearned for a more peadeful world.

Gillian M White
Professor of International Law
Director of the Melland Schill Fund
University of Manchester
December 1989

PREFACE

The aim of this work is to fill a lacuna in the area of international legal literature devoted to analysing the United Nations in its role of maintaining international peace and security.

Throughout its life the Organisation has been studied in two main forms. First, there is the approach, exemplified in *The Charter of the United Nations* (1969) by Goodrich, Hambro and Simons and more recently in *La Charte des Nations Unies* (1985) by Cot and Pellet, that utilises the Charter's Articles as its basic framework. Secondly, there is the method which takes a chronological or case study approach. Higgins' four volumes on *United Nations Peacekeeping* are a good example of this.

To adopt an Article by Article analysis fails to deal adequately with a great deal of United Nations' practice. For example, peacekeeping is only mentioned in passing in both the major commentaries which use this method. This approach also tends to label items of United Nations' practice as being derived from particular Articles, when such practices like peace-keeping or voluntary measures can either be said to be based on general powers rather than particular provisions, or can be placed equally well within several different Charter provisions. The point is that analysis by Article creates a conceptual straitjacket into which the commentators try to force all United Nations' practice when quite clearly a significant amount of it will not fit.

Generally, such commentaries are concerned with the whole of the United Nations' Charter and so go far beyond the Organisation's role of maintaining international peace and security. For such an undertaking it may be that a restrictive conceptual framework is needed in order to prevent the work from becoming unwieldy.

The case or conflict analysis approach has the advantage of looking in greater detail at United Nations' practice in this particular area. However, it fails to impose any overall conceptual framework on that practice. Each individual conflict, dispute or situation may be analysed, *inter alia*, in terms of constitutional powers, political considerations and effectiveness, but overall comparison and evaluation is missing.

This work represents an attempt at synthesising these approaches in order to produce a conceptually based but comprehensive analysis of the United Nations' powers, practice and effectiveness in the maintenance of international peace and security.

The first two Parts of the work, on the Security Council and the General Assembly, perhaps lean more towards the conceptual approach than the conflict analysis method. In Part 1, after an Introduction (which incidentally can be used as an historical introduction to the work as a whole, since in 1945 it was envisaged that the United Nations' role in the maintenance of peace would fall almost entirely on the Security Council) an attempt is made in chapter 1 to extract the powerful political factors operating on the Security Council.

The next chapter purports to examine constitutional limitations, free from the distorting effect of politics. It may be that this attempt to remove all political influences in order to leave the area free for legal examination is unduly idealistic. Realistically, the aim is to consider and identify the political factors in order that when the legal or constitutional issues are considered the reader is already cognisant with the political motivations, factors and influences behind them.

Part 1 then ends with an analysis of the effectiveness of the Security Council in terms of the powers it uses in practice. Most of these powers are derived from the provisions of Chapters VI and VII of the United Nations' Charter. However, because of the political factors operating on it, the Security Council has developed and expanded some of its powers whilst modifying, refining or virtually discarding others.

A similar approach is taken in Part 2 to the General Assembly, except that the political element is considered in general terms in the Introduction. Chapter 4 contains an analysis of the constitutional issues in order to ascertain, amongst other things, how the Charter deals with the problem of the separation of powers between the Security Council and the General Assembly in the field of international peace. Then the political factors are reintroduced to show the actual division of competence between the two bodies in chapter 5. Finally, in relation to the Assembly, chapter 6 examines the Assembly's development of a very general set of Charter provisions into a number of specific powers which are assessed in terms of effectiveness.

Part 3, on the peacekeeping function of the United Nations, veers more towards the casebook approach. However, the wide conceptual framework, in terms of considering first the operative political factors, secondly the legal issues, and finally the question of effectiveness, remains. Chapter 7 contains the political factors which limit the global ambit of peacekeeping. Chapter 8 then considers the legal questions by working through the various United

Nations' forces, and arrives at a considered conclusion as to the legal nature of peacekeeping. Finally, chapter 9 ascertains each force's effectiveness, not only in terms of fulfilling its mandate, but also in terms of its contribution to world peace.

The peacekeeping function is separated and analysed in this way because it was born of political necessity and is to a certain extent a constitutional oddity. Peacekeeping is also different from most of the other powers of the United Nations, which are sometimes rather cynically referred to as paper powers, because it involves a physical presence. These points led me to separate the peacekeeping function from the analysis of the Security Council and the General Assembly. The more case-orientated approach is utilised because of the *ad hoc* nature of each force. Generally, each force is different politically, legally, and in terms of effectiveness from the others.

Before entering into the substance, I would like to thank Professor Harris and Mr M. J. Bowman of the Law Department, Nottingham University, for their help and supervision of the Ph.D thesis upon which this book is mainly based. Finally, I am grateful to my wife for her patience and encouragement.

N.D. White
Nottingham
September, 1989

PART 1

The Security Council

INTRODUCTION

The main aim of the United Nations is to maintain international peace and security.[1] Throughout the complex Great Power negotiations which led to the conference at San Francisco, the emphasis was on a particular body within the United Nations – the Security Council – performing that role. Indeed, this is reflected within the provisions of the Charter, which, *inter alia,* grant the Security Council 'primary responsibility'[2] for the maintenance of international peace accompanied by comprehensive powers to enable it to fulfil that role. The Great Powers did not foresee the General Assembly having any substantive powers, intending merely to have it as a meeting place for the representatives of States. However, the smaller powers at San Francisco managed to secure sufficient provisions in the Charter to enable the Assembly to develop an increasingly important subsidiary role in the maintenance of international peace.

This introduction is mainly concerned with giving a background to the United Nations viewed in the light of the League experience and the Great Power negotiations which preceded the adoption of the Charter. It must be remembered that throughout these negotiations it was the Security Council which was intended to embody the principal aim of the United Nations, namely the maintenance of international peace through a system of collective security.[3]

The League of Nations[4] had failed to keep world peace primarily because the idea of collective security was far weaker than the individual States' desires to protect their national interests. One of the statesmen behind the creation of the League, President Wilson of the United States, saw the League replacing the previous balance of power system with a centralised body comprised of powerful States 'who shall be the trustees of the peace of the world'.[5] Paradoxically, it was the United States' refusal to join which could be said to be the first example of a powerful State believing that collective security was not in its best interests.

Although the Covenant of the League of Nations did contain provisions for collective security[6] and provided for the imposition of embargoes and possibly collective military sanctions against offending States,[7] the League was doomed to failure because sovereign States naturally saw national interests as paramount over collective interests. Such considerations of national power resulted in the dilution of the League's power to such an extent that the question of imposition of sanctions under Article 16 became not one for the consideration of the League's Council or Assembly, but for each individual member. Piecemeal and ineffective sanctions were imposed in this manner against Italy after its invasion of Abyssinia in 1935. The failure to impose any sort of collective measures against aggressors meant the inevitable demise of the League.

Sarkensa writes, 'the League experience was an abortive attempt to translate the collective security system into a working system'.[8] The United Nations, in particular the Security Council, represented the world's second attempt at developing a feasible system of collective security. The Organisation had its origins, indirectly, in the 'Declaration by the United Nations' of 1 January 1942[9] which did not refer to any world body, instead it concentrated on spelling out the Allied programme to be pursued against the Axis powers. Nevertheless, the idea of the United Nations continuing after the war was outlined in the Moscow Declaration of October 1943,[10] in which the Big Four – China, the United Kingdom, the United States and the Soviet Union – recognised 'the necessity of establishing, at the earliest possible date, a general international organisation based on the principle of sovereign equality of all peace loving States, and open to membership by all such States, large and small, for the maintenance of international peace and security'.

The ideal of collective security was behind this statement, though by juxtaposing the notion of a world body with that of State sovereignty, the clash between collective and national interest had not been removed. The major lesson of the League had not been learned. Nevertheless, to give collective interests primacy over national interests would be to have created a world government. In practice, the most that could be done was to give the world body, through the Security Council, greater powers for collective measures which might weigh more heavily on the scales against the counter-balance of national interests.[11]

Comprehensive proposals from the Big Four were discussed by those States at Dumbarton Oaks between August and October 1944, resulting in a far-reaching and detailed agreement concerning the Organisation.[12] They agreed that the Security Council should have the function of maintaining international peace through collective measures if necessary. However, they also decided that the Great Powers should have a special position on the Council consisting of permanent representation with special voting rights which would ensure that no substantive decisions would be taken by the Council without their unanimous concurrence. The right of veto was further refined at the Yalta Conference in February 1945.

Whether one regards the necessity of Great Power unanimity as an idealistic attempt to continue where the Allies finished after the end of the war, or more cynically, as a recognition by those Powers of each others' and their own national interests being paramount over any collective interests, it is realistic to state that without the power of veto the Organisation would probably not have been born, and even if created, it would not have been able to take enforcement action against the Great Powers, particularly the Soviet Union and the United States, without devastating effects. At San Francisco the right of veto was accepted by the other States with little challenge, possibly because most delegates preferred, at least publicly, to lean towards an idealistic vision of Great Power unity providing future collective security.[13]

Generally the delegates were enthusiastic about collective security but unduly optimistic about Great Power unanimity.

Hopes of great power co-operation had largely been based on Allied unity during the war, which left the misleading impression that international collaboration was easy to achieve. But actually Allied unity, so far as the Soviet Union was concerned, was a remarkable achievement due mainly to the intense opposition that Hitler aroused.[14]

Indeed, President Roosevelt recognised this in a speech in which he said that, 'the nearer we come to vanquishing our enemies the more we inevitably become conscious of the differences among the victors'.[15]

The marriage of convenience which resulted in unanimity during the war was terminated after a brief honeymoon in San Francisco. Within two days of the Council's first meeting the Cold War, in the form of a complaint by Iran of the Soviet Union's presence in its country, was on the Council's agenda, followed two days later by a Soviet complaint of the British presence in Greece.

The idea that the United Nations could prevent the resurrection of the balance of power system was not even achievable before the end of the war, a fact that was to be emphasised with great clarity when the Security Council began to function. Collective security was subservient to the national interests of the Great Powers, particularly the superpowers, who protected those interests by the power of veto. The geopolitical division of the world into two competing power blocs has effectively set the limits as to the areas in which the Security Council can properly carry out its functions of maintaining international peace and security. These global political considerations will be the subject of the first chapter.

Notes

1 Article 1(1) of the UN Charter.
2 Article 24(1) of the UN Charter.
3 K.P. Sarkensa, *The United Nations and Collective Security*, 4 (1974).

4 See generally F. S. Northedge, *The League of Nations: Its Life and Times*, (1986).
5 Sarkensa, *The United Nations*, 9.
6 Articles 10 and 11 of the League Covenant. UKTS 4 (1919), Cmd 153.
7 Article 16 of the Covenant.
8 Sarkensa, *The United Nations*, 23.
9 For text see R. B. Russell and J. E. Muther, *A History of the United Nations Charter*, Appendix C (1958).
10 For text see World Peace Foundation, *The United Nations in the Making: Basic Documents*, 9–10 (1945).
11 Russell and Muther, *A History of the United Nations*, 227–8.
12 For text see UNCIO, vol. 3, 2–17.
13 See for example UNCIO, vol. 1, 502–3, delegate from Luxembourg.
14 R. Hiscocks, *The Security Council: A Study in Adolescence*, 67 (1973).
15 Message on the State of the Union, 6 January 1945.

CHAPTER 1

A geopolitical analysis of the Security Council

Before analysing the jurisdiction of the Security Council in terms of the Charter, it will be helpful to identify the major geographical limitations imposed on the effective jurisdiction of the Security Council by political factors; factors arising, in particular, as a result of the global and strategic interests of the superpowers, which often cause a paralysis in the Council as those interests are protected by the veto. It must be remembered however, that the veto, along with another geopolitical limitation – regionalism – are provided for in the Charter. In this sense they are legal limitations, but they must be realistically viewed as geopolitical limitations because they are operated for political motives with the result that large areas of the globe are excluded from Security Council action. In addition, the use of the power of veto and of the various regional organisations is often in contradiction to the terms of the Charter so that one cannot really say that they are legal rather than geopolitical limitations.

The power of veto

The power of veto is contained in Article 27 of the Charter. After stating in paragraph 2 that 'decisions of the Security Council on procedural matters shall be made by an affirmative vote of' nine (previously seven) out of the fifteen (previously eleven) members,[1] paragraph 3 provides that 'decisions of the Security Council on all other matters shall be made by an affirmative vote of nine members including the concurring votes of the permanent members; provided that, in decisions under Chapter VI, and under paragraph 3 of Article 52, a party to the dispute shall abstain from voting.'

As has been brought out in the introduction, the power of veto had its genesis in the desire to prevent the permanent members from being the potential objects of collective measures. However, Article 27(3) was drafted on a much wider basis after the Yalta Conference. It was clear after Yalta that Great Power unity was destined to be an unachieved ideal with the power of veto extending beyond the enforcement provisions of Chapter VII, to Chapter VI, which granted the Council general, recommendatory powers for pacific settlement, unless one of the permanent members was a party to the dispute.

Indeed, the Yalta formula, presented to the San Francisco conference in explanation of the right of veto, illustrated the permanent members' desire to leave no loopholes to prevent their use of the veto. The Yalta formula introduced the prospect of the 'double veto', which meant that any 'decision regarding the preliminary question as to whether or not such a matter is procedural must be taken by vote of [nine] members of the Security Council, including the concurring votes of the permanent members'.[2]

However, the smaller powers' objections at San Francisco were not directed at the double-veto, but at the 'chain of events' theory outlined in the Yalta formula. The smaller powers demanded that the veto should be confined to questions concerning enforcement action. The Australian delegate argued that 'the Council has the duty rather than a right to conciliate disputants' and that it was essential that no member should have the right to veto resolutions aimed solely at pacific settlement of disputes.[3] The major powers stuck to the somewhat fallacious argument presented in the Yalta formula that any pacific measures 'may initiate a chain of events which might in the end require the Council under its responsibilities to invoke measures of enforcement'.[4] It might well be that such a chain of events could occur, but it did not appear necessary to allow the veto to occur at the pacific settlement stage as long as the permanent members could operate it at the enforcement stage. The 'chain of events' theory was, in reality, a mechanism whereby the whole field of Council action would be the subject of the veto. The smaller powers continued to object, but it became clear that Article 27 would have to be accepted as the 'Big Five decided to let it be known that unless the voting provision was accepted, there would be no Organisation'.[5] It was no longer a question of preserving Great Power unanimity but of preserving the Organisation.[6]

The applicability of the double veto and the chain of events theory peppered exchanges in the Council during its first decade. These have been thoroughly reviewed by Bailey[7] and it is not proposed to discuss them as a separate issue here. Such debates have, in any event, petered out in the face of the permanent members developing a practice which enables them to use the veto to defeat any sort of proposal under Chapter VI or Chapter VII, unless it is clearly procedural.

In stating the chain of events theory the sponsoring powers still deferred to their obligation to abstain if they were parties to a dispute being dealt with by the Council under Chapter VI. In practice the permanent members have disregarded this provision,[8] thus destroying the general aim of this aspect of Article 27(3) to separate 'law as it is invoked by the claimants to the dispute and law as it is employed by [the Council] when passing its decision'.[9] The drafting of the provision allows a member to argue, if it wants, that it only has an 'interest' in the dispute which is insufficient to make it a 'party' or that the proposed resolution is only dealing with a 'situation' and not a 'dispute',[10] or does in fact envisage Chapter VII rather than Chapter VI action. In practice the permanent members rarely raise such arguments. The power of veto is exercised according to considerations of interests rather than in accordance with the letter of the Charter.

Permanent member, particularly superpower, interests and influences have become so pervasive in the post-war world that the veto has effectively debarred the Security Council from taking action or recommending measures of any sort in many areas of the globe.[11] Indeed, in many cases, the super-powers operate the veto not to protect 'vital' interests but in order to curry favour with other States or as a reflex reaction to oppose the other super-power's voting intentions. The Indian invasion of Goa in 1961 is a reasonable example of the Soviet Union using its veto not for any vital protective purpose but to express support for India, the Third World and anti-colonialism.[12]

Even when a great power appears to be a 'party' to a 'dispute' within the spirit of Article 27(3), it has disregarded its obligation to abstain when faced with the possibility of being subject to a recommendatory Chapter VI-based resolution. The French and British could hardly deny that they were 'parties' to the Suez crisis in 1956, but they did not have to as they vetoed draft resolutions proposed by the United States and the Soviet Union calling for Israel to cease fire and withdraw.[13] The proposers of the draft resolutions deliberately refrained from invoking Chapter VII for fear of justifying Anglo/French intervention.[14] Nevertheless, the British and French vetoes were not challenged on the grounds of Article 27(3).[15]

During the Falklands crisis in 1982, the Panamanian representative thought that the last operative paragraph of resolution 502 placed it under Chapter VI, in that it called for pacific settlement of the dispute, in which case, he argued, the United Kingdom should be debarred from voting on the resolution. Sir Anthony Parsons stated that the resolution came under Chapter VII, namely Article 40, and so the obligation to abstain was not applicable.[16] Although no members challenged Sir Anthony further on this point, the very fact that he had to justify his vote was a rarity. Perhaps it can be explained by the fact that the Security Council approached the Falklands free from any overt superpower concern,[17] and consequently discussions and resolutions were clearly based on considerations of international and Charter law rather than on considerations of power and zones of interest.

Indeed, the Falklands represents one of the few occasions on which the Council briefly acted in a manner approaching that envisaged in 1945. In many other cases the Security Council is paralysed by considerations of power manifesting themselves in the form of the veto. The main areas from which the Security Council is effectively excluded, in terms of taking any positive measures, even recommendations, are the power blocs.

Intra-bloc situations

In a world dominated by two superpowers with their own hemispheric or bloc
domains there emerges a distinction between intra-bloc and inter-bloc conflicts.
In intra-bloc conflicts such as Guatemala in 1954 and Hungary in 1956, the
veto is operated by the relevant bloc leader to allow the dispute to be settled
within that bloc, combined, in the case of the United States, with arguments
in favour of the regional organisation.

Inter-bloc conflicts often occur on the 'power frontiers'[18] between the
'spheres of influence'[19] of the superpowers, usually as a consequence of a
miscalculation by one of them as to the ambit of its hemispheric control. Good
examples of such disputes are the Berlin blockade in 1948 and the Cuban
missile crisis in 1962. In these cases, it will be argued, the Security Council
did play a significant role. The polarised positions taken by each side before
the Council were gradually whittled down behind the scene until a common
ground was achieved. In inter-bloc conflicts the stark choice is between
annihilation or 'peaceful coexistence'.[20] Both superpowers have to make
concessions if peaceful coexistence is to continue.

As has been pointed out, there are few areas in the world where the superpowers do not exert an influence, particularly when taking into account
China's emerging superpower status.[21] The world is thus distilling into a
system of three superpowers, analogous to three continental plates sometimes
rubbing together, sometimes overlapping, sometimes drawing apart as their
influences alter; in each case, instead of producing earthquakes or volcanic
eruptions, they result in conflicts.

During the initial Cold War period (1945–55), the United Nations was
dominated by the West[22] which managed to manipulate the whole Organisation to further its political and strategic ends. The case of Guatemala in
1954 is illustrative of how that manipulation often occurred to protect
American interests. It also shows how the Soviet Union was often forced to
use its veto in the early years because of the American dominance of the
Council.

The Guatemalan episode involved the question of whether regional bodies
should have priority over the world body.[23] Articles 52(4) and 103 of the
Charter clearly answer the question negatively, and yet the Soviet Union was
forced to use its veto to uphold this view after Brazil and Columbia had
proposed a resolution which would have left the matter to the Organisation
of American States (OAS).[24] The United States was in such a strong position
in the Security Council that it did not have to use its veto to protect its interests
– it merely relied on its allies on the Council to outvote any proposal which
was deemed to be against Western interests. Its dominance of the Guatemalan
debate was highlighted when the US President of the Council effectively
prevented further consideration when he proposed to take a procedural vote

on the question whether to keep the item on the agenda. The item was duly removed despite the negative Soviet vote.[25]

As with several of the earlier intra-bloc disputes involving the United States, that country was so confident of its position on the Council that it did not feel it necessary to veto what appeared to be constructive Council resolutions. Resolution 104,[26] proposed by France, called for the 'immediate termination of any action likely to cause bloodshed, and requests all members to abstain from giving assistance to any such action'. It was essentially a neutral, valueless resolution but by voting for it along with the Soviet Union, the United States reinforced the view that it was the upholder of the Charter even where the principles contained therein seemed to be operating against American interests, whereas the Soviet Union was portrayed as only voting for resolutions criticising the United States and as using its veto when there was even a hint of criticism of its actions. Nevertheless, such illusions should not hide the real fact that the United States was manipulating the Council to protect its hemispheric interests. Its representative made this very clear by instructing the Soviet Union to stay out of the United States' 'hemisphere'.[27] This amounted to a reassertion of the Monroe Doctrine and constituted 'a declaration which reciprocal practice over the next two decades was to stamp with an almost jural quality'.[28]

The tacit agreement between the Great Powers at Potsdam that Eastern Europe was within the Soviet Union's sphere of influence was put beyond doubt after the Soviets intervened in Hungary in 1956.[29] The Western powers were unwilling to help Nagy when he announced on 1 November the withdrawal of Hungary from the Warsaw Pact accompanied by a declaration of its neutrality, and requested the United Nations and the four other permanent members to defend its neutral status. The Soviet Union also saw it necessary to protect its interests by using its veto in the Security Council to defeat a United States' sponsored draft resolution[30] calling for Soviet withdrawal and respect for 'the independence and sovereignty of Hungary'. Ambassador Sobolev of the Soviet Union explained the action in terms of defence of the Soviet Union's strategic zone.[31]

Just as the United States sees the creation of a 'communist' government – whether created by popular assent or by outside interference – as an attack on Western principles and interests, so the Soviet Union views 'capitalism' as an attack on its bloc solidarity. Both powers view the removal of each respective threat from their respective zones as a legitimate defence of their strategic interests.[32]

Intra-bloc interventions are often challenged by the other superpower in the Security Council to show rhetorical political support for the people of the country being intervened in. By allowing the other side to verbally vent its anger, it could be argued that the Security Council reduces the chance of that side counter-intervening leading to a global conflict. The United States complained of Soviet intervention in Hungary in 1956. The compliment was repaid in 1965 when the Soviet Union complained of 'armed intervention' by the United States in the Dominican Republic.[33] The Soviets introduced a draft resolution[34] condemning the intervention and demanding that the United States withdraw. Western support was still strong enough in the Council to ensure that the proposal only secured two votes in its favour.[35] The United States treated the situation on a similar basis to Guatemala a decade earlier by allowing resolutions to be adopted calling for a cease-fire but not prejudicing the OAS's role in the situation.[36] Again, the world saw the United States refraining from using its veto in contrast to the Soviet Union's use of its power to block resolutions on Hungary and later on Czechoslovakia. Nevertheless, it is clear that the United States would have used its veto to prevent criticism of its action, or to prevent proposals for peaceful settlement of the situation, or to prevent the establishment of machinery to facilitate a cease-fire such as peacekeeping – in other words anything that would have vaguely hindered or criticised the US/OAS operation. According to Ambassador Stevenson 'the establishment of a communist dictatorship' in the Dominican Republic was a matter for 'hemispheric action only'.[37]

On 28 August 1968, Western States brought the situation in Czechoslovakia to the attention of the Council.[38] The Soviet intervention led to the enunciation of the Brezhnev Doctrine of limited sovereignty within the Socialist commonwealth,[39] paralleling the various interventionist doctrines expounded by American Presidents. Ambassador Malik made a weak attempt to justify the intervention by referring to it as self-defence against an 'imperialist' attack. However, in the same speech the overt political reasons became apparent, in that 'the situation in Czechoslovakia affected the vital interests of the Soviet Union'.[40]

The Soviet Union views the use of the veto in the Council to prevent criticism of its actions as a necessary corollary to the protection of its vital interests by intervention. There is no question even of allowing weak, neutral resolutions to be adopted, an attitude that probably can be explained by a 'knee-jerk' reaction produced by its minority position on the Council plus the fact that it has no regional organisation equivalent to the OAS to give its intra-bloc actions an air of legality. The Soviet Union vetoed a Danish draft which condemned Soviet 'armed intervention' as well as a Canadian draft which was aimed at achieving limited measures and took the form of a request to the Secretary General to send a representative to Prague 'to ensure the personal safety of the Czechoslovak leaders under detention'.[41]

The Soviet intervention in Afghanistan in 1980 was different in geopolitical terms from its previous interventions in Czechoslovakia and Hungary because it represented the first time the Soviet Union had pushed its troops beyond the zone inherited after the Second World War.[42] This was reflected in the large number of States – Non Aligned as well as Western – which requested the convening of the Security Council to discuss the situation in Afghanistan.[43] A draft resolution was proposed by the Non Aligned group on the Council which deplored the 'recent armed intervention' and called for 'the immediate and unconditional withdrawal of all foreign troops from Afghanistan'. The vetoed draft resolution also called for respect for Afghanistan's non aligned status, reflecting the Western view that the Soviet Union had stepped beyond its zone as well as the Non Aligned movement's fear of its members being the subjects of superpower intervention.[44]

Afghanistan illustrates the fine line between intra-bloc conflicts in which the other superpower will be content with rhetorical confrontation, and inter-bloc conflicts which may escalate into a global military confrontation. The Carter Doctrine,[45] which warned the Soviet Union not to advance any further towards the Gulf, drew the line at the Afghan border, suggesting that the United States was treating the intervention as politically allowable. However, President Reagan redrew the power frontier closer to the Soviet Union by authorising material support for the Afghan rebels.[46] As we shall see, in cases of superpower confrontation on a power frontier, paralysis in the Security Council may lead to a climb down by one superpower in the course of diplomatic moves. This may, in part, explain the Soviet Union's withdrawal from Afghanistan in 1989 as a result of the Geneva Accords signed by Pakistan, Afghanistan, the Soviet Union and the United States and brokered by the United Nations.[47]

The intervention in Grenada in 1983 which was legally justified on three grounds by the United States – the protection of nationals (and wider arguments of humanitarian intervention to protect the whole population), the invitation of the Governor General, and regional action by the Organisation of Eastern Caribbean States (OECS)[48] – was, in reality, an application of the so-called Reagan Doctrine. This doctrine or policy encompasses support for anti-communists – whether established governments or rebels – not only in the American hemisphere but throughout the world. Consequently, the present United States' administration supports the Contras fighting in Nicaragua; the Khmer Rouge fighting the Vietnamese-imposed government in Kampuchea; the National Union for the Total Independence of Angola (UNITA) guerrillas fighting the Soviet/Cuban backed MPLA government in Angola, and the Afghan mujahedin. These interventions do not fit the historic pattern of superpower behaviour in that they are indirect and are sometimes extra-hemispheric. The Reagan Doctrine is offensive, it aims to 'recover communist controlled turf for freedom'[49] and so goes beyond the intra-bloc interventions so far discussed which were aimed at maintaining bloc cohesiveness.

In effect, the United States under President Reagan was trying to stand the dominoes back up. Thus, with at least one of the superpowers positively asserting influence in areas under the other's control, there existed the potential for more inter-bloc confrontations leading to further paralysis in the Security Council. Whether this trend will continue under President Bush is more doubtful, particularly when faced with a more conciliatory and open regime in Moscow. A more constructive, as opposed to rhetorical, exchange between the superpowers may lead to an expansion in the work of the Security Council. The United Nations' sponsored agreement on Afghanistan is one indicator. Another can be seen in the form of the United Nations' investigative team sent by the Security Council into Central America following a complaint by Nicaragua that there was a threat to the peace in the region as a result of the landing of United States' troops in Honduras.[50]

In the decade prior to this thaw in superpower relations, the United States had increasingly used its veto to protect its interests. In the debate over its Grenadan intervention, even the United States' closest ally – the United Kingdom – refused to support it in vetoing a draft resolution condemning the 'armed intervention' and calling for the withdrawal of foreign troops.[51] Unlike the cases of Guatemala and the Dominican Republic, the United States was unable to avoid using the veto to protect its interests.

Indeed, the United States has had to use its veto power increasingly since the late 1970s to prevent the Council adopting resolutions against what it believes are its strategic interests. Until recently it had vetoed any action by the Council as regards Central America unless the resolution expressly leaves the matter of pacific settlement to the Contadora group of States (Mexico, Colombia, Panama and Venezuela).[52]

After the International Court found that the United States had illegally intervened militarily against Nicaragua by, *inter alia*, supporting the Contras,[53] the United States predictably used its power of veto to defeat draft resolutions urgently calling for full and immediate compliance with the World Court's judgement.[54] The representative of the United States stated that his country's policy towards Nicaragua would continue to be based on the protection of the United States and of Nicaragua's neighbours due to Nicaragua's close military and security ties with Cuba, the Soviet Union and the Warsaw Pact.[55] The preponderance of strategic over legal justifications in the United States' argument before the Council highlights that State's view that any world bodies such as the International Court or the Security Council are to be excluded from acting within its bloc. Having said that, there are recent indicators, namely the Security Council's approval of a fact-finding mission to the area and the widely supported regional peace plan, which may suggest that hemispheric control by the United States is not absolute.[56]

Despite recent Security Council activity in the zones of influence of the two superpowers, it is still true to say that their interests represent a vast limitation on the Council's operative area. On the other hand the emerging superpower status of China represents a less severe hemispheric limitation on the Council. There is no doubt that China has a hemispheric influence over parts of the

Far East, an area where the Soviet Union has substantial influence, for example in Vietnam. Consequently, when in 1979, Vietnam invaded Kampuchea to overthrow the Chinese supported Pol Pot regime and to instal a puppet regime, the Chinese saw that as a threat to their security and part of a 'greater Soviet hegemonism'.[57] The Chinese resorted to a punitive attack against Vietnam.[58] The Security Council became a verbal battleground between the Soviet Union and China. The Soviet Union operated its veto on two occasions during the debate to protect Vietnam from criticism.[59] Interestingly, China did not use its veto, even though the second draft resolution referred obliquely to its attack against Vietnam. This is probably a part of China's policy of aligning itself with the Third World rather than regarding itself as a superpower. A denial of that status has probably led to Communist China limiting the use of its veto since taking the permanent seat.[60]

Inter-bloc situations

The superpowers' pervasive global interests mean that potentially there are very few areas in the world in which the Council can utilise fully the powers at its disposal. It is axiomatic that where there is a case of direct East-West confrontation there will be little possibility of a Security Council resolution. Nevertheless, there is evidence to the effect that in these inter-bloc disputes, the Security Council can sometimes play a significant role.

Great Power unanimity collapsed almost immediately with the inscription of the Iranian crisis on the Council's agenda on 28 January 1946.[61] The crisis arose out of the continued Russian occupation of the region of Azerbaijan in the north of Iran following the end of the Second World War. The Iranians supported by the United States desired to involve the Security Council. The situation concerned the extent of the Soviet Union's zone of influence which, in this area, was still in a state of flux. The United States saw a danger to the vital oil supplies and the threat of Soviet expansion to the Gulf.

The situation was the first classic case of East-West confrontation. The Secretary General, Trygve Lie, foresaw that debate in the Security Council would not produce anything concrete by way of settlement of the dispute.[62] Nevertheless, the Iranians requested a meeting of the Security Council, which prompted the Soviet Union to walk out saying that the dispute would be settled by bilateral negotiations between the Soviet Union and Iran.[63] The United States was left free to manipulate the Council into adopting a resolution which directed the Secretary General to discover the progress of negotiations and the Soviet intentions as to withdrawal.[64] Lie reported that the Soviets would withdraw on 6 May, at which point the Iranians wanted the question to be removed from the Council's agenda. However, the United States insisted on keeping the item on, illustrating that the situation was really a confrontation between the Soviet Union and the United States.[65] The Soviets withdrew.

Franck sees the Council's involvement with the Iranian question as harassing rather than facilitating the solution to the problem. He criticises the 'institutionalised crisis management technique' of the Council which 'conduces to the striking of poses and the taking of rigid positions' that seem to take on a 'metaphysical reality', which was heightened in this case by the 'agenda question'. Nevertheless, the manipulation of the Council by the United States indicated that country's serious intent. From the striking of poses in the public forum, the Soviet Union could climb down quietly in private under the aegis of the Secretary General's diplomatic efforts.[66]

One must not underestimate the role of the Council in one of the most dangerous situations to threaten world peace since 1945. In 1962 the Americans purported to use the forum as a tactical measure with no real intention of using it to negotiate with the Soviets over the withdrawal of missiles from Cuba.[67] The United States convened the Council and introduced a draft resolution which had no chance of being adopted.[68] It reasserted its demand 'for immediate dismantling and withdrawal from Cuba of all missiles and other offensive weapons' and the dispatch to Cuba of a 'United Nations' observer corps to assure and report on compliance'. Only after the affirmative 'certification of compliance' would the quarantine imposed by the United States be terminated. The call for withdrawal of the missiles was expressly stated to be 'under Article 40', that is a 'decision' of the Council having binding force under Article 25. The Soviet draft resolution[69] was equally uncompromising in that it condemned the actions of the Americans and called for the immediate revocation of the 'decision to inspect the ships of other States bound for' Cuba, and for an end 'to any kind of interference in the internal affairs of' Cuba.

There appeared little chance of settling the issue through these kind of polarised proposals, but the draft resolutions did overlap in one area; they both called for bilateral negotiations between the United States and the Soviet Union to remove the threat to the peace. Acting Secretary General U Thant seized on this common area in a letter to Kennedy and Khruschev in which he called for the 'voluntary suspension of all arms shipments to Cuba and also the voluntary suspension of the quarantine for a period of two to three weeks'.[70] On 26 October 1962 President Kennedy agreed to the proposal.[71] The Soviets indicated their willingness to accept by stopping the shipments. This eventually led to a tacit agreement by which the Soviets would remove their missiles already emplaced in Cuba in return for the American withdrawal of missiles from Turkey.

It may appear that it was the Secretary General's diplomatic moves which helped to settle the dispute, whereas moves in the Council were a failure. This view is founded on the belief that the Security Council is an adjudicative body. The Council, being a political organ, very rarely acts in this fashion, especially when the parties to the dispute are the Soviet Union and the United States.

In these situations it establishes the often extreme positions of the parties, which obviously cannot be reconciled in the public forum, so necessitating the supplementary aid of 'corridor' diplomacy. Rhetorical confrontation in the Council can be a forerunner to the successful settlement of the dispute by diplomacy.

The inter-bloc situations examined so far − the Iranian situation in 1946 and the Cuban missile crisis in 1962 − both involved, more or less, direct confrontation between East and West. However, a large preponderance of modern warfare concerns the indirect involvement of the superpowers, in which one or both will confront the other by the use of proxy armies − often in the form of national liberation fronts.[72] In these situations the danger of escalation is less because the superpowers are effectively two steps away from all out war − indirect confrontation must turn into direct confrontation which in turn must escalate. Thus, with this cushion the superpowers are less willing to compromise. As with the situation of direct East-West confrontation, this has rendered the Security Council a barren place, but unlike direct inter-bloc disputes, there is often little possibility of diplomacy filling the vacuum. Two conflicts will be examined to illustrate how indirect superpower confrontation limits Council action, namely Angola and Vietnam.

The conflict in Vietnam has lasted in various forms from 1946 to the present day if one includes the North's takeover of the South in 1975 and the Vietnamese expansion into Kampuchea in 1979. This analysis will be confined to the period 1946−73 when the conflict was an indirect confrontation between East and West.[73] It was a battle on the edge of the 'zones of influence', in this case the 17th parallel. The United States was determined to hold the line, for if Vietnam fell to communism the 'domino theory'[74] suggested that neighbouring countries would fall as communism spread through Indo-China. The United States did not distinguish between the Chinese and the Soviets who both supported the North Vietnamese, but, with hindsight, the American defeat can be seen as an expansion of the Soviet sphere.[75]

The period 1946−54 saw the French fighting the North Vietnamese communist movement until the French were heavily defeated at Dien Bien Phu. Although the French were fighting to maintain their colonial empire in this period, by 1954 the conflict was taking on a Cold War aspect with the United States paying seventy-five per cent of the French costs in fighting the war.[76] After Dien Bien Phu, a conference was held at Geneva in July 1954 to consider the future of French Indo-China.[77] A cease-fire agreement divided Vietman at the 17th parallel, while the Final Declaration of the Conference[78] provided for elections to be held leading to a single Vietnamese State. The elections did not come about, mainly because of South Vietnamese opposition,[79] and so the scene was set for a conflict between North and South with Sino-Soviet aid to the former and American military commitment to the latter.

The Security Council, indeed the United Nations, had little to do either

with the 1954 Conference or the preceding period.[80] After French involvement was replaced by American commitment the Security Council played a
peripheral role. It met inconclusively on four occasions, three of which
concerned aspects of the war rather than the whole situation. In 1959,
Laos complained of military incursions into its territory by the North Vietnamese.[81] The Security Council, using a procedural vote in the face of Soviet
objections based on the 'double-veto' and the 'chain of events' principles,
created an investigative sub-committee.[82] This committee reported that the
fighting was of a 'guerrilla character' and so did not constitute a crossing of
the frontiers of Laos by the North Vietnamese.[83]

In May 1964, the government of Cambodia complained to the Security
Council of alleged acts of 'aggression' directed against it by South Vietnamese
and United States' forces.[84] These two States denied the charge, and suggested that the non-demarcation of the boundary between Cambodia and
South Vietnam was the reason. The United States representative suggested
that the answer would be a role for a United Nations' force, emplaced to
observe the integrity of the boundary.[85] South Vietnam indicated its willingness to accept such an observer force on its territory, but Cambodia was
opposed to having it on its side of the border. No observer or peacekeeping
forces were sent.

In August 1964, the United States requested that the Council consider the
attacks on American vessels in the Gulf of Tonkin by the North Vietnamese.
The Hanoi regime was unwilling to state its case before the Council and
declared via the Soviet Union that consideration of the problem did not lie
with the Security Council, but with the members of the 1954 Geneva
Conference.[86]

It was not until 1966 that an attempt was made to bring the whole situation
before the Security Council, when the United States requested a meeting of
the Security Council and submitted a draft resolution calling for 'immediate
discussions without preconditions', with the priority being the arrangement
for a cessation of hostilities.[87] The Soviet representative objected to a Council
meeting to discuss the Vietnam war. He stated that the move by the United
States was a diversionary tactic to cover the expansion of its aggressive war
in Vietnam as evidenced by the resumption of its 'barbaric' air raids on the
North.[88] The overwhelming atmosphere of distrust between the superpowers
meant that the American proposal was not even voted on.

Although many other complaints and correspondence were directed to the
Security Council, Vietnam was discussed by the body only on the four
occasions outlined above, in which no concrete measures were adopted. Yet
the situation was so grave in Vietnam that, although it was not on the agenda
of the 21st session of the General Assembly, 107 out of 110 speakers referred
to it. It was a virtual poll of international public opinion. All of those who
spoke on the subject recognised the conflict in Vietnam as a serious threat

to international peace and security which had the potential to spread beyond south-east Asia and ignite a Third World War.[89]

There were certain factors which restricted the ability of the Security Council or General Assembly to deal with the threat to the peace which Vietnam posed. At the Geneva Conference in 1954, very few of the participants envisaged United Nations' involvement, particularly the North Vietnamese and Chinese.[90] These two countries maintained a strong desire to exclude the United Nations from being involved, seeing the United Nations as 'a tool for US aggression'.[91]

They had some justification for feeling this in that the West had dominated and, to a certain extent, had manipulated the United Nations in the early years, particularly, as regards the Chinese, in the case of Korea in 1950. The United States had also prevented the Communist Chinese from taking the permanent seat. The Chinese and North Vietnamese, not being represented at the United Nations, felt a deep distrust for the Organisation,[92] which, when combined with the mutual distrust between the Soviet Union and the United States during the Cold War, had the result of giving the United Nations little possibility of taking positive steps to solve the conflict in Vietnam.

The United States relied on a similarity between the Korean War and the conflict in Vietnam to justify its support for the South.[93] In the case of Korea, the United States was willing to turn its support for South Korea into a United Nations' action at the outset of the war, whereas in Vietnam, the United States showed a willingness to involve the United Nations only when the war was going against it, by which time the position of the opposing parties and their respective superpower backers had become too intransigent for the United Nations to intervene. While in the case of Korea, the Communist attack from the north was a clear breach of Article 2(4) and a 'breach of the peace' within Article 39, the Vietnamese situation was more complicated, evidenced by the fact that there was considerable support for the Vietcong in the South. There was no discernable initial aggression by the North and no significant event which would have enabled a collective response as in the case of Korea, and certainly the Soviet Union was not going to absent itself and so allow the collective response to become a collective United Nations' response. Vietnam could best be described as a gradually escalating, internationalised civil war which was a 'threat to the peace' rather than a clear 'breach of the peace' as in Korea. The gradual escalation of the conflict in Vietnam severely limited the potential of United Nations' action. It had not really dealt with the situation at its origin – either in 1946 or by participating in the 1954 Conference – and thereafter it was in the untenable position of having to deal with the conflict from the outside.

The Secretary General – U Thant – supported this view. In his New Year message in 1966, he pointed out that just as the parties to the conflict had decided in 1954 to negotiate the end of the war outside the framework of the

United Nations, the conflict could not be settled in 1966 under the auspices of the United Nations because only the United States, of all the parties to the conflict, was a member of the United Nations. U Thant preferred diplomacy rather than open debate in the Security Council and at several points in the conflict made proposals for settlement.[94]

The Vietnam War involved only one superpower directly and so the other – the Soviet Union – was quite content to block any diplomatic moves initiated by the Security Council or in the United Nations as a whole, because by indirectly encouraging the North Vietnamese, it was partly tying up the United States militarily and politically, and also embarrassing it. The North Vietnamese showed considerable independence, evidenced by the aid received from both the Soviet Union and the Chinese, whereas the South Vietnamese were to all intents and purposes 'puppets' of the United States. The Soviets did not control the North Vietnamese. The asymmetry of the conflict in Vietnam – in other words the difference in commitment between the two superpowers – meant that it was virtually impossible to solve in the United Nations.[95]

One must remember that at the outset of the Vietnam War, the United States was the dominant world power. It had a vast nuclear superiority over the Soviet Union and so felt able to draw power frontiers fairly close to the Soviet frontiers in òrder to prevent communism spreading. The Soviet Union's inferiority was reflected in the indirect manner of its support for North Korea and North Vietnam. It was only when nuclear parity was achieved in the late 1960s that the Soviets felt able to confront the United States in the intermediate areas between the power blocs – in the Middle East and Africa.[96]

Moscow saw an Angola ruled by the Popular Movement for the Liberation of Angola (MPLA) as giving it 'a promising zone of influence in a vast, rich and strategically located country just south of Zaire, a staunch US ally'.[97] Its initial intervention – using Cubans on the side of the MPLA in 1976 – was based on an accurate assessment of United States' reaction. The United States was unwilling to counter-intervene because of the so-called 'Vietnam syndrome' prevalent in the American public and government which effectively prevented the United States from intervening in foreign civil wars. By the 1980s, however, the United States' administration had sufficiently regained its confidence to repeal the Clark Amendment banning aid to Angolan insurgents as part of the so-called Reagan Doctrine.[98] The scene was set for another indirect superpower confrontation but this time the Soviets were the more committed.

The situation was made more complicated by the involvement of South Africa which since 1976 has, for lengthy periods, occupied parts of Southern Angola and has supported UNITA in its continuing attacks against the MPLA. The Security Council has repeatedly condemned South African 'aggression',[99] the superpowers finding that such resolutions are a useful smokescreen for covering up their own activities in the region. In their speeches before the Council the representatives of the Soviet Union and the United States recognised the underlying power conflict. The ambassador of the United States has criticised the presence of 13,000 Cuban troops as an example of foreign intervention in a civil war, and has abstained on resolutions which have recommended the furnishment of military assistance to Angola.[100] The United States did go so far as to publicly support the activities of Pretoria in relation to Angola, but tried to take the edge off any resolution which might go beyond condemnation. The Soviet Union, on the other hand, persistently criticised the United States and other North Atlantic Treaty Organisation (NATO) countries for supporting South Africa and for preventing the application of mandatory sanctions against that State. It still advocates sanctions, not only as a method of punishing South Africa for its aggressions but also as a means of ending apartheid.[101] It suited the Soviet Union to condemn South Africa and to urge effective measures against an economy in which it has very little interest, not only to curry favour with the Non Aligned, but also to strengthen and defend its base in Angola.

Superficially, the Security Council appeared not to be excluded from considering the situation in Angola. However, it only concentrated on the regional elements; it was effectively excluded from dealing with the fundamental problem – the power conflict between the United States and the Soviet Union. Indeed, it took an accord between Cuba, South Africa and Angola brokered by the United States and supported by the Soviet Union to end Cuban and South African intervention in Angola. Security Council involvement was limited to authorising the supervision requested by the parties to the agreement.[102]

Regionalism

So far we have seen how the influences and interests of the superpowers effectively preclude the Council from taking action in relation to disputes within large areas of the globe. Another *de facto* limitation on the Council's sphere of operation is regionalism, which is often, but not always, related to the spheres of influence claimed by the superpowers.

De jure, however, the United Nations' Charter does not permit regionalism to be paramount over globalism. The Charter, in Chapter VIII Article 52(1), recognises 'the existence of regional arrangements or agencies for dealing with such matters relating to the maintenance of international peace and security as are appropriate for regional action'. It even provides, in Article 52(3), that the Security Council 'shall encourage the development of pacific settlement of local disputes through such regional arrangements'. However, the provisions of Chapter VIII make it plain that the Security Council is supreme in matters relating to international peace and security. In relation to the pacific settlement of disputes, the Council's paramountcy is maintained by Article 52(4), whilst Article 53(1) provides that

the Security Council shall, where appropriate, utilise such regional arrangements or agencies for enforcement action under its authority. But no enforcement action shall be taken under regional arrangements or by regional agencies without the authorisation of the Security Council.

Articles 52(4) and 53(1) together mean that the Security Council retains supremacy over matters coming within Chapter VI or Chapter VII. Any lingering doubts about overall United Nations' supremacy are seemingly removed by Article 103: 'In the event of a conflict between the obligations of the Members of the United Nations under the present Charter and their obligations under any other international agreement, their obligations under the present Charter shall prevail.'

However, the compromise between regionalism and globalism attained in Chapter VIII (and Article 103) is itself compromised by Article 51. The insertion of this provision into the Charter at San Francisco arose from 'the fear that the veto power' preserved in Article 53(1) 'might cripple the functioning of regional arrangements'.[103] Consequently regional arrangements were granted the right of collective self-defence in Article 51, a right which could be exercised 'until the Security Council has taken measures necessary to maintain international peace and security'. Whereas Article 53(1) allows the Security Council to veto any proposed enforcement action by a regional organisation, Article 51 effectively removes action taken in collective self-defence from being vetoed, at least at the outset of the action.

Writers have tended to concentrate on the difference between regional organisations in the nature of collective self-defence pacts under Article 51 and regional organisations in the nature of 'arrangements' and 'agencies' under Chapter VIII, rather than looking to specific actions to see if they are of a defensive or an enforcement nature.[104] This writer takes the view that organisations such as NATO and the Warsaw Pact are not, *prima facie*, regional arrangements under Chapter VIII. Such arrangements are probably confined to those which have similar functions and powers to the United Nations as regards international peace, and perhaps as regards economic and social co-operation, except these powers are operated on a regional not a global basis. Organisations designed primarily to enhance the defence and military capabilities of power blocs do not fit this concept. This does not mean that such 'collective self-defence' pacts do not undertake enforcement action, but if they do, it should be authorised by the Security Council under Article 53(1). On the other hand, if a regional organisation, which primarily appears to come within Chapter VIII, operates, on occasions, solely in collective self-defence, it should not require such authorisation for it is acting under Article 51. Designating that a regional organisation comes within Article 51 or Chapter VIII is only a *prima facie* presumption that its actions will be based on those provisions, it does not prevent that organisation from taking collective self-defence action under Article 51 even if it is a regional arrangement under Chapter VIII; nor does it prevent a *prima facie* collective self-defence pact from taking enforcement action under Article 53(1) as long as it is authorised by the Security Council.

However, *de facto* the superpower dominated organisations – the OAS and the Warsaw Pact – ride roughshod over the provisions of Chapter VIII and Article 51. Even if the superpowers do make references to these Charter provisions, they are usually only using the Charter as a fig leaf to cover the naked abuse of power. However, whether this applies to regional organisations in the intermediate areas of the world – such as the Organisation of African Unity (OAU) – is doubtful. Nevertheless, there is one factor common to the OAS, the Warsaw Pact and the OAU, namely, that disputes in the areas of the world they cover are not usually the subject of Security Council action. In the case of the OAS and the Warsaw Pact this is because of the superpower veto, whereas, in the case of the OAU, it appears to be due to the fact that both superpowers are vying for influence that a 'hands-off' approach is taken.

The OAS appears to be a regional organisation for the purposes of Chapter VIII, not simply because its Charter specifically states that it is, but also because it is designed to perform similar functions to the United Nations on a hemispheric level. Nevertheless, it could act solely within Article 51 as a self-defence pact, a fact envisaged by its Charter.[105] Be that as it may, unfortunately the OAS has sometimes been used by its dominant member – the United States – in an attempt to legalise interventions aimed at purging 'ideological non-conformity' by one of the American States.[106]

A good example of a dispute in which the *de jure* supremacy of the Council gave way to the *de facto* supremacy of the OAS was the United States' intervention in the Dominican Republic in 1965. Originally solely a United States' operation, the OAS authorised the use of its own force,[107] which remained mainly composed of United States' troops. Predictably the Soviet Union took the view that, 'in order to cover up its armed intervention in the Dominican Republic' the United States was 'once more trying to retreat behind the screen of the Organisation of American States, which it long ago placed in the service of its imperialist aims'.[108]

The United States stated that the OAS action did not constitute 'enforcement' action within the meaning of Article 53(1) which required prior Council authorisation, arguing instead that the Organisation was undertaking a 'peacekeeping operation'.[109] Even if this were so, the Security Council, theoretically, was supreme and could only be disregarded initially if the action was in self-defence.

Nevertheless, considerable effort is put into arguments trying to circumvent Article 53(1). Chayes admits that since the quarantine imposed by the United States and rubber-stamped by the OAS during the Cuban missile crisis in

1962 was not in response to an 'armed attack', it could not be considered as self-defence. It was therefore enforcement action which was not forbidden by Article 53(1), according to Chayes, because that provision should be interpreted to allow regional enforcement action when the Council has failed to disapprove – a situation usually caused by the veto.[110]

Why does the United States manipulate the OAS and the provisions of the United Nations' Charter in attempts to legally justify its actions? It could, as the Soviet Union does, merely rely on spurious arguments of self-defence. Akehurst suggests that the reason for using the OAS is to give the action some degree of reasonableness, not necessarily legality.[111] United States' politicians seem to go further than this, evidenced by Robert Kennedy, then United States' Attorney General, commenting on the Cuban missile crisis: 'It was the vote of the Organisation of American States that gave the legal basis of the quarantine. It changed our position from that of an outlaw acting in violation of international law into a country acting in accordance with twenty allies legally protecting their position.'[112] Comments such as this suggest that in American matters the OAS is paramount over the Security Council, despite the provisions of the United Nations' Charter.

In its foreign policy, the United States puts a considerable amount of emphasis on legal justifications as evidenced by its manipulation of Chapter VIII. The Soviet Union has a much simpler approach. It uses its regional organisation – the Warsaw Pact – which, *prima facie*, is a self-defence pact, combined with a wide interpretation of Article 51, to maintain its hold on the Eastern bloc. This method circumvents the requirement of prior Security Council 'authorisation', for under Article 51, Council consideration and attempted measures follow any action taken in 'collective self-defence' and, of course, the Soviets are able to prevent any criticism by using the power of veto.

An example of the Soviet Union relying on Article 51 was during the Czechoslovakian crisis of 1968.[113] However, in the absence of an 'armed attack', the Soviets' reliance on Article 51 is transparent. In reality it represents a mechanism whereby intra-bloc disputes are kept from being the subject of Security Council measures.

So far the examination of regional organisations fits in with the previous analysis of intra-bloc interventions by the superpowers. One would have thought that in the intermediate areas of the world the Security Council would not be restricted by arguments in favour of regionalism. Africa and its regional body – the OAU – are the most striking examples. However, in the case of the OAU, it is true to say that after the United Nations' involvement in the Congo ended in 1964 there has been little Security Council interference in independent black Africa.[114]

There are remarkable similarities between the civil war in the Congo and the three-year-long Nigerian civil war (1967–70). Both involved problems of secession arising out of the artificial boundaries left by colonial powers, and both involved extensive suffering and loss of life. Yet the Congo produced a United Nations' involvement second only to Korea, whereas the Biafran tragedy was virtually ignored by the world Organisation. On no occasion was it discussed in the Security Council. The Secretary General of the United Nations had initially explored the possibility of exercising his good offices, but when he spoke before the 5th session of the OAU Assembly he stated that 'the OAU should be the most appropriate instrument for the promotion of peace in Nigeria'.[115]

Since the establishment of the OAU[116] in May 1963, the Security Council has avoided even discussing many significant conflicts within the continent. This cannot be due entirely to a 'hands-off' attitude from the permanent members because there is often a significant permanent member involvement in many of the conflicts. It might be that the permanent members, particularly the superpowers, are playing the regionalism card knowing that the OAU is powerless to stop them intervening in Africa.

In 1977–78, the Congo (renamed Zaire) again became an area of conflict with international repercussions. In March 1977 a force from Angola invaded the southern province of Shaba (formerly Katanga). President Mobutu of Zaire alleged that the insurgents were Soviet/Cuban backed with a core composed of remnants of the Katangese secessionists of the early 1960s. When a larger force invaded Shaba in May 1978, French and Belgian paratroops became involved, ostensibly to rescue Europeans trapped in the mining town of Kolwesi, although in so doing they helped to repel the invaders. The matter was not discussed before the Council, nor the OAU, probably in silent recognition of the fact that the conflict was a product of the uneasy and unstable spheres of influence in the area, with Soviet involvement in Angola and Western support for Zaire.[117] Before the area became a power frontier between East and West, in other words, when Angola was still a Portuguese colony, the Security Council expressly preferred that the OAU should seek a peaceful solution after the United States and Belgium had intervened in the Congo to rescue white nationals held hostage in Stanleyville in December 1964.[118]

The sometimes ephemeral nature of the superpowers' influence in the continent is illustrated by the conflict in the Horn of Africa in 1977–78. Prior to 1977 Ethiopia had received aid from the United States, whereas Somalia was heavily supported by Moscow pursuant to a Soviet/Somali Treaty of Friendship signed in 1974. However, when American aid to Ethiopia was withdrawn because of human rights abuses the Soviets started supporting Ethiopia as well as Somalia. Such was the situation when war broke out in June 1977 between the two countries in the disputed Ogaden desert. The conflict lasted until March 1978 when Somali troops withdrew from the Ogaden after a joint Cuban and Ethiopian offensive. The conflict appeared to be a 'breach of the peace' and should have involved the Security Council. It did not meet probably because of anticipation of a Soviet veto combined with an apparent general policy of leaving such matters to the OAU. The OAU produced little by way of positive measures. Its eight nation mediation committee merely reaffirmed the inviolability of frontiers inherited from the colonial era.[119]

Vestiges of colonialism are probably significant factors in determining why the Security Council has little involvement in black Africa. Significant Council intervention could upset African members who may see it as a form of neo-colonialism, and yet as we have seen, the superpowers are quite heavily involved in Africa. Even former colonial powers still play a role in African affairs. The French role in the decade-long conflict between Chad and Libya is but one example.[120] It is a paradoxical situation in which seemingly fiercely independent African States are only prepared to conciliate through the OAU and yet they are subject to superpower intervention. The fundamental reason for this is probably the economic dependence of many African States on Western and Soviet aid.

Most of the conflicts examined so far have involved permanent members, so making Council action unlikely. The major exception is the Biafran tragedy which indicates that even if there is no Great Power involvement the Security Council is still unwilling to intervene in black Africa. It may be argued that Biafra was essentially an internal dispute and so excluded from Council purview by Article 2(7). It will be seen later that situations such as Biafra, and Sri Lanka today, in which there are major atrocities and serious loss of life are of 'international concern' and as such escape the limitation in Article 2(7).[121]

Conclusions

The following is a brief summary of the geopolitical limitations on the competence of the Security Council.

Generally, in conflicts within the superpowers' respective blocs the Security Council will be prevented from taking action by the use of the veto. Similarly, in conflicts or disputes that are inter-bloc, in other words, which are cases of East-West confrontation, the Security Council will be paralysed. Nevertheless, the Council may perform a peripheral role in the settlement of inter-bloc disputes in that it sometimes is a prelude to a settlement by diplomacy. However, whether such open debates are a necessary prerequisite to successful settlement remains doubtful.

In the intermediate areas of the world beyond the power blocs, the Security Council may operate without geopolitical restriction, unless the superpowers are trying to establish a sphere of influence in that particular area; or even, in some cases, are merely protecting a State in which one of them has an indirect involvement or limited interest.

Intra-bloc disputes are often accompanied by arguments in favour of regionalism being paramount over universalism. *De jure*, the Charter of the United Nations maintains that the Security Council remains paramount; *de facto*, the superpowers have ensured that their regional organisations are supreme.

Even in the intermediate areas, the Security Council may show undue deference to a regional body. This may either be due to the fact that the super-powers are vying for control in these areas and are prepared to let a weak regional body provide the necessary veneer of pacific settlement while not getting to the substance of the problem, or it may be due to pure disinterest which amounts to a policy of leaving disputes in a particularly unimportant area to the relevant regional organisation. Thus, lack of Security Council concern could be due to the fact that the area is too strategically important or, conversely, too strategically unimportant.

The question remains: How could more areas of the world be opened up to the positive and objective scrutiny of the Security Council?

It would be unrealistic to expect the permanent members of the Security Council to cast their votes in favour of the abolition of the veto power as required by Article 109.[122] The most that could be expected would be a gentlemen's agreement between the permanent members to veto only when their vital interests are affected, instead of vetoing in situations where they have only a limited concern. In the light of the recent thaw in East–West relations this scenario, from being remote, now appears to be a possibility.

A realistic reform would be to alter the rules of procedure to ensure that the Security Council is forced to scrutinise all international conflicts. At the moment the methods of seizing the Security Council of a dispute rely on the initiative of States which allows for the non-discussion of certain disputes for geopolitical reasons. Procedural reform, of course, would not prevent the operation of the veto but it might lead the Council not to think in terms of resolutions and of potential vetoes but in terms of providing accommodation and conciliation.[123]

Sohn has suggested a method whereby the Council would have to consider all disputes or conflicts endangering international peace, by taking the initiative of complaining to the Security Council out of the hands of States under Article 35, and putting it into the hands of the Secretary General and people appointed by him. These people or 'regional monitoring groups' would be placed strategically so as to be able to report on international violence. They would co-ordinate with regional organisations so that the Council and these regional organisations could act together, instead of at odds, in the settlement of disputes. The reports of these groups would be submitted by the Secretary General under Article 99 and so would, in all probability, have to be discussed by the Council.[124]

Notes

1 L. M. Goodrich, E. Hambro and P. S. Simons, *The Charter of the United Nations*, 215, 2nd ed. (1969).
2 UNCIO, vol. 11, 713. S. D. Bailey, *Voting in the Security Council*, 16–17 (1969).
3 H. V. Evatt, *The United Nations*, 53 (1948).
4 UNCIO, vol. 11, 714.
5 See R. B. Russell and J. E. Muther, *A History of the United Nations Charter*, 766 (1958).
6 UNCIO, vol. 11, 592.
7 Bailey, *Voting*, chapter 3.
8 But see SC Res. 188, 19 UN SCOR Resolutions 9 (1964).
9 R. Higgins, 'The Place of International Law in the Settlement of Disputes by the UN Security Council' 64 *A.J.I.L.*, (1970), 1, at 1.
10 But see J. P. Cot and A. Pellet, *La Charte des Nations Unies*, 607 (1985).
11 E. Luard, *The United Nations*, 26 (1979).
12 SC 987–8 mtgs, 16 UN SCOR (1961). UN doc. S/5033 (1961).
13 SC 749 mtg, 11 UN SCOR 31 (1956). UN docs S/3710 (1956), S/3713/REV 1 (1956).
14 I. S. Pogany, *The Security Council and the Arab-Israeli Conflict*, 55–78 (1984).
15 See also Bailey, *Voting*, 81.
16 SC 2350 mtg, 37 UN S/PV 81–84 (1982).
17 See E. McWhinney, *United Nations Law Making: Cultural and Ideological Relativism and International Law Making for an Era of Transition*, 88 (1984).
18 J. Fawcett, *Law and Power in International Relations*, 67 (1982).
19 See P. Keal, *Unspoken Rules and Superpower Dominance*, 7–33 (1983).
20 See G. I. Tunkin, 'Coexistence and International Law', 95 *Recueil des Cours* (1958), 49.
21 See J. Gittings, in Chomsky, Steele and Gittings, *Superpowers in Collision: The New Cold War of the 1980s*, chapter 4, 2nd ed. (1984).
22 E. Luard, *A History of the United Nations: Vol. 1 The Years of Western Domination 1945–1955*, (1982).
23 See 'Regionalism' at pp. 21–6ff.
24 UN doc. S/3232 (1954).
25 See SC 676 mtg, 9 UN SCOR (1954).
26 SC Res. 104, 9 UN SCOR Resolutions 4 (1954).
27 SC 675 mtg, 9 UN SCOR (1954).
28 See I. Dore, *International Law and the Superpowers: Normative Order in a Divided World*, 55 (1984).
29 See generally the report of the UN Special Committee on the problem of Hungary, 11 UN GAOR Supp. (No. 18) (1956).
30 UN doc. S/3730/REV 1 (1956).
31 SC 754 mtg, 11 UN SCOR (1956).
32 A form of defence not envisaged by Article 51, Cot and Pellet, *La Charte*, 787.
33 UN doc. S/6316 (1965).
34 UN doc. S/6328 (1965).
35 SC 1214 mtg, 20 UN SCOR (1965).
36 SC Res. 203 and 205, 20 UN SCOR Resolutions 10 (1965).
37 SC 1196 mtg, 20 UN SCOR 19 (1965); paralleling the Johnson Doctrine, 52 *US Dept of State Bulletin* (1965), 29.
38 UN doc. S/8758 (1968).
39 20 *Current Digest of the Soviet Press*, No. 46, 3–4.
40 SC 1441 mtg, 23 UN SCOR 8 (1968).

41 UN docs. S/8761, S/8767 (1968), Denmark, Canada.
42 But see Dore, *International Law in a Divided World*, 87.
43 UN doc. S/13724 (1980).
44 UN doc. S/13729 (1980). SC 2190 mtg, 35 UN SCOR (1980).
45 16 *Weekly Compendium of Presidential Documents* (1980), 197.
46 See W. M. Reisman, 'Critical Defence Zones and International Law: the Reagan Codicil', 76 *A.J.I.L.* (1982), 589.
47 See 27 *I.L.M.* (1988), 577 for Geneva Accords. See UN doc. 17 February 1989 for withdrawal.
48 78 *A.J.I.L.* (1984), 645.
49 S. Rosenfeld, 'The Guns of July', 64 *Foreign Affairs* (1986), 698, at 699.
50 S/19638 (1988). SC 2802 mtg, 43 UN S/PV (1988).
51 UN doc. S/16077/REV 1 (1983).
52 UN doc. S/14941 (1982). SC 2347 mtg, 37 UN S/PV 56 (1982). But see SC Res. 530, 38 UN SCOR Resolutions 10 (1983).
53 *Case Concerning Military and Paramilitary Activities in and Against Nicaragua*, I.C.J. *Rep* 1986, 14.
54 UN docs. S/18250, S/18428 (1986).
55 SC 2716 mtg, 41 UN S/PV 6–16 (1986).
56 26 *I.L.M.* (1987), 1164. 27 *I.L.M.* (1988), 922.
57 SC 2108 mtg, 34 UN SCOR 9–11 (1979).
58 See SC 2129 mtg, 34 UN SCOR 8 (1979).
59 UN docs. S/13027, S/13162 (1979).
60 See generally D. Nicol, 'The People's Republic of China in the Security Council' in Nicol (ed.), *Paths to Peace*, 128–9 (1981).
61 SC 4 mtg, 1 UN SCOR (1946).
62 Trygve Lie, *In the Cause of Peace*, 75 (1954).
63 See UN doc. S/1 (1946).
64 SC Res. 3, 1 UN SCOR Resolutions 2 (1946).
65 See SC 22 mtg, 1 UN SCOR 437 (1946).
66 T. M. Franck, *Nation against Nation*, 27–33 (1985).
67 See generally A. Chayes, *The Cuban Missile Crisis*, (1974). B. Urquhart, *A Life in Peace and War*, 192–3 (1987).
68 SC 1022 mtg, 17 UN SCOR (1962). UN doc. S/5182 (1962).
69 UN doc. S/5187 (1962).
70 UN doc. S/5191 (1962). SC 1024 mtg, 17 UN SCOR 21 (1962).
71 UN doc. S/5197 (1962).
72 See generally T. M. Franck, 'Who killed Article 2(4)', 62 *A.J.I.L.* (1970), 809. J. F. Murphy, *The United Nations and the Control of International Violence*, 135–206 (1985).
73 See C. Bown and P. J. Mooney, *Cold War to Detente*, 93, 97, 2nd ed. (1986).
74 See D. D. Eisenhower, *Mandate for Change*, 333 (1963).
75 See Bown and Mooney, *Cold War*, 115–30.
76 *Ibid.*, 50–2.
77 See generally R. F. Randle, *Geneva 1954: The Settlement of the Indochinese War*, (1969).
78 Misc. 20 (1954), Cmnd 9239.
79 Eisenhower, *Mandate*, 372.
80 See generally M. S. Rajan, and T. Israel, 'The United Nations and the Conflict in Vietnam' in the American Society of International Law, *The Vietnam War and International Law*, vol. 4, 114–43 (1976).

81 UN doc. S/4212 (1959).
82 SC Res. 132, 14 UN SCOR Resolutions 2 (1959). SC 847 mtg, 14 UN SCOR (1959).
83 UN doc. S/4236 (1959).
84 UN doc. S/5697 (1964).
85 SC 1126 mtg, 19 UN SCOR 11 (1964).
86 UN doc. S/5888 (1964).
87 UN doc. S/7106 (1966).
88 SC 1273 mtg, 21 UN SCOR 3 (1966).
89 See GA plen. mtgs 1411–14, 1416, 1418, 1420–4, 1426, 1430, 1432, 1434–8, 1440–7, 1501, 21 GAOR (1966).
90 See generally, *Documents on International Affairs*, 121–42 (1954).
91 *Peking Review*, 16 April 1965.
92 UN doc. A/8401/ADD 1 (1971).
93 60 *A.J.I.L.* (1966), 565.
94 See *United Nations Yearbook* (1966), 147, 152. *UN Monthly Chronicle* (1967), 69.
95 For 1973 Paris conference peace agreement, see 67 *A.J.I.L.* (1973), 389.
96 See Steele, *Superpowers in Collision*, 59–60.
97 Dore, *Intenational Law in a Divided World*, 77.
98 See *The Guardian*, 30 April 1986.
99 From SC Res. 387, 31 UN SCOR Resolutions 10 (1976), to SC Res. 606, 42 UN SCOR Resolutions 13 (1987).
100 See SC 1906 mtg, 31 UN SCOR 20 (1976). SC 2767 mtg, 42 UN S/PV (1987).
101 See SC 2607 mtg, 40 UN SCOR 28 (1985).
102 See Keesing's *Contemporary Archives* (1988), 36380, referred to as *Keesing*.
103 E. Berberg, 'Regional Organisations: A United Nations Problem', 49 *A.J.I.L.* (1955), 166 at 169.
104 M. Akehurst, 'Enforcement Action by Regional Agencies with Special Reference to the OAS', 42 *B.Y.I.L.* (1967), 175. H. Kelsen, 'Is the North Atlantic Treaty a Regional Arrangement?', 45 *A.J.I.L.* (1951), 162. A.L. Goodhart, 'The North Atlantic Treaty of 1949', 88 *Recueil des Cours* (1951), 187. E.W. Beckett, *The North Atlantic Treaty, the Brussels Treaty and the Charter of the United Nations*, (1950).
105 Articles 1–3 and 27 of the OAS Charter. 119 UNTS 4.
106 Franck, *Nation against Nation*, 824.
107 UN doc. S/6333/REV 1 (1965).
108 UN doc. S/6317 (1965).
109 SC 1200 mtg, 20 UN SCOR 33 (1965).
110 Chayes, *The Cuban Missile Crisis*, 61.
111 Akehurst, 42 *B.Y.I.L.* (1967), 222.
112 R. Kennedy, *Thirteen Days*, 121 (1969).
113 SC 1441 mtg, 23 UN SCOR 8 (1968).
114 Here 'black Africa' excludes the white minority regimes both past and present in southern Africa.
115 See UN Press Release SG/SM/998, 13 September 1968.
116 See generally B. Andemichael, *The OAU and the UN*, (1976).
117 See *Keesing* (1977), 28397–8400.
118 See SC Res. 199, 19 UN SCOR Resolutions 12 (1964).
119 See *Keesing* (1977), 28421–3, 28633–4; (1978), 28760, 28989, 29537.
120 Discussed in SC 2060 mtg, 33 UN SCOR (1978).
121 See W.M. Reisman and M. McDougal, 'Humanitarian Intervention to protect the

Ibos' in Lillich (ed.), *Humanitarian Intervention and the United Nations*, 167 (1973).
122 But see D. Nicol, *The UN Security Council: Towards Greater Effectiveness*, appendix 2 (1982).
123 See E. Luard, *The United Nations*, 27 (1979).
124 L. B. Sohn, 'The Security Council's Role in the Settlement of International Disputes', 78 *A.J.I.L.* (1984), 402 at 404.

CHAPTER 2

The competence of the Security Council as provided by the Charter

Chapter 1 contained an examination of the geopolitical limitations on the competence of the Security Council. However, it would be wrong to say that these limitations were extra-legal, at least in their origins. The two principal geopolitical limitations, the power of the veto and the power of regional organisations, are both recognised in the Charter – in Article 27 and Chapter VIII respectively. They therefore remain legal limitations. It is the use of these powers in the Security Council that has created limitations which are strongly influenced, if not solely determined, by political and strategic considerations – considerations which often go beyond the powers provided by the Charter for the operation of the veto and of regional organisations. This chapter will contain an examination of the Charter provisions as to jurisdiction which provide the detail within the framework of the larger scale, global limitations elucidated in chapter 1. The difference is essentially one of scale for it will be seen that many jurisdictional questions examined by the Security Council, for example the determination of a 'threat to the peace' within Article 39, are, in essence, political decisions. That is not to say that legal considerations do not play an important role on occasions, but such considerations only provide a counter-weight to the permanent members' interests which, if sufficiently strong, will predominate.

This chapter will consider the relative openness of the Charter system regarding the maintenance of international peace and security through the Security Council; in other words whether there is any equivalence between the norm of *jus cogens* contained in Article 2(4) and the situations contained in Article 39 which give the Security Council jurisdiction under Chapter VII. Perhaps this may help us to distinguish between the type of situation, dispute or conflict which gives the Council competence under Chapter VI, and the type which gives it jurisdiction under Chapter VII. We may discover that there is no essential difference and that what determines competence under each Chapter are political factors. To elucidate whether there is a distinct type of situation which is dealt with under Chapter VII an attempt will be made to find a consistent practice of the usage of, and perhaps even arrive at definitions of, the terms used in Article 39 — 'threat to the peace', 'breach of the peace' and 'act of aggression'. The analysis will then be concerned with whether the domestic jurisdiction limitation contained in Article 2(7) has any effect on the Council's competence. Once we have distinguished between the elements which spark off jurisdiction under Chapter VI and Chapter VII, the question of whether there is an essential difference in the nature of resolutions adopted under each Chapter will be examined. In essence, this will involve an exami-nation of the mandatory/ recommendatory dichotomy.

The essence of this chapter is to define the factors which give, and the limitations upon, the Council's jurisdiction as contained in the Charter. It is not concerned with the powers that are at the Council's disposal once it has jurisdiction. An examination of the powers and effectiveness of the Council is left to chapter 3.

Whether the Security Council's jurisdiction is limited by Article 2(4)

Article 2(4) is a peremptory norm of international law and a fundamental provision of the Charter.[1] It states that all 'Members shall refrain in their international relations from the threat or use of force'. Since Article 2(4) purports to control the use of force by stating a norm of international law to which States must conform, and the Security Council is concerned with maintaining international peace by taking action against States using force in contravention of Article 2(4), one might think that there would be a correlation between Article 2(4) and the competence of the Security Council. In other words, one might argue that the Security Council can only deal with actual or potential breaches of Article 2(4). Chapter VI may be seen to deal with potential breaches, whereas Chapter VII deals with actual breaches of Article 2(4). To agree with this hypothesis would be to accept a direct relationship between 'threat or use of force' under Article 2(4) and a 'threat to the peace', 'breach of the peace' and 'act of aggression' under Article 39. In other words 'threat of force' corresponds with 'threat to the peace' and 'use of force' is equivalent to a 'breach of the peace' and 'act of aggression'. This necessarily would entail limiting the Security Council to situations which are or potentially could be breaches of Article 2(4). Such a thesis envisages that the Charter established a 'closed' rather than an 'open' system. The Security Council's competence would be defined, at its limits, by Article 2(4); to go beyond that and, say, determine that a situation was a 'threat to the peace' when it was not a 'threat of force' would be *ultra vires* the Charter.

The above analysis contains an inherent weakness in the arguments for a closed system, in that equating Article 2(4) with Article 39, it pushes to one side potential breaches of Article 2(4) which may be caught under Chapter VI or under Article 39. The introduction of a wide, discretionary concept such as a potential breach of Article 2(4), weakens the argument beyond repair, because it would allow the Council to deal with a wide range of disputes that may theoretically breach Article 2(4) in time, but in reality, are unlikely to do so.

The main advocate of a closed Charter system by which the Security Council's ultimate competence is defined by international law in the form of Article 2(4) is Arntz.[2] Kelsen, on the other hand, states that it is 'completely within the discretion of the Security Council as to what constitutes a threat to the peace'.[3] Kelsen and Higgins[4] state that because the Council is not fettered in its powers of determination under Article 39, such a determination, in a case where no obligation stipulated by customary international law or Charter law is breached, can create new law as to what constitutes a threat to or breach of the peace. In other words, the Security Council's jurisdiction is not limited by international law.[5]

As is to be expected from a politically orientated body, the Security Council has, in practice, manifested a preference for the open system. In particular it has applied the concept of a 'threat to the peace' to essentially internal situations. Arntz argues that internal situations are not within the ambit of Article 39 because they do not constitute a 'threat of force' against another State within the meaning of Article 2(4). He argues that the text of the Charter, particularly the preamble and Article 1, indicate that 'peace' is the antithesis of war, and so the Charter deals only with threats to or breaches of inter-state or international peace, and not to intra-state or internal peace. However, the evidence is that if an internal situation or civil war is serious enough the Security Council will become involved, subject, of course, to political limitations. This is sufficient, in itself, to destroy the closed Charter theory.[6]

For instance, in 1966 the Council determined that the 'situation in Southern Rhodesia constitutes a threat to international peace and security'.[7] It cannot really be denied that the only 'threat or use of force' arose from the activities of the guerrillas infiltrating Rhodesia from the frontline African States. Nevertheless, the Council decided that the situation in Southern Rhodesia itself constituted a 'threat to the peace', evidenced by its policy of imposing sanctions against Rhodesia.[8]

In 1977, the Security Council determined 'having regard to the policies and acts of the South African Government, that the acquisition by South Africa of arms and related matériel constitutes a threat to the maintenance of international peace and security'.[9] It could be argued that the 'acts' referred to are the frequent punitive attacks against the frontline countries of Botswana, Angola, Zambia, Zimbabwe, Mozambique and Lesotho, and so the 'threat to the peace' has the international character that Arntz's formulation requires. Indeed, the resolution makes reference to South Africa's 'persistent acts of aggression against neighbouring States'. However, the resolution also refers to the 'policies' of the South African government and calls for the elimination of apartheid and racial discrimination within the country. Given that the resolution was adopted against a background of riots and killing in the black townships, it is submitted that it is the internal system of apartheid that constitutes the 'threat to the peace' with the border conflicts being manifestations of that threat.[10]

A parallel can be drawn with the arrival of oil tankers at Beira carrying oil for Rhodesia − an event which the Security Council seemed to view, in resolution 221,[11] as being, in itself, a 'threat to the peace'. However, the real threat was the situation in Southern Rhodesia itself, a fact later recognised by the Council in resolution 232. The Council initially made a limited finding of a threat because of political factors.[12] The same can be said of South Africa, where the Western members refuse to allow a general finding of a threat.[13]

It is often forgotten that the Council determined that there was a 'threat to the peace' arising from the crisis in the Congo[14] after the situation had deteriorated so badly as to constitute a civil war. It is arguable whether this was an internal situation as such with Belgian support for Tshombe and Soviet aid to Lumumba. However, there was certainly no direct 'threat or use of force' by one State against another. At the time the Council found a 'threat to the peace' in resolution 161 the main foreign element of force consisted of the few hundred mercenaries employed by Tshombe to maintain Katanga's secession. The crisis had international repercussions in that the civil war could suck in outside forces, including the superpowers, and that was why the internal civil war in the Congo was a threat to international peace. The linkage of the civil war in the Congo and the threat to international peace was emphasised in resolution 161.

The Security Council's measures against the Smith regime in Southern Rhodesia is the main thorn in the side of the advocates of a closed Charter system, although the situations in South Africa and the Congo are sufficient, in themselves, to cast doubt on this view. All three situations involved international repercussions of varying degrees, but it must be remembered that these repercussions derive from the internal situation itself. To be sure, the Council often refuses to find a 'threat to the peace' in situations that seem to fit the Rhodesian model. Portugal's failure to implement the General Assembly's 'Declaration on the Granting of Independence to Colonial Countries and Peoples'[15] is one example. The Council went as far as to adopt a resolution in Addis Ababa which found that the 'situation resulting from the policies of Portugal both in its colonies and in its constant provocations against neighbouring States seriously disturbs international peace and security'.[16] Although this falls short of a finding under Article 39, there is evidence to suggest that a finding of a 'threat to the peace' might eventually have been made as a result of international pressure against Western members had the Salazar regime survived in 1974.[17]

The above analysis suggests that a finding of a 'threat to the peace' is, to a large degree, a political decision on the part of the Council, and so such a finding as regards a wholly internal situation is not precluded. Generally, however, the permanent members are not going to exercise this discretion unless the situation has potential international repercussions which could affect their interests, or even involve them in an escalating conflict. An alternative and no less plausible viewpoint would be to say that changing political views shape and change the legal meaning of concepts such as 'threat to the peace'.

The difference between a 'danger to international peace and security' and a 'threat to the peace'

The provisions of Chapter VI refer, in several instances, to a 'dispute' or 'situation' which is 'likely to endanger the maintenance of international peace and security'.[18] To save repeating this ungainly formula, the phrase 'danger to international peace' will be used to signify the set of circumstances to be dealt with using the pacific settlement powers of the Council contained in Chapter VI of the Charter. The title of Chapter VII reads 'action with respect to threats to the peace, breaches of the peace, and acts of aggression'. These terms are repeated in Article 39 which make it clear that the set of circumstances to be dealt with under Chapter VII are threats to or breaches of international peace.

This section will be concerned with determining whether there is any objective difference between situations or conflicts dealt with under Chapter VI and those dealt with under Chapter VII, or whether the Security Council treats the powers contained in the two Chapters as one continuum, using them selectively and interchangeably as political factors, including the need for consensus, dictate. The main area of this analysis will concern the fine distinction, if one can be drawn, between a 'danger to international peace' and a 'threat to the peace'.

So close is the relationship between a 'danger' and a 'threat' that it will become clear from the following analysis that there is often no substantive factual distinction between the two. They are, in effect, often merely 'labels' put into the resolutions to indicate the political climate in the Council. Conceptually, however, there is a legal distinction between a 'danger' and a 'threat'. The latter, for example, is often used as a legal tool to facilitate the imposition of mandatory measures under Chapter VII, a function which the label 'danger' is not legally qualified to perform.

To say that there is little practical difference between a 'danger to international peace' and a 'threat to the peace' is not so radical as it may first appear. At San Francisco, the Dumbarton Oaks proposals had provided for a link between Chapters VI and VII. The proposals had a provision at the beginning of what emerged to be Chapter VII of the Charter which empowered the Council to find a 'threat to the maintenance of international peace and security' if the procedures in what is now Article 33(1) or recommendations in Article 36(1) had failed or had been ignored.[19] In other words, the scale and the nature of the conflict may not have altered significantly since the Council had purported to deal with it under Chapter VI. The factor which converted a danger to international peace under Chapter VI to a threat to the peace under Chapter VII was not necessarily a change in the nature of the conflict (except its prolongation) but a failure by the Council to end it under Chapter VI. The provision was dropped at San Francisco, not because it brought the concepts of danger and threat too close together, but because it fettered the Council's operation of its powers,[20] that is it might have prevented the complete unfettered discretion of the Council in determining whether a situation was a 'threat to the peace' or not. This was despite the fact that the proposed provision would have been of relative insignificance in practice for it was, itself, discretionary.

Nevertheless, in its formative years the Council did seem to develop a jurisprudence purporting to differentiate between a danger and a threat to international peace, revealed most clearly by the Spanish question in 1946. The Council adopted a resolution establishing a sub-committee of five members[21] to determine whether the existence and activities of the Franco regime in Spain endangered international peace and security. The sub-committee reported that the situation was of 'international concern' but not yet a 'threat to the peace' within Article 39. There was a 'potential menace to international peace' and therefore 'a situation likely to endanger international peace' within Article 34.[22]

The sub-committee thus created a distinction between a potential threat to the peace which corresponds to a danger within Chapter VI and an actual or real threat within Article 39. There is no further development of the distinction in the report except the factual findings that Spain had no imminent warlike intentions, which suggests that the test is the relative immediacy of the war or conflict. However, the probable reason for distinguishing between a potential and an actual threat was that the sub-committee was labouring under an understandable view that Chapter VII was a 'very sharp instrument'[23] which enabled the United Nations to wage war if necessary. This belief meant that it was reluctant to find a threat unless there was a very real and immediate danger to international peace which there was not in Spain.

However, the powers of Chapter VII have been revealed to be not as formidable as believed in 1946. This has resulted in the relaxation of the distinctions between a danger and a threat. Nevertheless, the motivating factor behind the Council's finding or not finding a 'threat to the peace' remains, in most cases, the reluctance by some members to impose economic sanctions under Chapter VII.

The development of the Security Council's arms embargo against South

Africa is interesting for it reveals that often the difference between a potential threat and an actual threat or a danger and a threat is not an increase in the level of violence of a dispute or conflict, but the ephemeral motives and interests of the members of the Council. The Western members see the protection of their economic interests in South Africa as vital, and therefore their general aim is to stop a mandatory set of sanctions being imposed against the Pretoria government. Nevertheless, the international pressure on South Africa, and consequently on Western governments, has forced them to grant some concessions. Thus, changing political factors affect the Council's jurisdictional finding often to a greater extent than any legal criteria.

In 1963 the Council called upon all States to cease the shipment of arms and military material to South Africa after expressing its conviction 'that the situation in South Africa is seriously disturbing international peace and security'.[24] The call was only voluntary, with the phrase 'seriously disturbing' seemingly equivalent to 'likely to endanger'. As we have seen, this was eventually made mandatory in 1977 with a determination that the supply of arms to South Africa constituted a 'threat to the peace'. The finding of a 'threat' accompanied by a partial embargo was delayed by the intransigence of Western States until 1977 mainly because it was not until this time that South Africa had become fully armed.[25] There may have been a change in the nature of the situation due to an increased level of violence within South Africa which may have influenced the Council in its determination of a threat, though by far the most significant factors were the political interests of the Western States.[26]

The gradual change in the Council's collective will can be traced in the language of its resolutions on South Africa. By 1970, the determination was that, 'the situation resulting from the continued policies of apartheid and the constant build up of the South African military and police forces constitutes a potential threat to international peace and security'.[27] The original draft resolution sponsored by the Non Aligned members of the Council[28] contained the phrase 'serious threat', but with Western opposition the second and final draft amended this to 'potential threat'. The representative of the United Kingdom expressed the West's opposition to the earlier drafts using the language of Chapter VII, whereas the phrase 'potential threat' was not objectionable on those grounds.[29] With the prevention of Chapter VII achieved, the resolution's call for an arms embargo was generally accepted to be only recommendatory, even though it also referred to a 'real threat to the security' of surrounding African States due to the arms build up in South Africa.

'Likely to endanger international peace',[30] 'seriously disturbing international peace', 'threats to the security' of neighbouring States, 'potential threat to international peace' and a 'threat to international peace' are terms used by the Council. They could be said to be arranged here in a scale of ascendancy with the last being the most serious and the only one which is recognised as representing an implied finding under Article 39. The factors which produce a move up or down the scale are a combination of factual and determinable change in the level and nature of the conflict and also political and strategic adjustments by the members of the Security Council, particularly the permanent members. The political factors being the stronger, the phraseology used should be seen as an indicator of a change in political will rather than providing any significant criteria by which one can legally define the difference between a danger to international peace and a threat to international peace. Nevertheless, political factors primarily influence the timing of a finding of a 'threat to the peace'. Once a finding is made it is possible to determine why a situation is a 'threat to the peace' and to construct a legal definition. In doing this one should try to ignore the political factors which influenced the designation of the situation as a threat to the peace at a particular time, for it may well be that, legally speaking, such a threat had existed for many years prior to the finding.

The influence of political factors in finding a 'threat to the peace' in the Rhodesian situation illustrates the influence a solitary permanent member can have. Resolution 216, adopted on 12 November 1965, condemned the Unilateral Declaration of Independence (UDI) and called upon States not to recognise the 'illegal regime' or render any assistance to it. The resolution contained no determination of a danger to international peace nor of a threat to the peace because it arose from the desire to find a compromise between a British draft resolution,[31] which determined that the 'continuance of the resulting situation is likely to endanger the maintenance of international peace and security', and a draft resolution proposed by the Ivory Coast[32] which stated that the declaration of independence constituted a 'threat to international peace and security'. The difference in terminology arose principally because of the British and Western view that Rhodesia should not be subjected to punitive sanctions but to a policy of gradually escalating sanctions to urge peaceful change, whereas the Afro-Asian and Communist view was that Rhodesia should be the subject of immediate and punitive mandatory sanctions and possibly the use of military force.[33] This divergence was not primarily due to different perceptions of the nature of the situation in Rhodesia. According to the General Assembly a 'threat to the peace' had existed in 1963,[34] and since the Assembly's resolutions are also politically motivated to a great extent, it may well be that a 'threat to the peace' had existed for some years prior to the Assembly so deciding.

Due to the United Kingdom's hold over the other members of the Council in the form of its veto, the Council's resolutions reflected the British policy rather than that of the Afro-Asian States.[35] The Council gradually moved towards a finding of a threat to the peace with a corresponding move from voluntary to mandatory measures which were eventually made comprehensive.

Resolution 217, adopted on 20 November 1965, determined that the 'continuance in time' of the Rhodesian situation 'constitutes a threat to international
peace and security'.[36] This phrase appears to be akin to a 'potential threat'
and so it was no surprise when the Council found a 'threat to the peace' specifically in relation to the oil tankers arriving at Beira,[37] then a general finding
of a 'threat to the peace' as regards the Southern Rhodesian situation as a
whole,[38] accompanied by the imposition of mandatory sanctions which were
later made comprehensive.

An intermediate finding of a potential threat is generally indicative of the
Council members' first consensual step towards an implied finding under
Article 39. Ambassador Goldberg of the United States summarised the state of
the Council's deliberations when voting on resolution 217, stating that it did 'not
mention whether Chapter VI or Chapter VII is brought to bear. My Government agrees with this interpretation of the text'.[39] This bizarre comment
merely reflects the mid-point between the polarised views of the other Council
members. For example, the Ivory Coast believed that resolution 217 imposed
mandatory sanctions, whereas the British viewed it as 'not falling under
Chapter VII'.[40]

The phrase 'potential threat', which conceptually appears to be no
different to a danger to the peace, is a product of the requirement of
the need for consensus in a body dominated by the veto power. If some
members want a finding of a threat accompanied by Chapter VII action,
whilst others, for equally political reasons, desire only a finding of a
danger and a recommendation of peaceful settlement under Chapter
VI, in order to produce some sort of resolution a compromise is often
achieved by the use of 'potential threat', accompanied perhaps by voluntary measures. If a compromise is not achieved the veto will inevitably
be used.

The need for consensus may produce a jurisdictional finding of a potential
threat or it may result in no finding being made at all,[41] or it may manifest itself in the appearance of two different types of finding. After considering a
complaint by Senegal of armed attacks by Portugal from its colony in Guinea-
Bissau,[42] the Council adopted resolution 294 on 15 July 1971 in which it was,
on the one hand, 'conscious of its duty to remove threats to international peace
and security' and, on the other, gravely concerned that such incidents 'might
endanger international peace and security'. The resolution created a Special
Mission to investigate the complaint. The resolution was a compromise between
Western members who desired to protect their NATO ally from more than just
formal censure and the Non Aligned and Socialist States desiring Chapter VII
action.[43]

Such resolutions give rise to charges of inconsistency being levelled
against the Council, even that it has not developed any coherent policy
or norms to guide States' behaviour.[44] One must remember that the Council

is a political body in which the national interests of States are going to be paramount over any consideration of creating any international policies.

Probably the most hurtful action the Council can take against a State is of a mandatory kind under Article 41. Such mandatory action usually follows a finding of a 'threat to the peace', which means that such a finding will only be made exceptionally because of the possible serious consequences. The result is that an implied finding − whether a threat to or breach of the peace or an act of aggression − under Article 39 is unlikely to be made, particularly if accompanied by mandatory measures.[45] Given the unlikelihood of the Council utilising mandatory measures, it has developed the range of its 'lower order' recommendatory powers to include areas designated in the Charter as coming under Chapter VII. These include the power to recommend a cease-fire and a power to ask for voluntary measures. The conceptual home for these powers is Chapter VII − Articles 40 and 41 respectively − but because the Council has developed them as recommendatory it is common for them to be attributed to Chapter VI − namely Article 36.[46] Whether one designates them as coming within Article 36 or Article 40 or 41 is relatively unimportant; the significant factor is whether they are mandatory or recommendatory. As we shall see in chapter 3, the powers of the Security Council contained in Chapters VI and VII have become, in practice, one continuum, which creates a situation in which most, but not all, of the powers can either be mandatory or recommendatory.

Distinctions between and usage of 'threat to the peace', 'breach of the peace' and 'act of aggression'

'Threat to the peace'

We have seen in the above section that because of a delay caused by political factors in a finding of a 'threat to the peace' there appears to be little factual difference between a situation 'likely to endanger international peace' and a 'threat to international peace'. Undoubtedly, a 'threat to the peace' is a very flexible concept, covering anything from intra-state situations to inter-state disputes.[47] Nevertheless, if we ignore for a moment the confusion caused by political delay, it can be seen that, on the limited occasions of its use, the term 'threat to the peace' is taking on a conceptual form.

The most extensive use of the term, undoubtedly, was during the meetings of the Security Council between 1965 and 1968, although very few of the speakers explained why the situation in Southern Rhodesia was a threat to the peace. Perhaps the decision was a political one requiring no rational or conceptual deliberations by the members of the Council. However, the meeting of 16 December 1966, at which the first mandatory resolution of a more general nature was adopted, reveals that at least some of the representatives had applied their minds as to why an essentially internal situation was a threat to the peace. The representative of Jordan stated that UDI amounted to 'an invasion of the rights of the majority. It is an act of aggression that cannot be condoned. The answer to such invasion and aggression is Chapter VII.'[48] *Prima facie* he appears to be referring to an inter-state conflict rather than an internal situation; however, the 'invasion of the rights of the majority' clearly shows the primary reason for the situation being a threat to the peace, namely, the gross deprivation of human rights by the Smith regime, although, as the following analysis shows, another element in a threat to the peace is the potential spillover effect — the likelihood of internal violence spreading to become international violence. This writer believes that the spillover element in a finding of a threat is greatly overplayed because any situation where there is a significant deprivation of human rights has the potential to ignite international violence, for example through misconceived unilateral humanitarian intervention. Thus revealed it is the deprivation of human rights that is the true basis of a finding of a threat.

The threat to the peace in Rhodesia justified the Security Council undertaking collective humanitarian intervention using the weapon of mandatory sanctions. Is is unlikely that such a situation would have justified unilateral humanitarian intervention before 1945 because traditionally the pre-condition of such an intervention was the large scale loss of life not the deprivation of other human rights. It could be argued that the UN Charter has replaced the misused doctrine of humanitarian intervention with collective measures which may be used in a wider range of situations, because a power of collective humanitarian intervention is not generally subject to the political machinations of individual States.

Nevertheless, the violations of human rights by Smith's black successors in Zimbabwe's Matabeleland,[49] and the indifference shown by the United Nations to the Biafran rebellion in 1967, indicate that although the factual considerations may be present, political factors will often predominate to prevent such a finding — indeed, to prevent any finding whatsoever. These factors may limit a finding of a threat to colonialist, neo-colonialist or 'white racist' regimes.

It could be argued that in Matabeleland and Biafra the denial of human rights threatened only internal and not external peace, and that for a threat to the peace to be found an internal conflict must have the potential to ignite a wider conflict. This argument has already been dismissed, but even if correct, it would not exclude a factual finding of a threat to the peace as regards the form of government in South Africa. The Council has not made such a finding in general terms, although resolutions passed in condemnation of the system of apartheid have said as much without using the term. For example, resolution 473 of 13 June 1978 reaffirmed that, 'the policy of apartheid is a crime against the conscience and dignity of mankind and is incompatible with the rights and dignity of man, the Charter of the United Nations and the Universal Declaration of Human Rights and seriously disturbs international peace'. The last phrase appears to be added to keep the resolution within the bounds of Chapter VI. Nevertheless, designating apartheid as a 'crime against mankind' indicates that there is sufficient 'international concern' to rebut any arguments of domestic jurisdiction, even when the Council is acting within Chapter VI. However, only a finding of a threat to the peace will be sufficient if the Council is going to operate within Chapter VII.[50]

Such a finding would entail a political decision on the part of Western members of the Council for the legal requirements have existed for many years, not only in the form of gross deprivations of human rights, but also, until recently, by its illegal presence in, and practice of apartheid in, Namibia — a situation which the Council labelled a 'mounting threat'.[51] The evidence is that Western members are willing to allow findings of aggression and threats to the peace[52] as regards South African attacks on neighbouring States, but not to allow any mandatory measures to be directed against the perpetrator. The Western political lines are apparently being re-drawn to allow findings of individual incidents being categorised as threats, but not permitting a general finding nor any concrete Chapter VII measures.[53]

It appears that a 'threat to the peace' is the term the Council has shaped to use in situations of non-traditional international violence[54] in which the main danger to international peace is not a conflict between two or more States, but instead arises primarily from the internal events in one State, which may, as in the case of South Africa, manifest itself in the form of attacks upon other States. Whereas South Africa and Rhodesia are cases of human rights abuses caused by racist regimes, the crisis in the Congo was more akin to a civil war situation.[55] The problems of civil strife and human suffering were, in themselves, sufficient to warrant a finding of a threat to the peace,[56] although the Council tended to combine this with the menace caused by Belgian and mercenary military intervention.

In other conflicts the question of civil strife is often overshadowed by foreign intervention. In 1974, a Greek-backed coup against Archbishop Makarios followed by the Turkish invasion of the northern part of Cyprus led the Council to adopt resolution 353,[57] which stated that there was a 'serious threat to international peace and security' and demanded 'an end to foreign military intervention'. The threat to international peace was inherent in the civil strife between the Greek and the Turkish Cypriots, a fact recognised by resolution 186, adopted in 1964, which classified the violent eruptions on the island as 'likely to threaten international peace'. The Turkish invasion in 1974 was a manifestation and realisation of the threat.

Earlier practice of the Council does not reveal the same usage of 'threat to the peace' as does later practice, which is probably a reflection of the increasingly organised influence of the Non Aligned group of members sitting on the Council. In early years, a finding of a threat to the peace was viewed as a preliminary to a finding of a breach of the peace. The invasion of Palestine by the surrounding Arab countries after the proclamation of the State of Israel on 14 May 1948, eventually led the Council to classify the situation as a 'threat to the peace within the meaning of Article 39', and to order that 'pursuant to Article 40', there should be a cessation of hostilities which should take place 'not later than three days from the date' of the resolution. Any failure to comply 'would demonstrate the existence of a breach of the peace within Article 39'.[58] The Council was not saying that the Arab countries were threatening to breach the peace, for hostilities had already begun − it was the continuance in time of the conflict which would convert a threat into a breach of the peace.

Through its later practice the Council had developed a more complex and wide-ranging concept of threat. In 1969, Ireland requested a meeting of the Security Council[59] to consider the situation in Northern Ireland with a view to sending a United Nations' peacekeeping force to the province because of the serious disturbances caused by the alleged denial of civil rights to the Catholic community. Although the question was not even adopted on the agenda, it is interesting to note that Lord Caradon was sufficiently perturbed by Irish references to southern Africa that he not only relied on Article 2(7) as would be expected, but also denied that the situation in Northern Ireland was a threat to international peace.[60]

This illustrates that members do have in mind the wide concept of a threat to the peace. It must be noted, however, that whereas South Africa and Southern Rhodesia involved, *inter alia*, the suppression of the fundamental rights of the majority, justifying collective humanitarian intervention by the United Nations, in Northern Ireland it is only the minority that allege this suppression. Thus, Northern Ireland cannot be a threat to the peace even if the Irish view that Northern Ireland is a part of the Republic is subscribed to, because it still involves only the suppression of the rights of a minority − those Catholics in the six provinces.

As we have seen, in the earlier practice, threat to and breach of the peace were not always distinguishable, even though Kelsen's early commentary had contained a strikingly prescient differentiation.[61] He cites the case of Korea, saying that if the North Korean forces had not been the forces of a State, but a revolutionary group or insurgents making the Korean war a civil war, then there could be only a threat to the peace not a breach of the peace. Unlike the Council in the case of Palestine, Kelsen distinguished between the peace between States and the peace between one and the same State. A threat to the peace only applies to the latter, whereas a breach only applies to the former. Subsequent practice shows that Kelsen was essentially correct, with the proviso that a threat is not only applied to civil wars but to a much wider range of situations involving considerations of human rights and the principle of self-determination.

'Breach of the peace'

In practice, a breach of the peace has rarely been found, the recent preference being for findings of aggression. This is surprising for aggression is merely a special case of breach, Article 1(1) speaking of 'acts of aggression or other breaches of the peace'. Although a finding of aggression is much more condemnatory, often, as shall be seen, it produces little by way of sanctioning measures. 'Breach of the peace', although a much more neutral expression when applied to traditional international violence, has, on the three occasions on which it has been found, been accompanied by positive Council action.

The Australian representative attempted a reasonable definition of a breach of the peace during discussion of the Indonesian question, when he assumed that it meant 'a breach of international peace and applies to cases where hostilities are occurring, but where it is not alleged that one particular party is the aggressor or has committed an act of aggression'.[62] He advocated such a finding in relation to the conflict occurring in Indonesia.

The Dutch representative objected on the grounds that, 'what happened in Indonesia was not a breach of international peace but rather a breach of internal peace. Breaches of internal peace are and remain the exclusive responsibility of the Members of the United Nations on the territory of which those unfortunate occurrences take place.'[63]

A finding of a threat to the peace may have been more applicable if the situation was indeed a breach of internal peace. As will be seen later, a finding under Article 39 generally renders nugatory the application of Article 2(7). However, the Council did not make such a finding, neither at the beginning of the conflict nor at any stage throughout it, in order to gain Dutch consent to its resolutions. Council practice in the late 1940s had not evolved the wider concept of a threat to the peace, which in retrospect could have been applied to the Indonesian question.

There have been three findings of a breach of the peace in cases before the Council. The first concerned the conflict in Korea in 1950. On 25 June, the Council was rapidly convened at the request of the United States,[64] after massive North Korean forces had crossed the 38th parallel which had divided the country since the Japanese surrender to Soviet forces north of that line and to American forces south of it. The Soviet Union had been absent from the Council since 30 January 1950 in protest of the failure to install the Chinese Communists in the permanent seat instead of the Nationalists. If the Soviet Union had been present any Council moves would probably have been vetoed, possibly on the grounds that the armed conflict in Korea was a civil war or war of national liberation involving only that country. However, the rest of the Council viewed the North Korean attack as a 'breach of the peace'.[65] The resolution referred to the General Assembly resolution 293[66] which recognised the government of the Republic of Korea based in South Korea, and so the

Council was able to view the attack as akin to an armed attack by one State against another.

The Secretary General had viewed the attack as a 'threat to international peace', whereas the United States had labelled it as a 'breach of the peace and an act of aggression'.[67] Secretary General Lie's use of 'threat' is possibly because he was thinking of a civil war situation which was serious enough to warrant a finding under Article 39. He may have viewed Korea as a single State temporarily divided at the 38th parallel, with the result that the conflict was, if anything, a threat to the peace, or he may have been influenced by the fact that the Council would have been entering upon a new era with a finding of a breach or indeed of aggression. Indeed, he might have been advocating a finding of a threat as a preliminary finding which might be followed by a determination that by continuing the attack the North Koreans had breached the peace. The Council viewed the situation differently, although a finding of aggression would have been more suitable as the Secretary General had received a report from United Nations' observers that the attacks had been launched in strength by North Korean forces.[68] The finding of a breach of the peace was sufficient, however, to allow the Council to adopt some of the most strident resolutions in its history. Suffice to say, for the moment, that the operation in Korea was, arguably, the only military enforcement action undertaken by the United Nations.

The second occasion on which a breach of the peace has been found in a resolution was during the Falklands conflict in 1982. On 3 April, after Argentina had invaded the Falklands, the British introduced resolution 502 which determined that there was a 'breach of the peace in the region of the Falkland Islands'. The resolution did not condemn Argentinian aggression to ensure that it did not incur the veto of an otherwise indifferent Soviet Union. It then introduced certain provisional measures which, although not complied with, were, in the circumstances, probably the best that could be expected.

The third occasion upon which the Security Council determined that a breach of the peace existed was on 20 June 1987 when it unanimously adopted resolution 598. The breach was found in relation to the Gulf war between Iran and Iraq which had been continuing for seven years before the Council found that a clear case of inter-state conflict came within Article 39. This illustrates the political nature of such a finding because during those years the Council was unwilling to step into Chapter VII. As it is, a cease-fire has been established and resolution 598 has formed the basis of protracted negotiations towards a permanent peace.[69]

'It would seem logical that any resort to armed force would come within the meaning of the phrase' breach of the peace.[70] Even if the phrase is defined more narrowly as referring to international and not internal peace, it appears, at the very least, incongruous that a body established with 'primary responsibility for international peace and security'[71] has found a breach of the peace on only three occasions. It has been calculated that in the period 1946 to 1981 there were seventy-three instances of conflict between or among States.[72] In the study only inter-state conflict was examined so findings of threats to the peace in relation to intra-state conflicts would not be encompassed in the seventy-three instances. In other words, 'breach of the peace' and 'act of aggression' together should, objectively speaking, have been employed by the Council in over seventy cases. Although 'aggression' has been applied by the Council in relation to South African attacks against neighbouring States and as regards several Israeli reprisals, a fairly accurate estimate of its overall use would not exceed a dozen. As shall be illustrated, a finding of aggression is more condemnatory than constructive, whereas, in the rare instances of its use, a finding of a breach of the peace has entailed positive Security Council action.

'Act of aggression'

As has been suggested above, an act of aggression is a special form of a breach of the peace. In particular it labels or condemns one of the States involved in a conflict as the guilty party. Whilst it is not surprising that the term 'aggression' is used quite frequently in exchanges in the Council chamber, the body as a whole is unlikely to agree to use it on a regular basis.

Indeed, before the adoption of a definition of aggression in 1974,[73] there had been no formal findings of aggression; since, there have been several against South Africa[74] and Israel.[75] However, Western members are still cautious about allowing a finding of aggression against two friendly States, only allowing such determinations as long as they are not accompanied by positive measures. They can ease their consciences as well as deflecting international pressure to introduce sanctions against these countries by allowing the occasional condemnatory but paper resolution to be adopted.

Indeed, when an attempt is made to link a finding of aggression with a mandatory measure under Chapter VII, the alleged aggressor is protected by its superpower backer. The Middle Eastern theatre of conflict tends to produce these predictable reactions. In 1967, during the Six Day War, the Soviet Union submitted a draft resolution condemning Israeli aggression and demanding the immediate withdrawal of Israeli troops from the Arab territories occupied by the Israelis.[76] This attempt to introduce a binding resolution under Chapter VII after an implied finding under Article 39 was too much for the pro-Israeli members of the Council. After much negotiation a consensus was reached on a recommendatory resolution, with no condemnatory overtones.[77]

Although it appears that the 1974 definition of aggression has produced an increase in the number of formal findings of aggression, the question remains whether it has resulted in objective findings or whether they are predominantly caused by political factors.

During the drafting of the Charter at San Francisco, both Bolivia and the Philippines[78] proposed to include definitions of aggression. The Bolivian definition was similar to the Soviet proposal submitted to the Disarmament Conference in 1933,[79] in that it combined the enumeration of acts of aggression with a recognition of the Council's power to determine that other acts also constitute aggression.

At San Francisco, the committee concerned rejected the idea of a definition, stating that it would not be able to envisage or encompass developments in warfare, besides which it might lead to the 'premature application of enforcement measures' through 'automatic Council action'.[80] Despite these objections the United Nations struggled for years to find an acceptable definition of aggression. When this finally happened on 14 December 1974 the formulation was similar to the Bolivian proposal.

The definition is a compromise between those States who favoured a generic definition and those who favoured an enumerative approach. The problem was resolved by the adoption of a mixed definition. Article 1 contains the generic definition: 'Aggression is the use of armed force against the sovereignty, territorial integrity or political independence of another State, or in any other manner inconsistent with the Charter of the United Nations.' This is similar to Article 2(4) of the Charter. Unlike Article 2(4), the definition makes it clear that for the purposes of a determination of aggression under Article 39 the Council is considering the use of armed force only.

Article 3 enumerates the acts that may qualify as aggression. Invasion, attack, bombardment, blockade and occupation are cases of direct aggression, whereas allowing territory to be used by another State to perpetrate aggression against a third State, and the sending of armed bands to carry out acts of force against another State are really cases of indirect aggression. The latter are additions to the already well-settled cases of direct aggression.

However, although the definition introduces indirect aggression, it has never been found in a Security Council resolution, for as Broms points out, 'the case of aggression must be exceptionally clear and reprehensive before the term aggression has a chance of being adopted by consensus'.[81] Cases of indirect aggression are more likely to be unclear. In addition, such cases often involve elements of national liberation. The introduction of such elements often negates the possibility of a finding of aggression. As has been pointed out, South Africa has been condemned frequently for its incursions into Angola and other neighbouring African States. The South Africans argue that these were punitive raids aimed at preventing the incursions of SWAPO and the African National Congress (ANC) into Namibia and South Africa,[82] but the Council condemned only South African aggression not Angolan or Botswanan.

Even where Socialist or Non Aligned support for a particular war of national liberation does not exist it is still difficult to reach a finding of indirect aggression. The United States-backed Contra guerrillas fighting to overthrow the Sandinista government in Nicaragua is a case of indirect aggression which does not enjoy the support of the national liberation lobby at the United Nations. Nevertheless, when Nicaragua introduced a draft resolution[83] which obliquely referred to indirect aggression by the United States by using such language as 'covert' and 'destabilising' action, the United States used its veto power, although it was not directly named. If indirect aggression does not involve the support of the national liberation lobby, it more often than not involves one of the superpowers, so paralysing any attempt in the Council to label the actions as aggression.

Articles 2 and 4 of the definition preserve the discretionary powers of the Council. Article 2 states that the 'first use of armed force by a State in contravention of the Charter shall constitute *prima facie* evidence of an act of aggression', although the Council, in the light of all the evidence, may decide otherwise. Article 4 further states that acts enumerated in Article 3 'are not exhaustive and the Security Council may determine that other acts constitute aggression under the provisions of the Charter'.

Although the use of the term aggression in Council resolutions has increased since 1974, the definition has not resulted in a consistent and objective use of the term. The findings are mainly motivated by selective, discretionary and political factors and so the fears expressed by some[84] that the definition would lead to a proliferation of unhelpful, condemnatory resolutions have not been realised. The loopholes provided in the definition by retaining a balance in favour of the discretion of the Council and by the tacit encouragement of wars of national liberation in Article 7 of the definition, have proved sufficient to save the Council the embarrassment of making an objective finding of aggression.

Although the Council may appear to be acting within the definition when it condemns South Africa and Israel, it is being somewhat selective because, irrespective of their treatment of blacks and Palestinians within their countries or territories under their occupation, they too are being subjected to aggression of an indirect nature. There has been no attempt to define the Lebanese acquiescence of the Palestine Liberation Organisation (PLO) in its country as a case of indirect aggression against Israel. The United Nations is so hostile to Israel that it has managed to equate Zionism with racism,[85] so allowing the PLO to be designated as fighting a racist regime in an attempt to exercise the Palestinian right of self-determination, and making it as legitimate as the ANC and SWAPO guerrillas in southern Africa.

The extent of the domestic jurisdiction limitation on the competence of the Security Council

Article 2(7) of the Charter provides that 'nothing contained in the present Charter shall authorise the United Nations to intervene in matters which are essentially within the domestic jurisdiction of any State ... but this principle shall not prejudice the application of enforcement measures under Chapter VII'. The meaning of Article 2(7) is unclear. It has been argued that the limitation was intended to exclude all Security Council review, whether discussion or resolution, either under Chapter VI or by its recommendatory powers under Chapter VII when the situation it is faced with is essentially internal.[86]

An examination of the process whereby the exception to Article 2(7) in favour of enforcement measures was arrived at will show that the delegates intended that the exception be wider. The French had hoped to limit Article 2(7) further by proposing that the domestic jurisdiction principle would apply 'unless the clear violation of essential liberties and human rights constitutes itself a threat capable of compromising peace'.[87] The problem was finding the correct words to express the view that 'it would be proper in the interests of peace and justice, and in the preservation of human rights to interfere in the internal affairs of Member States'.[88] The Australian amendment that the domestic jurisdiction principle 'shall not prejudice the application of enforcement measures under Chapter VII' was rather clumsy. It did not fully express the views of the delegates and gave rise to technical difficulties.

In practice, the Security Council has developed its own interpretation as to what constitutes intervention and domestic jurisdiction.[89] Of course, a finding under Article 39 accompanied by the application of enforcement measures under Article 41 or Article 42 is exempt by the terms of Article 2(7) itself. The Council has taken the next logical step by adopting the practice that any finding under Article 39, whether or not combined with enforcement measures, is sufficient to internationalise the situation and so escape the grasp of Article 2(7). In fact this probably does no more than the delegates at San Francisco had in mind for Article 2(7).

For example, it has been argued that if it is accepted that the ONUC operation was taken pursuant to Article 40 (which is the non-enforcement provision of Chapter VII) it should have been subject to the domestic jurisdiction limitation.[90] It must be remembered that the Council eventually made a finding of a threat to the peace in relation to the situation within the Congo.[91] Resolution 169[92] referred to resolution 161 which contained the finding of a threat while authorising the Secretary General to take vigorous action, including the requisite measure of force, in order to 'apprehend all foreign troops and mercenaries'. The resolution also declared that 'all secessionist activities against the Republic of the Congo are contrary to the

Loi Fondementale and Security Council decisions' and specifically demanded 'that such activities which are now taking place in Katanga shall cease forthwith'. This certainly appears to be interference in the internal affairs of the Congo, which is the sort of activity *prima facie* prohibited by Article 2(7). Certain members expressed reservations about setting a dangerous precedent for the future, by putting the United Nations 'at the beck and call of any State faced with a problem of a dissident minority within its own borders'.[93]

The International Court advised that ONUC was not an enforcement measure under Article 42,[94] which leaves open the question, considered in chapter 8, whether it came instead within the terms of Article 40. If Article 40 is the correct Charter base for ONUC, according to a literal reading of Article 2(7), the exception to the domestic jurisdiction limitation for enforcement measures is inapplicable. However, this ignores the fact that when a situation is designated a threat to the peace it is inevitably out of the domestic realm into the international sphere, effectively rendering redundant the exception contained in Article 2(7) itself. Any action within Chapter VII, whether enforcement or not, is not limited by Article 2(7).

It is also true to say that the limitation contained in Article 2(7) is circumvented not only by a finding of a threat to the peace, but also by the finding that the situation is one of 'international concern'. 'This doctrine of international concern has seen service in the guise of a potential threat to the peace.'[95] Thus, a finding of a potential menace can be seen not only as a link between Chapters VI and VII, but also as a means by which the Council can utilise the provisions of Chapter VI and the power to ask for voluntary measures in the face of the provisions of Article 2(7).

Indeed, as early as 1946, the Council interpreted Article 2(7) as allowing it to establish a Commission of Investigation under Article 34 in order to report on aspects of the Greek civil war.[96] Further, in the Spanish question, the Security Council set up a sub-committee to investigate the situation in Spain.[97] These two early examples highlight the facts that an investigation to ascertain the facts and, in the latter case, to make substantive recommendations, do not constitute examples of intervention. The sub-committee found the situation in Spain to be of 'international concern' and a 'potential menace to international peace'. It recommended action under Chapter VI in the form of a voluntary termination of diplomatic relations. Although no such resolution was adopted, the view that Article 2(7) was inapplicable in cases of international concern prevailed, the proposed resolution being vetoed by the Soviet Union on the ground that the situation was a threat to the peace and should have been dealt with by mandatory measures.[98]

A more recent example of the Council using its recommendatory powers in a superficially domestic situation is as regards South Africa. The Council has not found a general threat to the peace in relation to the system of apartheid in South Africa. However, it has adopted many resolutions of a recommendatory natule, including a recent call for selective voluntary measures[99] after 1985 witnessed killings at Crossroads, further political detentions, suppression of freedom, and the declaration of a state of emergency. South African objections based on Article 2(7) have proved fruitless, because by characterising apartheid as a 'crime against humanity', the Council has recognised the situation as one of sufficient international concern to warrant collective humanitarian intervention using recommendatory measures.

Article 2(7) was a rather clumsy attempt to reconcile the doctrine of State sovereignty with the need to intervene in cases of international concern, which historically connotes the gross deprivation of human rights. However, it has been pointed out that the concepts of international concern and domestic jurisdiction are 'incapable of capture and crystallisation for all time. What is truly domestic today will not necessarily be so in five years time.'[100] For the moment we can conclude that the deprivation of the human rights of the majority of the population of a State is not within the domestic jurisdiction of the State despite first appearances. Maybe, in the future, the deprivation of the human rights of the minority will be of sufficient international concern to be outside the limitation of Article 2(7).[101]

However, one must not forget the political limitations on the competence of the Security Council, in that international intervention via the United Nations only occurs in the areas 'outside the direct zones of influence of the two superpowers'. If there is internal strife in countries within the superpowers' 'areas of security interest or in States closely allied to them', then Council 'intervention' is likely to be non-existent.[102] To disguise their own political intentions the superpowers will often rely on *ex post facto* legal justifications based on Article 2(7).[103]

Whether the Security Council's ability to adopt mandatory decisions is limited to Chapter VII

The topics of this chapter are the limitations placed upon the Security Council's competence and powers by the provisions of the Charter itself and the Council's interpretation by its subsequent practice of those provisions. The different types of power will be examined in the next chapter. A problem which spans both chapters is the mandatory/recommendatory dichotomy. This section is concerned with the question of whether the Council's use of mandatory decisions is limited to Chapter VII.

Article 25 of the Charter declares that the 'Members agree to accept and carry out the decisions of the Security Council in accordance with the present Charter'. This provision is contained in Chapter V of the Charter and immediately follows the *lex generalis* of the Council contained in Article 24(1), which confers on that body primary responsibility for the maintenance of international peace and security. A layman reading the Charter may believe that any decision of the Security Council relating to a matter within Article 24(1) would be binding on member States, whether it was taken under Chapter VI or Chapter VII – which contain the *lex specialis* of the Council. If the Council desired to make a recommendation in accordance with its powers, this would be clear from the resolution and so would not constitute a mandatory decision of the Council within the meaning of Article 25. A binding decision under Chapter VI may be rare because it is mainly concerned with recommendatory powers,[104] although it is not impossible. Article 39 allows the Council to make non-binding recommendations as well as mandatory decisions within the framework of Chapter VII.

Different factions of the Security Council have interpreted Article 25 in varying ways. The situation in Namibia has highlighted the controversy over Article 25. During a Council debate on the situation, the British representative stated that 'as a matter of law, my Government considers the Security Council can only take decisions generally binding on Member States only when the Security Council has made a determination under Article 39 ... only in these circumstances are decisions binding under Article 25'.[105] In this statement he was disagreeing with the opinion of the International Court of Justice on Namibia which was delivered after being so requested by the Council.[106] The Court opined that Article 25 was not restricted in its application to Chapter VII.[107] The Council resolution to which the British objected was resolution 269 of 12 August 1969, which 'decided' that 'the continued occupation of the Territory of Namibia by the South African authorities constitutes an aggressive encroachment on the authority of the United Nations' after reminding members of the content of Article 25. The resolution did not contain an express or implied determination under Article 39, in spite of the suggestion that the United Nations was in some way the object of some sort of aggression. An express determination would, for example, be 'an act of aggression within the meaning of Article 39'. An implied finding would merely refer to an 'act of aggression'. Similar language – for example, 'an aggressive encroachment' – is not usually sufficient to constitute an implied finding. Nevertheless the resolution invoked Article 25. All the Western powers on the Council abstained on this resolution, indicating that the collective view of the West is to equate Article 25 with Chapter VII.

The views of the United States were also enunciated in the initial Council dealings with Namibia after the termination of South Africa's mandate by the General Assembly.[108] Initially, the Council concerned itself with the essentially peripheral matter of the trials by the Pretoria government of members of SWAPO. Although resolutions 245 and 246[109] originally contained references to Article 25, these were deleted on the insistence of the United States, whose representative explained that 'among these changes is the omission of the reference to Article 25 of the Charter which we would have regarded as inappropriate for a resolution which was to be adopted under Chapter VI'.[110]

The Western view has been taken for granted in several books written on the Security Council's dealings with international conflicts. Both Murphy[111] and Pogany expound a simple view, summarised by the latter, who writes, 'resolutions under Chapter VI do not constitute decisions within the meaning of Article 25'.[112]

The Western view is probably based on the desire to provide a rough and ready, convenient and simple guide to the drafting of resolutions, which through constant reiteration by its adherents has taken on, for them, the status of international law.[113] However, it is probably true to say that only the British have taken a rigid view as to the application of Article 25; the United States has recently shown itself a little more flexible when it is in its interests to do so.

After the Israelis had invaded southern Lebanon in March 1978, the Council adopted resolution 425 which established UNIFIL, while remaining, like most resolutions on peacekeeping, ambiguous as to the Charter base of the force. When Israel and other factions in southern Lebanon prevented the implementation of UNIFIL's mandate, the American ambassador called upon all concerned to comply with Article 25.[114]

There is a strong argument that peacekeeping is not consonant with Chapter VI or VII, instead it is an implied power deriving from Article 24. The International Court viewed Council resolutions on Namibia as also coming within this power,[115] so it may be said that the Council can make binding decisions outside of Chapter VII if it is using the general principles of Article 24. The United Nations' operation in the Congo accords with this view. Before the Council had determined that there was a threat to the peace it had invoked Article 25 in a resolution,[116] when it called on Belgium to withdraw its troops from the province of Katanga. The operation of ONUC and the activities of the Council in relation to the Congo can be viewed as an extension of the powers contained in Article 24, although the later finding of a threat to the peace complicated the matter.

The Soviet Union, while not always citing Article 25, has made suggestions that decisions of the Council may be made outside of the framework of Chapter VII.[117] A good example of this can be seen during the debates of the Council on the Yom Kippur War in 1973. The East–West deadlock which had prevented the Council acting at the beginning of the war was overcome by the invitation of Secretary of State Kissinger to Moscow. The result was a resolution virtually forced through the Council by the superpowers[118] which simply called on the parties to the conflict to 'terminate all military activity' no later than twelve hours after the adoption of the resolution, followed by the implementation of resolution 242. Non-compliance with the cease-fire resulted in another joint superpower-sponsored resolution[119] which confirmed the Council's 'decision' in the previous resolution and urged the combatants to 'return to the positions they occupied at the moment the cease-fire became effective'. Although both resolutions had the appearance of being provisional measures under Article 40, an application of the Western view, supported by Pogany, would mean that without a finding under Article 39 there can be no decision within the meaning of Article 25, and consequently the resolution can only be a recommendation adopted within the parameters of Chapter VI.

The Soviet Union, while not actually citing Article 25, seemed to view both the resolutions as binding decisions,[120] although it must be pointed out that it was in the political interests of the Soviet Union to refer to 'decisions' in order to put pressure on Israel to comply because at the time the Arab States, favoured by the Soviet Union, were in retreat.

Higgins has pointed out that the British view of Article 25 would effectively retitle Chapters VI and VII as 'Recommendations for the settlement of disputes' and 'Decisions with respect to the breakdown of peace' respectively. She suggests that although this may provide a good working basis, an equally good working basis would be 'achieved by looking to see whether a resolution was intended as a recommendation or a decision'.[121] This more flexible approach seems to be adopted by the majority of the Council. If a resolution simply 'calls upon', 'urges' or generally is asking for voluntary co-operation or compliance, then it is probably a recommendation, whereas in the Middle East crisis in 1973, the Council, particularly the sponsors, intended resolutions 338 and 339 to be binding without aggravating the situation by making a determination of a threat to or breach of the peace. Often political compromise will not allow a finding to be made under Article 39. However, this absence does not, on occasions, prevent the production of a resolution which is a binding decision. Similarly, a recommendation can be made under Article 39. This is expressly provided for in that provision. The United Nations' recommendation of enforcement action against North Korea in 1950 provides a somewhat unusual example.[122]

Generally, until the Western States drop their equation of Article 25 with Chapter VII, the observer must take this into account when analysing resolutions. Nevertheless, there is a growing tendency to ignore the West's working rule in some critical situations where a binding resolution is essential but an express or implied finding under Article 39 is not feasible, possibly due to the fear that a cease-fire resolution, for example, accompanied by a finding of a threat to or breach of the peace may lead to the later application of collective measures. A finding under Article 39 is essential for the application of enforcement measures, it is not a prerequisite for the resolution to be binding under Article 25. This leads to the conclusion that a cease-fire resolution may be binding in the absence of a determination under Article 39, but a resolution calling for sanctions could never be mandatory in the absence of such a finding.[123]

Notes

1 J.P. Cot and A. Pellet, *La Charte des Nations Unies*, 113–25 (1985).
2 J. Arntz, *Der Begriff der Friendensbedrohung in Satzung und Praxis der Vereinten Nationen*, (1975).
3 H. Kelsen, *The Law of the United Nations*, 727 (1951).
4 R. Higgins, *The Development of International Law through the Political Organs of the United Nations*, 266 (1963).
5 M. McDougal and W.M. Reisman, 'Rhodesia and the United Nations: The Lawfulness of International Concern', 68 *A.J.I.L.* (1968), 1 at 11.
6 Cot and Pellet, *La Charte*, 655.
7 SC Res. 232, 21 UN SCOR Resolutions 7 (1966).
8 J.C. Nkala, *The United Nations, International Law and the Rhodesian Independence Crisis*, 163–76 (1985).
9 SC Res. 418, 32 UN SCOR Resolutions 5 (1977).
10 O.A. Ozgur, *Apartheid: the United Nations and Peaceful Change in South Africa*, 99–105 (1982).
11 SC Res. 221, 21 UN SCOR Resolutions 5 (1966).
12 Nkala, *The Rhodesian Independence Crisis*, 77–90.
13 UN Doc. S/18785 (1987), vetoed on 9.4.1987; see SC 2747 mtg, 42 UN S/PV (1987).
14 SC Res. 161, 16 UN SCOR Resolutions 2 (1961).
15 GA Res. 1514, 15 UN GAOR Supp. (No. 16) 66 (1960).
16 SC Res. 312, 27 UN SCOR Resolutions 10 (1972).
17 See SC 1639 mtg, 27 UN SCOR 14 (1972), India.
18 Articles 33 and 34. See Cot and Pellet, *La Charte*, 607, and Kelsen, *Law of the UN*, 360, for 'dispute' and 'situation'.
19 See UNCIO, vol. 3, 13.
20 See R.B. Russell and J.E. Muther, *A History of the United Nations Charter*, 669–70 (1958).
21 SC Res. 4, 1 UN SCOR Resolutions 8 (1946). Australia, Brazil, China, France and Poland.
22 Report of the Sub-Committee on the Spanish Question, 1 UN SCOR Special Supp. (No. 2) 5 (1946).
23 *Ibid.*, 4.
24 SC Res. 181, 18 UN SCOR Resolutions 7 (1963).
25 Ozgur, *Apartheid*, 102.
26 In 1965, the General Assembly found that the situation in South Africa was a threat to the peace; GA Res. 2054, 20 UN GAOR Supp (No. 14) 26 (1965).
27 SC Res. 282, 25 UN SCOR Resolutions 12 (1970).
28 UN doc. S/9882 (1970).
29 SC 1549 mtg, 25 UN SCOR 3 (1970).
30 See also the Eichmann case in 1960, when the Security Council considered that Israel's kidnapping of Eichmann from Argentina, 'if repeated ... may endanger international peace and security', SC Res. 138, 15 UN SCOR Resolutions 4 (1960).
31 UN doc. S/6928 (1965).
32 UN doc. S/6929 (1965).
33 See H. Strack, *Sanctions: The Case of Rhodesia*, 23–36 (1978).
34 GA Res. 1889, 18 UN GAOR Supp. (No. 15) 46 (1963).
35 See Nkala, *The Rhodesian Independence Crisis*, 229.
36 This resolution seemed poorly drafted. To make sense 'constitutes' should be replaced by 'will constitute'.
37 SC Res. 221, 21 UN SCOR Resolutions 5 (1966).

38 SC Res. 232, 21 UN SCOR Resolutions 7 (1966).
39 SC 1265 mtg, 20 UN SCOR 15 (1965).
40 *Ibid.*, 6 and 16.
41 See SC Res. 216, 20 UN SCOR Resolutions 8 (1965).
42 UN doc. S/10251 (1971).
43 See SC 1572 mtg, 26 UN SCOR (1971).
44 See E. Luard, *The United Nations*, 30−31 (1979).
45 Cot and Pellet, *La Charte*, 649.
46 *Ibid.*, 614, 682, 686.
47 McDougal and Reisman, 68 *A.J.I.L.* (1968), 8−9.
48 SC 1340 mtg, 21 UN SCOR 4 (1966).
49 See Keesing's *Contemporary Archives* (1984), 3315−37.
50 SC Res. 556, 39 UN SCOR Resolutions 4 (1984), condemned the system of apartheid as a 'crime against humanity'.
51 SC Res. 539, 38 UN SCOR Resolutions 13 (1983).
52 See SC Res. 567, 571, 574, 40 UN SCOR Resolutions 16−18 (1985).
53 UN doc. S/18087 (1986), vetoed at SC 2686 mtg, 41 UN S/PV 131−32 (1986).
54 See generally J.F. Murphy, *The United Nations and the Control of International Violence* (1983).
55 T.M. Franck, 'Who killed Article 2(4)', 64 *A.J.I.L.* (1970), 809 at 810.
56 SC Res. 161, 16 UN SCOR Resolutions 2 (1961).
57 SC Res. 353, 29 UN SCOR Resolutions 7 (1974).
58 SC Res. 54, 3 UN SCOR Resolutions 22 (1948).
59 UN doc. S/9394 (1969).
60 SC 1503 mtg, 24 UN SCOR 1 (1969).
61 Kelsen, *Law of the UN*, 930.
62 SC 171 mtg, 2 UN SCOR (1947).
63 SC 417 mtg, 4 UN SCOR (1949).
64 SC 473 mtg, 5 UN SCOR (1950).
65 SC Res. 82, 5 UN SCOR Resolutions 4 (1950).
66 GA Res. 293, 4 UN GAOR Resolutions 15 (1949).
67 SC 473 mtg, 5 UN SCOR 3−7 (1950).
68 See S.D. Bailey, *How Wars End: The United Nations and the Termination of Armed Conflict 1946−1964*, 396, vol. 2 (1982).
69 SC Res. 598, 42 UN SCOR Resolutions 5 (1987). UN docs. S/195511, S/20094 (1988).
70 L.M. Goodrich, E. Hambro and P.S. Simons, *The Charter of the United Nations*, 296, 2nd ed. (1969).
71 Article 24(1) of the UN Charter.
72 G.P. McGinley, 'Ordering a Savage Society: A Study of International Disputes and a Proposal for Achieving their Peaceful Solution', 25 *Harvard International Law Journal* (1984), 43.
73 GA Res. 3314, 29 UN GAOR Supp. (No.31) 142 (1974).
74 Three examples are: See SC Res. 387, 31 UN SCOR Resolutions 10 (1976) re Angola; SC Res. 466, 35 UN SCOR Resolutions 17 (1980) re Zambia; SC Res. 568, 40 UN SCOR Resolutions 20 (1985) re Botswana.
75 SC Res. 573, 40 UN SCOR Resolutions 23 (1985) re PLO base in Tunis; SC Res. 611, 43 UN S/PV (1988), re assassination of Abu Jihad.
76 UN doc. S/7951/REV 2 (1967).
77 SC Res. 242, 22 UN SCOR Resolutions 8 (1967).
78 See UNCIO, vol. 3, docs. 577−79, 535−42.

79 See 5 Records of the Conference for the Reduction and Limitation of Armaments, League of Nations publication, Ser. D, 535–42.
80 UNCIO, vol. 12, doc. 505.
81 B. Broms, 'The Definition of Aggression', 154 *Recueil des Cours* (1977), 299 at 378.
82 See for example SC 2597 mtg, 40 UN S/PV 22 (1985).
83 UN doc. S/16463 (1984).
84 J. I. Garvey, 'The UN Definition of Aggression: Law and Illusion in the Context of Collective Security', 17 *Virginia Journal of International Law* (1977), 177 at 178.
85 GA Res. 3379, 30 UN GAOR Supp. (No. 34) 82 (1975).
86 D. R. Gilmour, 'The Meaning of Intervene Within Article 2(7) of the United Nations Charter' 16 *I.C.L.Q.* (1967), 330 at 349.
87 UNCIO, vol. 3, 386.
88 Report of the Conference held at San Francisco by the Rt Hon. Peter Frazer, Chairman of the New Zealand delegation, NZ Dept of External Affairs publication, No. 11, 28.
89 Cot and Pellet, *La Charte*, 158.
90 N. T. Kasser, 'The Legal Limits on the Use of International Force through United Nations Practice', 35 *Revue Egyptienne de Droit International* (1979), 163 at 207.
91 SC Res. 161, 16 UN SCOR Resolutions 2 (1961).
92 SC Res. 169, 16 UN SCOR Resolutions 3 (1961).
93 SC 976 mtg, 16 UN SCOR para. 15 (1961), UK.
94 *Certain Expenses of the United Nations* case, I.C.J. *Rep.* 1962, 151.
95 Higgins, *The Development of International Law*, 77.
96 SC Res. 15, 1 UN SCOR Resolutions 8 (1946).
97 SC Res. 4, 1 UN SCOR Resolutions 8 (1946).
98 SC 47 mtg, 1 UN SCOR (1946).
99 SC Res. 569, 40 UN SCOR Resolutions 8 (1985).
100 Higgins, *The Development of International Law*, 61.
101 See also 'Human Rights and Sovereignty, the Secretary General's view', 22 *UN Chronicle* (1985), 23.
102 O. Schachter, 'The United Nations and Internal Conflict' in Moore (ed.), *Law and Civil War in the Modern World*, 415 (1974).
103 See for example Soviet reliance on Article 2(7) after its intervention in Czechoslovakia, UN doc. S/8759 (1968).
104 But see Articles 37(2) and 34.
105 SC 1598 mtg, 26 UN SCOR 5 (1971). France expressed a similar view at 2.
106 By SC Res. 284, 25 UN SCOR Resolutions 4 (1970).
107 *Legal Consequences for States of the Continued Presence of South Africa in Namibia (South West Africa) Notwithstanding Security Council Resolution 276 (1970)*, I.C.J. *Rep.* 1971, 16 at para. 113.
108 GA Res. 2145, 21 UN GAOR Supp. (No. 16) 2 (1966).
109 SC Res. 245 and 246, 23 UN SCOR Resolutions 1–2 (1968).
110 SC 1397 mtg, 23 UN SCOR (1968).
111 Murphy, *The Control of International Violence*, 21.
112 I. S. Pogany, *The Security Council and the Arab Israeli Conflict*, 9, 125 (1984).
113 R. Higgins, 'The Advisory Opinion on Namibia. Which UN resolutions are Binding under Article 25 of the Charter?', 21 *I.C.L.Q.* (1972), 270 at 283.
114 SC 2085 mtg, 33 UN SCOR 3 (1978).
115 *Namibia* case, I.C.J. *Rep.* 1971, para. 110.
116 SC Res. 146, 15 UN SCOR Resolutions 6 (1960).
117 SC 2097 mtg, 33 UN SCOR 2 (1978).

118 SC Res. 338, 28 UN SCOR Resolutions 10 (1973).
119 SC Res. 339, 28 UN SCOR Resolutions 11 (1973).
120 SC 1751 mtg, 28 UN SCOR 8–10 (1973).
121 Higgins, 21 *I.C.L.Q.* (1972) 283.
122 But see J. W. Halderman, 'Some Legal Aspects of Sanctions in the Rhodesian Case, 17 *I.C.L.Q.* (1968), 672 at 675 and 688. See generally Halderman, *The Political Role of the United Nations*, (1981).
123 Supported in UNCIO, vol. 11, 393.

CHAPTER 3

Powers, practice and effectiveness of the Security Council

Having examined the limitations on the competence of the Security Council, both in terms of politics and law, we will now examine the development and use of the Council's powers, within those limitations. As has been suggested in chapter 2, there has been some blurring of the distinction between Chapters VI and VII and this will be reflected in the analysis below. Nevertheless, the basic structure of the Charter in terms of the Council's powers remains intact after forty years of that body's practice. The array of powers available to the Security Council has been described in terms of 'une gradation d'intensité des pouvoirs'[1] culminating in the provisions of Chapter VII.

The development of the Charter provisions concerning collective measures was the main preoccupation of the sponsoring powers at San Francisco in their quest for collective security. As we have seen, the contents of Chapter VII were not greatly questioned by the smaller powers. The only significant amendments to the Dumbarton Oaks proposals were the removal of the provision linking Chapter VI to Chapter VII; and to readily accept a Chinese proposal for the insertion of a provision enabling the Council to adopt provisional measures. The proposals regarding pacific settlement were to prove more novel and problematic, both to the sponsoring powers and to the other delegates at San Francisco.

Chapter VI of the United Nations' Charter arose out of Chapter VIIIA of the Dumbarton Oaks proposals. The latter had 'the doubtful distinction of being regarded as one of the most poorly drafted sections' which necessitated a multitude of amendments.[2] In fact the amendments probably created more confusion than the untouched proposals. The proposals were firmly based on the concept of the Security Council as a policeman. This was emphasised in the proposals by placing the Council's powers of investigation at the head of the section containing powers of pacific settlement.

The main action the Council could take under the proposals for pacific settlement was primarily to call on the parties to the dispute to settle it by the peaceful means enumerated in the third paragraph of Chapter VIIIA. If the dispute continued the Council could then utilise its powers in paragraph 5 to 'recommend appropriate procedures or methods of adjustment' or move into the enforcement powers contained in section B[3] by means of paragraph 1 of section B.

The original proposals did recognise a 'situation' as well as a 'dispute'[4] but the possible measures outlined above applied only to 'disputes'. The amendments to the proposals extended to the Council powers to give it a somewhat quasi-judicial or arbitral role. One of the amendments to this effect was to empower it to 'recommend appropriate procedures and methods of adjustment' to 'situations' as well as 'disputes'.[5] Theoretically it is the Council only which can recognise a 'situation likely to endanger the maintenance of international peace and security',[6] for the obligation placed on members to settle their disputes by peaceful means contained in Article 33 applies only to 'disputes'. This extends the Council's powers of determining the nature of events that endanger peace and hence is an enhancement of its judicial powers. Practically, however, States will often refer situations as well as disputes to the Council under Article 35, and although the Council could, by itself, determine jurisdiction under Article 34, it rarely does so, nor has it attempted to distinguish between a dispute and a situation.

Goodrich, Hambro and Simons summarise the major changes in the Dumbarton Oaks proposals for pacific settlement made at San Francisco. The proposals were rearranged so as to 'give pride of place to the obligation of the parties to seek a solution to their disputes by peaceful means'. The primary emphasis of the members' obligation to settle in Article 33(1) not only recognises that without some co-operation by the parties to the dispute settlement will be hard to obtain; it also illustrates the greater emphasis on the envisaged judicial role of the Council. If the parties fail to settle out of the Council, they may be subject to settlement not necessarily by the Council but with the (perhaps unwelcome) help of the Council; a process broadened by the second major amendment of enabling the Council to recommend 'terms' as well as 'procedures' for settlement.[7] In fact, the addition of Articles 37 and 38 to the proposals were intended to invest the Council with quasi-judicial powers. The confusion is created because the change of emphasis from policeman to judge did not involve a wholesale revision of the Dumbarton Oaks proposals; instead the judicial provisions were tacked on so that the fundamental role the Council should play in relation to international disputes is unclear. Only an examination of the Council's practice will help us to understand the role it has actually played.[8]

The Council's supervision of the members' obligation to settle their disputes by peaceful means

Article 33(1) of the Charter imposes upon members an obligation to settle by peaceful means disputes 'the continuance of which' are 'likely to endanger the maintenance of international peace and security'. It lists some examples of methods whereby this obligation could be fulfilled, such as negotiation, mediation, arbitration and resort to regional arrangements. Article 33(2) states that, 'the Security Council shall, when it deems necessary, call upon the parties to settle their disputes by such means' as contained in paragraph (1). Despite the inclusion of the word 'shall' instead of 'may', this provision does not purport to impose a mandatory obligation on the Council to enforce in some way the provisions of Article 33(1), for it operates only when the Council deems it necessary, which in theory should be when it has found the basic requirement of a danger to international peace and security. The Council's role under Article 33 is one of supervision of the obligation to settle placed on members.[9]

The most effective use of this power would be not only as a reminder to States of their duties under the Charter, but also as a warning of future Council action under the other provisions of Chapter VI or, if the States concerned continue to be in breach of their obligation, of the possibility of Council action under Chapter VII. A Presidential statement, made with the unanimous support of the Council, is often preferable, for it can be made quickly and is illustrative of the mood of the Council towards a continuance of the conflict, or, if the Council is purporting to take preventative measures, towards future breaches.

In 1982, with an Argentinian invasion of the Falklands imminent, the President of the Council made a statement on the same day that the Council was convened at the request of the United Kingdom.[10] It called upon Britain and Argentina 'to exercise the utmost restraint at this time and in particular to refrain from the use or threat of force in the region and to continue to search for a diplomatic solution'.[11] Although a balanced reminder, the statement was a warning to Argentina not to invade. The Argentinians needed a fair degree of international support if they were to maintain their hold on the islands, but the statement reflected unanimous Council opposition to invasion. The Argentinians misread the signs and carried out their threat to the almost unanimous condemnation of the Council.[12]

The Council then found a breach of the peace and demanded withdrawal,[13] which although not complied with, effectively put Argentina in the wrong, helped to isolate it internationally, and contributed to Argentina's defeat in that it tacitly supported the British stance in support of principles of international law, though not necessarily the use of force in defence of those principles.

The Falklands conflict was in an area free from superpower or regional interests. In other cases, where such influences predominate, the Council's use of the power contained in Article 33(2) is limited to a statement of concern, with no immediate prospects of further Council action. The Presidential statement calling on Chad and Libya to utilise the pacification machinery of the OAU in 1983[14] represented a token gesture by the Council to placate the Chadians, whose complaints have been heard on various occasions over the past decade. There remains little possibility of more constructive Council action despite the Chadians' insistence that they have exhausted all possible diplomatic, regional, and other peaceful means of settlement under Article 33(1).[15]

The use of Article 33(2) is sometimes the only measure available when the Council is faced with superpower intervention. In 1983, the Americans' objection to any Security Council interference in the Central American region relaxed slightly with the introduction of the OAS-supported Contadora group's peace efforts. This proved to be sufficient regionalisation to enable the United States to support resolution 530[16] which expressed the Council's concern at 'the danger of military confrontation between Honduras and Nicaragua'. Although the resolution was similar to the previously vetoed draft resolution,[17] it put more emphasis on the efforts of the Contadora group and so represents a particular application of the Council supervising the obligation imposed by Article 33(1) − of 'resort to regional agencies or arrangements'. It represents a minimum measures resolution aimed at securing the support of the United States.[18]

The fact that Article 33 is likely to be the only possible measure utilised in the face of superpower involvement is to be expected, although not condoned. However, it must be pointed out that in the Falklands conflict the United Kingdom, a permanent member, encouraged the adoption of a more forceful resolution (502) after initial use of Article 33(2) because it had international law on its side. Maybe the United States lacks the support of law and so is wary of any further Council action beyond Article 33, a view which is emphasised by the International Court's judgement against the United States in a case brought before it by Nicaragua.[19]

Sometimes each superpower is concerned not to let the other gain a foothold in an intermediate area, particularly one which would alter the strategic balance of power such as the Persian Gulf. Hence the relative Council inaction towards the Gulf war. The aim is not to protect their interests but to prevent each other from taking advantage of a change in the situation which may result from more positive Council action. Although the initial Council call to Iran and Iraq within the meaning of Article 33(2)[20] was supplemented by other recommendatory Chapter VI resolutions,[21] it took seven years of bloody conflict before the necessary consensus could be achieved to enable the Council to unanimously adopt resolution 598 on 20 July 1987, which contained a mandatory demand for a cease-fire within the terms of Chapter VII.

Goodrich, Hambro and Simons state that Article 33(1) is intended to operate only at the pre-conflict stage.[22] It has been pointed out by Arend[23] that the obligation contained in Article 33(1) has been extended beyond the pre-conflict stage − the period of tension preceding the outbreak of armed conflict − to operate during the whole period of hostilities. He suggests that the obligation to settle before and during hostilities is becoming a norm of contemporary international law.[24] He points to the Council activities during the Gulf war and the Falklands conflict as recent evidence of this trend. Both cases involved acts of aggression by Iraq and Argentina respectively − though the Council diplomatically avoided such factual determinations − but they provoked no collective enforcement measures by the Security Council; instead they produced calls to the parties to settle their disputes peacefully. Arend argues that this development has occurred to successfully fill the void created by the lack of enforcement muscle in the Council. The evidence does suggest that he is right, but a failure to arrive at a settlement other than by the use of force in the Falklands, and for many years, in the Gulf, suggests that this development will not increase the effectiveness of the Council; instead it will provide it with the excuse of not having to consider the application of enforcement measures at all, which in turn may result in further breaches of the peace.

Investigation

Investigatory bodies established by the Security Council to ascertain the facts of a dispute are relatively rare. The Charter basis for such bodies is to be located in a combination of Articles 34 and 29, although they are rarely cited in the enabling resolutions. Often the body's function will go beyond mere fact finding and enter the realm of good offices and peacekeeping. In this section an attempt will be made to keep the discussion centred on investigatory bodies, the true basis of which is Article 34. Good offices committees and peacekeeping bodies have different constitutional bases and are discussed later. Article 34 provides that 'the Security Council may investigate any dispute or any situation in order to determine whether the continuance of the dispute or situation is likely to endanger the maintenance of international peace and security'.

During the early years of Council practice, some confusion arose from the fact that this provision did not confer a general power of investigation on the Council. The power appears to be confined to ascertaining whether the dispute or situation came within the parameters of Chapter VI. Indeed, the subcommittee on the Spanish question established in 1946 was directed to ascertain whether the activities of the Franco regime constituted a situation within the meaning of Article 34 or Article 39.

However, very soon after, the Council showed its willingness to go beyond a strict interpretation of Article 34 when, in 1946, it established a Commission of Investigation to examine certain frontier incidents on the Greek borders.[25] The Commission not only ascertained the facts but made several wide-ranging recommendations[26] which, unfortunately, were not adopted by the Council because of Soviet opposition.[27]

Of course geopolitical factors have limited the ability of the Council to establish investigatory bodies. In the Greek case above, the Commission of Investigation was prevented from examining the situation further because of the Soviet Union's dislike of the Commission's findings which tended to blame Yugoslavia, Bulgaria and Albania. Similarly, as regards disputes in the American hemisphere, proposals for investigation of the conflict will not be adopted because of the opposition of the United States. Guatemala's complaint, in 1954, of aggression by neighbouring Honduras and Nicaragua,[28] allegedly inspired by a United States' concern (the United Fruit Company), cried out for an impartial investigation. Indeed, the Guatemalan representative asked for one,[29] but none was forthcoming. However, there are suggestions that the recent thaw in the Cold War has allowed the Security Council to step beyond its lowest level power and investigate intra-bloc situations in Central America. In 1988 a fact finding mission was sent to Nicaragua.[30]

A method of circumventing the superpower veto is by applying a procedural vote to the establishment of such a body. This was done in 1959 to establish a sub-committee to investigate a complaint by Laos despite the negative Soviet vote. The legality of this method is doubtful and it has not become an established feature in the practice of the Security Council. An alternative method would be to provide for continuous investigation independent of the whims of the voting of the members of the Council, perhaps under the control of the Secretary General. Reports would be sent to the Council from the various UN centres around the world, a scenario which would not only force the Council to consider all conflicts but would also make any permanent member involved in the conflict answerable to the other members when faced with independently obtained facts. It may be argued that criticism of a superpower will not alter its foreign policy. This may be true, but one may point to the great lengths to which the superpowers go to prevent criticism of their actions by the Council or by potential subsidiary bodies. An automatic investigation of all conflicts or potential conflicts might be one small factor in deterring the actions of actual or potential aggressors.

Such reforms would also enhance the investigatory potential of the United Nations as regards potential conflicts which would enable the Security Council to adopt preventative measures. At present, even in the intermediate areas where Council investigation is possible, the body established to undertake the task is often faced with a *fait accompli*. After alleged attacks by Portuguese forces on the independent African States of Guinea in 1970 and Senegal in

1971, the Council established Special Missions to ascertain whether such attacks occurred.[31] The Mission's report on Guinea led to the Council finding a threat to the peace.[32] However, since the attacks were over, the Council could only condemn them, warn Portugal against further attacks, and demand that Portugal pay compensation to Guinea.

Often in these cases where the aggression is short-lived and the *status quo* has been re-established, the investigation's only purpose is to find the guilty party, which proves virtually impossible in the case of mercenary aggression and difficult in the case of guerrilla activities. After a mercenary attack in 1977 aimed at overthrowing the government of Benin, a Special Mission could report only that the attackers worked for pecuniary motives and that the financiers could not be found.[33] This resulted in a general Council condemnation of mercenary aggression.[34]

It is doubtful whether, strictly speaking, the Council's powers under Article 34 go beyond investigating and reporting on a factual basis.[35] Sometimes the Council uses Article 34 in other senses which often are better covered by other provisions of Chapter VI. For example, in resolution 377, adopted on 22 October 1975, the Council, purportedly 'acting in accordance with Article 34', requested the Secretary General 'to enter into immediate consultations with the parties concerned' in the dispute over Western Sahara, with the intention of providing the Security Council with the basis upon which it could recommend a settlement. However, the Secretary General's report[36] did not produce any positive Council recommendation.[37] Nevertheless, fourteen years later the process continues and has produced a set of peace proposals formulated by the Secretary General of the UN and the Chairman of the OAU, and endorsed by the Security Council.[38]

Nevertheless, 'good offices' resolutions do sometimes produce a framework for settlement and as such should be classified within the powers provided by Article 36. Indeed, in the Kashmir case, the Council established a Commission on India and Pakistan (UNCIP) in 1948 to investigate the facts pursuant to Article 34.[39] UNCIP became more than a fact finding body when the Council set out the modalities for conducting a referendum under UNCIP auspices after 'considering that the continuance of the dispute is likely to endanger international peace and security'.[40] This recommendatory resolution, which was probably adopted with Article 36 rather than Article 34 in mind, was not complied with and UNCIP concentrated on demarcating the cease-fire line and placing observers along it.

Kashmir illustrates the flaw in the Council's powers of pacific settlement. Even if a successful investigation is carried out, a settlement based on the impartial findings is often not possible, which on occasions results in the Council accepting the 'lesser custodial role' of peacekeeping to maintain the *status quo*.[41]

The settlement of disputes

Article 36(1) of the Charter provides that 'the Security Council may, at any stage of a dispute of a nature referred to in Article 33 or of a situation of a like nature, recommend appropriate procedures or methods of adjustment'. Paragraph 2 of the Article directs the Council to 'take into consideration any procedures for the settlement of the dispute which have already been adopted by the parties'. This is a reversal of the procedure envisaged by Article 33, but it is also a recognition that the Security Council can recommend 'appropriate procedures or methods of adjustment' to 'situations' as well as 'disputes'.

The terms of Article 36 can be applied to a variety of situations in the absence of any statement in the resolution of its Charter base. Cease-fire and withdrawal resolutions can be seen as 'appropriate procedures or methods of adjustment', as can recommendations of settlement. This latter power can also be derived from Article 37(2) which empowers the Council to recommend 'such terms of settlement as it may consider appropriate'. When the Council makes a recommendation for settlement it does not state which provision in the Charter it is using, and so one must assume that, in practice, the Council's powers as regards settlement have been amalgamated. However, it could be said that Article 36 empowers the Security Council to establish the modalities for settlement or the framework within which a settlement process may be undertaken, whereas Article 37 enables it to directly recommend the terms of settlement.

Before examining the Council's use of these powers, it is worth mentioning the little utilised but potentially wide power conferred on the Council by Article 38, which provides that the Council 'may, if all the parties to any dispute so request, make recommendations to the parties with a view to a pacific settlement of the dispute'. The dispute does not have to cross the threshold of being a danger to international peace and security. However, despite the fact that by means of this provision the Council could involve itself in any kind of dispute, it has never been used in this way. During the Indonesian question, the Council appeared to have Article 38 in mind when it adopted resolution 31 on 21 August 1947, which resolved to tender the Council's 'good offices' in the form of a Committee of Three if the parties so requested. There can be little doubt, however, that the Indonesian situation was, at the very least, a danger to international peace and security, although the Council did not make such a determination, nor did it make one under Article 39.

'Good offices' resolutions

The phase of the Indonesian question which ended in a truce between the Netherlands and Indonesia with the signing of the Renville Agreement[42] in 1948 represented a relative success for the Council in its role as a peacemaker.

Resolution 27 of 1 August 1947,[43] called for a cease-fire and called on the parties 'to settle their disputes by arbitration or by other peaceful means'. The Council then began to build on the fragile cease-fire that ensued. Resolution 30[44] noted with satisfaction the steps taken by the parties to implement resolution 27, steps which included a Dutch statement that it intended to implement the Linggadjati Agreement.[45] It also noted the request by Indonesia for the creation of a commission of observers. On this last point the Council acted quickly by requesting, in the same resolution, that governments with consuls in Batavia jointly prepare reports on the state of the cease-fire for the Council. Then came the creation of the Committee of Three by resolution 31. The Council was creating the machinery to facilitate the reaching of an agreement; it did not, at this stage, recommend one itself, although its resolutions implicitly favoured the implementation of the Linggadjati Agreement. After clarifying the meaning of the earlier resolutions, the Council urged the Committee of Three (alternatively called the Committee of Good Offices) to help the parties reach an agreement.[46]

On 24 December 1947, the Committee of Good Offices addressed an informal message to the parties, containing suggested terms for a truce agreement. The Renville Agreement between the Netherlands and Indonesia provided for an immediate cease-fire, the establishment of demilitarised zones, and the supervision of arrangements by the military assistants of the Committee of Good Offices. It also contained principles governing negotiations towards a political settlement. The effectiveness of the Council depended, to a great extent, on the participation and co-operation in good faith of both parties to the dispute. The Dutch, although still denying the Council's jurisdiction, viewed use of the Council as the only viable means of achieving a peaceful solution.[47] Good offices resolutions do not work when the parties refuse to co-operate or give only token co-operation. This may be a truism, but it illustrates the inherent and unavoidable weakness of the Council in its pacification role as a whole.

Sometimes the parties to a dispute may appear willing to reach an agreement with the help of the United Nations. In the Cyprus question the two main disputants, Greece and Turkey, have consented, as has the Cypriot government, to the good offices of the Secretary General.[48] However, even since Perez de Cuellar commenced his task, the Turkish government has gone about consolidating its grip on the northern part of the island. 'Good offices' implies that the Secretary General should help the parties to reach an agreement. In the Cyprus case, it is the Secretary General who has, so far, made proposals for settlement. Several plans have failed.[49] The disputants display token, not genuine, consent to the settlement process. They feign consent because of international pressure, which in the case of Greece and Turkey, is heightened by their membership of NATO.

The quasi-judicial role of the Security Council in the settlement of disputes

Although it may be argued that some of the provisions of Chapter VI and the general principles contained in Article 1(1) create a quasi-judicial role for the Council, an examination of most Council debates leading to the adoption of a recommendation towards the pacific settlement of a dispute will illustrate that it is arrived at by political consensus, and that law is often merely a 'tactical device' and a 'weapon in the armoury of rhetoric'.[50] The law of nations could be said to play a residual role in the work of a political body such as the Security Council.

The argument that whilst the Council does not decide cases in accordance with international law as does the World Court, it is constrained by a 'broad framework of legally acceptable solutions',[51] appears flawed in that some Security Council-inspired pacification attempts seek solutions which appear to contradict the tenets of international law. For example, the Council-supervised negotiations on the Gulf war are premised on the non-identification of the aggressor – Iraq.[52] It may be said in contradiction to the example just given, that the Security Council fails to identify breaches of international law but it does not adopt resolutions which are themselves in breach of international law. However, this is a long way from the position that law plays an important role in the Council's pacification function.

The Council's failure to establish a solution is mainly due to it often being faced with the situation of an aggressor country gaining, with little possibility of it handing back its gains, when faced with a Council recommendation. This is an inevitable flaw in any system based on recommendation and voluntary acceptance. Nevertheless, in order to ensure that the recommendation has a chance of success, it should be clear and unambiguous. Unfortunately, the necessities of consensus dictate that clarity is often unattainable. Resolution 242, adopted on 6 November 1967, is an example of an ambiguous recommendation. The resolution stated, *inter alia*, that the Council,

Affirms that the fulfilment of Charter principles requires the establishment of a just and lasting peace in the Middle East which should include the application of both the following principles:
(i) Withdrawal of Israeli armed forces from territories occupied in the recent conflict;
(ii) Termination of all claims or states of belligerency and respect for and acknowledgement of the sovereignty, territorial integrity and political independence of every State in the area and their right to live in peace within secure and recognised boundaries free from threats or acts of force.

This appears to be a reasonable framework for the settlement of the Middle East problem, although the two principles outlined in the resolution miss the root of the problem – the homeless Palestinians. Nevertheless, the resolution is based on legal principles, namely, the implication that Israel has the right to exist, the non-use of force, and the return of territories occupied by Israel in the Six Day War. However, the fact that the resolution does not state whether this means 'all' or 'some' of the territories detracts from its value.

Law and justice point to the former interpretation, otherwise the Israelis would be gaining by the use of force, although it could be argued that the occupied territories, or at least some of them, are essential for the security and self-defence of Israel. Although Perry argues[53] that if an advisory opinion of the International Court were sought, there would be no doubt that resolution 242 would be interpreted to mean 'all' the territories, the doubt and confusion created by the British proposed text has not helped to end the conflict. Besides, although the World Court may opt for this solution, it is not unforseeable that the Council may promote peace on the basis of Israel handing back some of its territories but not all. One must not forget that international law is greatly tempered by political considerations in the Council forum.

When attempting to settle a dispute the Security Council tends to adopt recommendations which are aimed at not causing offence to either party in order to induce them to come to an agreement. Determinations of legal guilt may come later if the parties remain recalcitrant. Usually, these determinations will contain a finding under Article 39 without the accompaniment of enforcement action. The initial recommendations are usually based on broad principles of international law and justice centred around the *jus cogens* contained in Article 2(4) and the principle that a State should not gain from its breach. It may be argued that more concrete legal determinations should be made even under purely recommendatory Chapter VI resolutions. There are both pitfalls and advantages in this approach. A 'once and for all' legal determination may make a State more intransigent and so work against the settlement process, and at the same time it may mobilise international opinion which will work in its favour. Discussions of this nature miss the point somewhat, for it is the regular flouting of the principles of international law and those contained in the Charter, particularly the principle on the non-use of force, which undermines the effectiveness of the Council. All Council resolutions, whether recommendations or decisions of a substantive nature, are based primarily on this fundamental principle. Yet most nations pay only lip-service to Article 2(4); force is used illegally by States on a regular basis. In the cases of Goa, East Timor, Western Sahara, the Middle East, Kampuchea and West Irian, States have gained territory by the use of force. In many of the cases mentioned, which by no means constitute an exhaustive list, other principles of international law have been flouted, for example the principle of self-determination.

The relative ineffectiveness of the Council is due to a combination of the failure of some members to respect basic principles of law and a failure by the members of the Council to operate its powers in accordance with the objectives of the Charter rather than an inherent flaw in the Council's powers.

No power to impose a binding settlement

Despite isolated suggestions to the contrary,[54] neither the Charter nor the practice of the Security Council can be used to evince the possibility of a power to impose a mandatory or binding settlement by a combination of Article 25 and Chapter VI (Articles 36 and 37). Nevertheless, on occasions, the Council's recommendations for settlement based on a combination of Article 24 and Chapter VI, are more comprehensive and detailed so that they suggest a more intense and concerted effort by the Council to achieve a settlement than do the recommendations which outline a framework for settlement discussed above. However, they are not binding on non-complying parties.

The conclusion of the Renville Agreement between the Netherlands and Indonesia represented a success for the Security Council and its Committee of Good Offices. However, although the truce arrangements were put into effect, the political discussions broke down despite the efforts of the above-mentioned Committee. In December 1948, a Dutch surprise attack enabled it to capture most of the principal cities in the territory of the Republic, which, combined with a more intransigent approach by the Dutch,[55] signified that the Council could no longer persevere with its good offices approach. Nor did it venture into Chapter VII. Instead it adopted resolution 67 on 28 January 1949, which represented a much more comprehensive approach by the Council aimed at achieving a political solution.

The resolution uses, in its preamble, the language of Article 24, and then goes on to outline a more detailed recommendation for settlement, presumably with Article 36 or Article 37 in mind. The use of Article 24 is possibly to impress upon the intransigent parties the desire of the Council to fulfil its primary responsibility. By the resolution the Council established the United Nations' Commission for Indonesia in the place of the Good Offices Committee, a move which indicated the Council's increased commitment to a more comprehensive settlement. In operative paragraph 3 the Council recommended the establishment of an interim federal government which was to have internal powers until the transfer of sovereignty by the Netherlands which was to be achieved by 1 July 1950. Elections for the Indonesian Constituent Assembly were to be completed by 1 October 1949. The Commission was established to help the parties to implement the resolution.

The resolution was recommendatory only, but it had the value of being so comprehensive that it was almost 'decision like' in its content. Nevertheless, the Belgian representative made it clear that the resolution remained under Chapter VI.

With regard to the settlement of the substance of a question, the Council can only make recommendations, and it could not be otherwise. To acknowledge the Council's right to decide on the liberation of the peoples of Indonesia, or of any other people, would be the equivalent of granting it the authority to settle the fate of a territory, to determine likewise its allegiance, in a word, to settle categorically the question whether a State should or should not be created.[56]

Nevertheless, the combination of Article 24 and the obvious commitment of the Council to the independence of Indonesia led to the Dutch government notifying its general acceptance of the resolution with a few exceptions.[57] On 27 December 1949 the Netherlands transferred sovereignty to the Republic of Indonesia.

In the Namibian case, the Council 'decided' that the 'continued occupation of the Territory of Namibia by the South African authorities' was illegal and that its mandate over the territory was terminated.[58] However, this was only a decision on legality, it was not a political solution, although it provided a base for the United Nations' plan for Namibia. Subsequent resolutions on Namibia, dealing with settlement, can be viewed as coming under Chapter VI.

The current basis for the settlement of the Namibian problem is resolution 435, adopted on 29 September 1978, which endorsed the proposals in the Secretary General's report[59] providing for internationally supervised elections leading to the independence of the disputed territory, a plan which after over a decade of South African inspired frustration, now looks like coming to fruition.[60] It took an accord negotiated outside the United Nations and containing concessions towards South Africa, particularly by linking Cuban withdrawal from Angola with South African withdrawal from Namibia, before the South Africans would agree to the United Nations' plan.

The Security Council itself was unable to coerce the South Africans into implementing the plan because Western members were unwilling to back the UN plan with anything more than voluntary measures of a limited nature called for in resolution 566 of 1985.[61] The original text supported the implementation of mandatory sanctions against Pretoria if the Namibian Independence Plan had not been put into operation by a certain date, but the United Kingdom and the United States could not support this and they later vetoed a Non Aligned draft[62] which would have determined that the 'continued illegal occupation of Namibia by South Africa constitutes a breach of international peace and an act of aggression', and would have imposed mandatory sanctions against South Africa under Article 41, Chapter VII.

The use of Chapter VII action to enforce the provisions of a settlement proposal ostensibly made under Chapter VI and Article 24 would have represented the most effective method of operation for the Council short of the use of force. The two Western powers did not commit themselves to this when, paradoxically, they were two of the original drafters of the Namibian Plan for Independence.[63]

The lack of complete support for the Council's resolutions makes them ineffective. The same effect has been felt as regards the South African situation as a whole. The most effective method of bringing about change in the form of a comprehensive recommendation to end apartheid combined with the modalities necessary to replace it by majority rule under Chapter VI and Article 24, which, if not complied with, would be backed up by mandatory economic sanctions, has been prevented by Western States. Nevertheless, the tone of the Council's resolutions is beginning to reach this point as the Western powers begin to buckle as a result of the international outrage shown towards the continuing violence and repression in South Africa. In 1984 the Pretoria government introduced a new constitution giving 'coloureds' and those people of Asian origin some political franchise. The Security Council merely condemned the new constitution and declared it invalid, while expressing support for the continued struggle for self-determination.[64] By 1986, the Council was able to suggest a 'threat to the peace' in South Africa and demanded 'the immediate eradication of apartheid as a necessary step towards the establishment of a non-racial democratic society based on self-determination and majority rule through the full and free exercise of adult suffrage in a united and non-fragmented South Africa'.[65] And to this end it demanded, *inter alia*, the dismantling of bantustans, the release of political prisoners, and the lifting of the state of emergency.

The Security Council cannot impose a binding settlement under Chapter VII for two reasons; first, such a power is not envisaged in the Charter and secondly the settlement process is only conducive to recommendations. However, the Council could pass a forceful recommendation under Chapter VI or under the non-mandatory powers contained in Article 39, Chapter VII. The above resolution approaches this position but fails because it lacks the support of the United Kingdom and the United States who abstained and who would prevent any pressure being brought to bear on South Africa by the use of the powers of Chapter VII.[66]

The dysfunctional effect of the Council's attempts at conflict resolution
Jeanne Kirkpatrick, former United States' ambassador to the United Nations, has expressed some interesting points on the problems of conflict resolution. Her conclusion is that 'the UN has on occasion made conflict resolution more difficult than it would otherwise be'. She cites the Camp David Accords as an example of a successful settlement which would not have occurred through the United Nations. The negotiations between Israel and Egypt with mediation by the United States were, she states, 'pragmatic and non-ideological'. She argues that because only the parties to the dispute were involved, with assistance from the mediator, the settlement process was made much easier. On the other hand, at the United Nations 'the debates are intensely ideological, as are the resolutions that are ultimately adopted. The objective instead is to isolate and denigrate Israel and ultimately to undermine its political legitimacy.'

She states that bringing the conflict before the United Nations, by which she presumably means the Security Council or the General Assembly, actually has the effect of spreading the conflict by extending the number of parties to it. Certainly, in the case of the Security Council, the number of invited

speakers has proliferated over the last two decades, which inhibits the settlement process, but it remains doubtful that by involving the United Nations
the conflict is in danger of escalating. Speaking against Israel is not akin to
a declaration of war against Israel, although Kirkpatrick says that it amounts
to a 'war by other means'. She explains that as well as extending the conflict,
the United Nations exacerbates and polarises the conflict by discouraging
neutral stances which would give rise to negotiation attempts.[67]

Several of these points are valid, but one must remember that the Camp
David Accords dealt with only a small fraction of the Middle Eastern problem
– the conflict between Israel and Egypt – and then did not deal successfully
with the problem of the Gaza Strip. The Security Council had attempted to
establish a framework for the solution of the whole in resolution 242, when
perhaps it might have been better to take it piece by piece. However, the
polarisation talked about by Kirkpatrick is not solely caused by the Socialist
and Non Aligned blocs, but equally by the United States. Continual American
blocking of any effective Council moves to stop the Israeli advancement into
Lebanon in 1982 meant that when the Israelis left Beirut, the Americans had
only themselves to blame when in December 1985 the Syrians stepped in and
backed a peace plan encompassing all the various factions in Beirut.[68]
Sometimes it is the attitude of the United States which forces the settlement
or attempted settlement of a conflict outside the United Nations, in particular,
the Security Council.

Reference to the International Court

Article 36(3) of the Charter states that 'in making recommendations under
this Article the Security Council should also take into consideration that legal
disputes should as a general rule be referred by the parties to the International
Court'.

Many factors militate against increased reference by the Council to the
International Court. Many countries are not willing to gamble losing a dispute
in an all or nothing legal ruling; they prefer, if anything, political compromises.
In addition, a strict delineation between the Council and the International
Court on the basis of whether the dispute is political or legal fails to take
account of the fine and often blurred distinction between law and politics and
the fact that the Council has, by other provisions in Chapter VI, a quasi-
judicial role anyway.

In fact the Council has made little use of Article 36(3). In the dispute
between Albania and the United Kingdom over aspects of passage through
the Corfu Channel in 1947, the Security Council recommended that the parties
'immediately refer the dispute' to the International Court.[69] That the
Council, under Article 36(3), can do no more than make a recommendation
which the parties are free to accept or reject was made clear by the World

Court. The United Kingdom argued that the Council's resolution had established the Court's jurisdiction. Although the Court found it unnecessary to rule on this point, a majority pointed out that Article 36(3) did not introduce a new case of compulsory jurisdiction.[70]

The only other use of Article 36(3) by the Council occurred in 1976 when Greece complained of 'flagrant violations by Turkey of the sovereign rights of Greece on its continental shelf in the Aegean' which has 'created a dangerous situation threatening international peace and security'.[71] Resolution 395 was adopted on 25 August 1976 by consensus; it called for negotiations and invited the parties to refer the question to the International Court.[72]

Article 36(3) is really an example of settlement by pacific means and so should be associated with Article 33(1). It is not generally used by the Security Council because it only entails a recommendation. If the parties are willing to refer their dispute to the International Court they do not generally need the Council to remind them to do so. The infrequent use of Article 36(3) is a consequence of the limited use of the World Court in resolving conflicts.

Provisional measures

Article 40 provides that,

In order to prevent the aggravation of the situation, the Security Council may, before making the recommendations or deciding upon the measures provided for in Article 39, call upon the parties concerned to comply with such provisional measures as it deems necessary or desirable. Such provisional measures shall be without prejudice to the rights, claims or positions of the parties concerned. The Security Council shall duly take account of a failure to comply with such provisional measures.

By placing this provision in Chapter VII, which deals mainly with mandatory measures, there has been a tendency to view recommendations of provisional measures (usually a call for a cease-fire and withdrawal) as coming within Chapter VI, usually Article 36, with Article 40 measures being exclusively mandatory following a finding under Article 39 or by the invocation of Article 25.[73] However, as we have seen, provisional measures can be binding without references to Article 39 or Article 25 if the language of the resolution is peremptory and the discussions in the Council so indicate.

Once one accepts some degree of flexibility in the nature of provisional measures as developed in the practice of the Security Council, one can see that Article 40 is the natural basis for them whether their invocation is recommendatory or in the form of a decision under Article 25, just as Article 41 is the basis for sanctions whether voluntary or mandatory. The question to be discussed here is whether overtly mandatory provisional measures are more effective than recommendatory ones. First of all we will examine certain situations in which the call for a cease-fire and withdrawal was viewed as recommendatory.

In Palestine in 1948, the fighting between the Jewish Haganah and the Palestinian Liberation Army caused the Council to adopt several resolutions calling for a cessation of hostilities and a truce.[74] These are generally viewed as recommendatory because there was a refusal in the meetings of the Security Council to make a finding under Article 39.[75] These calls continued with little success even after the surrounding Arab countries invaded the newly proclaimed State of Israel,[76] until the conflict was brought clearly within Chapter VII. The question whether the later resolutions adopted under Chapter VII were more effective will be examined later.

The reason why the Council so often has to resort to cease-fire calls is obviously due to the fact that it is badly prepared. Often the cease-fire resolution is the first Council action in a conflict, whereas if it had heeded the warnings it could have attempted to defuse the situation at an earlier stage. The Middle East is again illustrative of the Council's poor crisis management. In the build up to the outbreak of the Six Day War on 5 May 1967, the Council showed an unwillingness to prevent what appeared to be at least 'a very serious potential threat to the peace'.[77]

The withdrawal of UNEF and the military build up of Egyptian, Syrian and Jordanian forces appeared to be a threat to the peace but pro-Arab members of the Council blocked any attempted move to prevent war.[78] Yet when the war broke out the Council managed to adopt a unanimous resolution which called upon 'the Governments concerned as a first step to take forthwith all measures for an immediate cease-fire'.[79] This was disregarded, so on 7 June the Soviet Union, concerned about Arab losses, proposed a more forceful draft which was adopted as resolution 234. In it the Council demanded a cessation of hostilities. A similar resolution was adopted when fighting intensified on the Syrian front.[80] By 10 June all the disputants had accepted the cease-fire.

These latter resolutions appear to have been more effective, perhaps because of their more peremptory language. However, this is deceiving for the Israelis accepted the cease-fire only when they had gained the Sinai, the West Bank and the Golan Heights, whereas the Arabs were in no position to refuse when their armies started losing severely. Cease-fire resolutions are often combined with or are followed by a call for the withdrawal of occupying troops. In the case of the Six Day War it was some months before the Council adopted resolution 242,[81] which, *inter alia*, called for Israeli withdrawal.

Although a cease-fire may be complied with, a call for withdrawal is less likely to be obeyed for it is often an intrinsic part of the settlement process. The Security Council quickly adopted both a cease-fire resolution[82] and a resolution calling for the withdrawal of Israeli troops[83] soon after the Israelis had launched their invasion of Lebanon in 1982. Neither call was complied with until the Israelis had achieved their aims of eradicating the PLO from Lebanon and establishing a security zone in the southern part of the country.

The Middle East illustrates how the Council is often unable to step beyond the establishment of a cease-fire. Even compliance with such a call is illusory of Council effectiveness, in that it will only be accepted when both sides are simultaneously ready because of their relative military positions. Withdrawal calls are not generally complied with because the party in the strongest position will lose most. Settlement in terms of international law or justice is unlikely while countries are able to benefit territorially by the use of force.

Potentially, the Security Council's role in a conflict, if one excludes mandatory enforcement measures, can be summarised as calling for or demanding a cease-fire, then a withdrawal to prior positions, and then an outline of settlement. The first two stages may be facilitated by the inter-positioning of a peacekeeping force. On several occasions the Council has been unable to go beyond a cease-fire call. For example, the sole Council resolution on the dispute between France and Tunisia in 1961 was a call 'for an immediate cease-fire and a return of all armed forces to their original positions'.[84] Similarly, for many years the Council called on the participants in the Gulf war to establish a cease-fire.[85]

On 20 July 1987 the Council finally adopted a mandatory demand for a cease-fire between Iran and Iraq in resolution 598 after expressly referring to Articles 39 and 40 of Chapter VII, as well as determining that there existed a 'breach of the peace as regards the conflict between Iran and Iraq'. The evidence is that a mandatory call for provisional measures is more effective since a cease-fire was established in August 1988.[86] However, the cease-fire was as a result of the failure of the Iranian offensive and of economic exhaustion which led it to accept the resolution, Iraq having already accepted resolution 598 because of its tenuous position.[87] The mandatory call may have provided the necessary diplomatic handle for both parties to grasp, but they were only prepared to grasp it when they both realised that the war was truly stalemated.

Often the effectiveness of any mandatory call under Article 40 is reduced because the Council dithers between Chapter VI and VII. The delay and political in-fighting which occur in the Council as various factions argue whether to make a determination under Article 39 or not, encourages the parties to a conflict to ignore the call, whether mandatory or recommendatory, because it obviously lacks the necessary solidarity, having been arrived at only when the various groups on the Council have simultaneously arrived at the conclusion that the party they favour would benefit from a cease-fire.

The Bangladesh crisis in 1971 took this process to the extreme. The Council met one day after the outbreak of hostilities. A plethora of draft resolutions did not result in a consensus, in fact it was five days after the hostilities had ceased that the Council managed to adopt a resolution which appeared to be a mandatory call for provisional measures. Resolution 307[88] made an indirect finding under Article 39 by stating that the situation on the sub-continent 'remains a threat to international peace' and then demanded that 'a durable cease-fire and cessation of hostilities be strictly observed'. The resolution noted that a cease-fire had already taken place; in fact a political solution had occurred through India's victory in the war, and by the creation of the independent State of Bangladesh. The Council was guilty of shutting the gate after the horse had bolted.

In other cases, the Council has acted less ineptly but still too slowly in its usage of a mandatory call under Article 40. The Gulf war is one modern example. The first Arab-Israeli conflict in 1948 is another. From 5 March 1948 to 7 July 1948[89] the Security Council could only produce mere cease-fire calls as hostilities intensified in Palestine. The Soviet Union and the United States favoured the newly born State of Israel and so pressed for a finding of a threat to the peace under Article 39 combined with provisional measures under Article 40 to try and stem the Arab advance, but with the British and Chinese being sympathetic to the Arab nations any such move was blocked.[90]

Eventually with the Arab countries losing, the United Kingdom and China felt unable to continue to prevent a determination under Article 39. Resolution 54[91] at last classified the situation as a 'threat to the peace within the meaning of Article 39' and ordered that 'pursuant to Article 40' a cessation of hostilities should take place 'not later than three days from the date' of the resolution. A truce was established within the specified time. However, with the Israelis strengthening militarily in the breathing space created by the truce, the Soviet Union and the United States blocked any attempt to make a further resolution (resolution 61) binding[92] by refusing to allow a finding of a threat to or breach of the peace. Resolution 61 called for the withdrawal of forces to positions held on 14 October and for the establishment of permanent truce lines. The Soviet Union and the United States realised that only Israel would lose by such an action. The Israelis ignored the resolution. The Council then entered into Chapter VII again with the adoption of resolution 62[93] which cited Article 39 and decided that to eliminate the threat to the peace an armistice should be established. It called upon the parties, 'as a provisional measure under Article 40' to negotiate with a 'view to establishing an armistice'. An armistice was eventually established.

From this brief account it appears that when the Council does place itself squarely under Articles 39 and 40, the cease-fire is established, whereas a mere recommendatory call is, all too often, readily ignored by the parties. However, this is too simplistic a view. Although the Israelis certainly viewed the mandatory calls of the Council with great concern,[94] the major factor in their acceptance of the cease-fire calls was the state of hostilities in each case. Resolution 54 produced a cease-fire because the Arabs were losing and the Israelis, unknown to the Arabs, desperately needed time to re-group and re-equip. Resolution 62 calling for armistice negotiations was initially ignored by the Egyptians who resumed an offensive in the Negev in December.

It was Israel's counter-offensive which forced the eventual negotiations of an armistice, while the Council ineptly returned to the use of a recommendatory resolution calling for a cease-fire.[95]

Mandatory resolutions may be marginally more successful than their recommendatory counterparts, but they still have the same inherent flaw when they are successful; they tend to freeze the dispute and usually to one of the parties' advantage. Even fairly rapidly arrived at resolutions, although sometimes effective, work to the advantage of one of the parties. When violence erupted between the two Cypriot communities in 1974, the Council was rapidly convened on 16 July.[96] With a Turkish invasion occurring the Council adopted resolution 353[97] which found a 'serious threat to international peace and security' and demanded an 'end to foreign military intervention'. The resolution called for both a cease-fire and for the co-operation of the parties with the peacekeeping force, present since 1964. The cease-fire was eventually complied with after the call had been reiterated.[98] Further provisional measures created a security zone between Turkish forces in the north of the island and Greek Cypriot forces to the south.[99] The effect of this was to cement the solution sought by Turkey and the Turkish Cypriots by the partition of the island.

The drafters of the Charter inserted the provisional measures provision as an optional stop-gap before the application of enforcement measures under Articles 41 and 42. The Security Council has used Article 40 more in the way of a holding measure while pacific settlement is sought. The Secretary General's attempts at mediation in the Cyprus situation have been mentioned. In the Falklands war, the Council speedily adopted a call for provisional measures after a finding of a breach of the peace[100] and then encouraged the Secretary General in his good offices mission.[101]

The call for provisional measures was quickly adopted in the Falklands war, but was ignored by Argentina. Similarly, after the North Korean forces had invaded the South, the Council quickly found a breach of the peace and called for a cessation of hostilities and a withdrawal of North Korean forces to the 38th parallel;[102] a call which was also ignored.

This suggests that even when quickly adopted, mandatory provisional measures are not much more effective than those adopted without a finding under Article 39. This is probably because the Council has very rarely adopted effective enforcement of the provisional measures it has called for, with the exception of the UN operation in Korea.

Voluntary sanctions

The powers contained in Article 41 were intended to be mandatory enforcement measures following a finding of a threat to or breach of the peace under Article 39. However, on occasions the Council is unwilling to take mandatory action, with the consequence that it settles for a call for voluntary measures or sanctions. Such action can be viewed as a reinterpretation of Article 41 to allow recommendations, or as merely a recommendation under Chapter VI, or a recommendation of enforcement action under Article 39. Although the Charter base for such powers is inconclusive there is no doubt that the Council has developed such a power, the evolution of which lies in political compromise. In almost every case in which voluntary measures have been called for, the Western powers have objected to a finding under Article 39 combined with mandatory sanctions. Voluntary sanctions, as the term implies, are breached with impunity and so are relatively ineffective except for a certain symbolic role plus being a reflection of international opinion.

In the Rhodesian situation the Council initially called for an arms, oil and petroleum embargo to be imposed against the Smith regime.[103] The Western powers viewed this as a voluntary call, although others thought that it was 'only under Chapter VII that economic sanctions are mentioned'.[104] With at least two of the permanent members regarding the call as voluntary, the resolution must be regarded as recommendatory.

International pressure sometimes has the effect of turning voluntary measures into mandatory ones. In the case of Rhodesia this happened relatively quickly when the Council first imposed selective mandatory sanctions[105] and then more comprehensive sanctions.[106] Nevertheless, over two years elapsed between the call for voluntary measures and the call for comprehensive mandatory measures, a fact that decreased the effectiveness of the sanctions for it allowed the Rhodesian economy time to prepare. It was almost as if certain members were dragging their feet to allow this to happen. The same can be said as regards the arms embargo placed on South Africa. This was originally a voluntary call made in 1963;[107] fourteen years later it was made mandatory,[108] giving the Pretoria regime ample time to stockpile and to work out alternative supply routes. The arguments against sanctions, which are prevalent in the West, will be examined below, although it can be said at this stage that sanctions are not going to be effective unless they are imposed immediately.

In the South African situation, the United Kingdom and the United States have prevented the application of mandatory sanctions. The most these countries accept is a voluntary call for limited economic sanctions.[109]

Mandatory economic sanctions

Article 41 of the United Nations' Charter reads,

The Security Council may decide what measures not involving the use of armed force are to be employed to give effect to its decisions and it may call upon the Members of the United Nations to apply such measures. These may include the complete or partial interruption of economic relations and of rail, sea, air, postal, telegraphic, radio and other means of communication or the severance of diplomatic relations.

Given that the military measures envisaged by Articles 42 and 43 are defunct, the application of economic sanctions under Article 41 probably represents the greatest extent of the Council's armoury. Voluntary sanctions have been mentioned and generally dismissed as purely notional and ineffective. Mandatory measures under Article 41 following an express or implied finding under Article 39 have been used only twice by the Council. They were imposed against the Smith regime in Southern Rhodesia in 1966, and were finally terminated in 1980[110] with the emergence of Zimbabwe. The only other mandatory use of Article 41 was a limited one − to impose an arms embargo against South Africa in 1977, which is still in force.[111] Thus, in the following examination we have only the Rhodesian experience to illustrate the effectiveness of a full economic embargo under Article 41. The attempts to introduce mandatory sanctions against South Africa provide a chance of comparing the effectiveness of sanctions in the Rhodesian case with the effectiveness of sanctions if applied with the purpose of ending the system of apartheid in South Africa.

If Article 41 sanctions prove to be ineffective, then the Security Council's ability to fulfil its primary role is similarly reduced. Potential aggressors and international law breakers are not going to be deterred by a toothless Security Council whose ultimate power is the application of ineffective enforcement measures in the form of economic sanctions. Indeed, the fact that the Council has used its power under Article 41 in only two situations suggests that it might be reluctant for fear of revealing its inadequacies. However, the main reason for its limited use is the perceived economic interests of the members, particularly the permanent members.

There have been varying assessments of the effectiveness of the mandatory economic measures imposed against Rhodesia.[112] The figures suggest that after initially struggling, after 1968 the Rhodesian economy improved.[113] These figures have been used to deny the effectiveness of economic measures. Nevertheless, there is evidence to suggest that after 1974, with the combined effects of Mozambique's independence (Portugal, the colonial power, was a major sanction breaker), the guerrilla war and the sanctions, the Rhodesian domestic situation as a whole began to decline. Thus, although the application of sanctions did not immediately achieve the primary goals of the Security Council of either ending UDI by forcing Smith to negotiate, or ruining the Rhodesian economy and thus forcing internal change, it did achieve certain subsidiary goals which must be viewed as a success. These were, namely, the prevention of an all out civil war in Rhodesia after the proclamation of UDI, the prevention of foreign military intervention to end UDI and possibly escalation, and the inducement, as opposed to the coercion, of the white regime to negotiate.

Nevertheless, the use of economic statistics to point to the alleged failure of sanctions against Rhodesia has led to arguments against applying sanctions against South Africa,[114] particularly by the West. Unless the West is willing to enforce sanctions they will be ineffective, but that is not an inherent fault in the nature of sanctions but the fault of the Western States.[115] Indeed, it has been suggested, by the former South African ambassador to London, that the mandatory, global application of those sanctions mentioned by the Eminent Persons Group[116] would have a 'very major effect' on South Africa.[117]

Nevertheless, in the Rhodesian case, sanctions were mandatory and so binding on member countries, including Western States. So the question remains as to why the Rhodesian economy was not affected more rapidly. One major reason for this is the poor timing of the imposition. Pokalas summarises the effect of this in the case of Rhodesia.

Such anticipatory actions as stockpiling materials, developing alternative supply sources to obviate over-dependence on any one source, diversifying domestic production, planting crops that were readily exportable, conserving key commodities and establishing new trade routes were utilised by Southern Rhodesia even prior to Security Council action.[118]

Comprehensive economic sanctions were imposed one and a half years after the Unilateral Declaration of Independence, which in terms of the United Nations was relatively quickly. However, it was six years since the United Nations had taken cognisance of the situation[119] and so the country had ample time to prepare. For sanctions to be effective they must be immediate, mandatory and comprehensive. In other words, a resolution should have been adopted by the Council on the day of UDI or even before, containing a determination of a threat to the peace and the imposition of mandatory, comprehensive measures. In the Rhodesian case sanctions were applied in a 'gradual crescendo of severity',[120] creating many loopholes which the Security Council gradually filled in a piecemeal fashion. Above all, for sanctions to be effective, they must have the full support of the members of the United Nations, in particular the permanent members of the Security Council.

On the basis outlined above, sanctions against South Africa would not be effective in bringing about an internal change because the Pretoria regime has been given over twenty years' warning of their possible implementation and so has had more than adequate time to prepare. In addition, it is doubtful whether the United States and Britain would commit themselves to sanctions even if they decided not to veto their mandatory application. In 1980, the United States was South Africa's number one trading partner, with an increase in two-way trade of 24% from 1979,[121] while British interest in South Africa comprises 45% of all foreign investment there.[122] Thus, these two Western powers have the most to lose after South Africa if sanctions are imposed, not only by losing investments and valuable minerals in South Africa but also by affecting their own economies.

Nevertheless, pragmatic arguments aside, and despite the fact that South

Africa has been given warning, sanctions applied fully by all the United Nations' members would deal a severe blow to the morale of South Africa and shorten its life, though not bringing it to its knees. Thus, sanctions would not cripple South Africa and so possibly cause a civil war in the ensuing vacuum; instead the increased pressure would force the minority regime to negotiate radical political reforms rather than the piecemeal ones it has adopted so far to placate its Western trading partners. As with the Smith regime in Rhodesia, the object of a full array of economic sanctions against South Africa must be to cause peaceful internal change not bloody revolution, economic collapse and possible escalation.

Given the scenario that the Council decided unanimously to adopt mandatory sanctions against a certain State and the members acted diligently to observe the binding obligation placed on them, there can be little doubt that even the strongest, well-prepared economy, such as South Africa's, would be damaged. Such damage would lead to negotiations, whereas destruction of the economy would probably lead to conflict. As regards observance, the permanent members, in particular, could apply their sophisticated intelligence and surveillance networks to ensure that no country was breaking the sanctions.

In the Rhodesian situation sanction breakers went unpunished in many instances, which led the Council to adopt resolution 333.[123] This called for the 'enactment and enforcement of legislation providing for the imposition of severe penalties on persons natural or juridical that evade or commit breach of sanctions'. Admittedly, in the case of Rhodesia the two countries which openly defied sanctions − South Africa and Portugal − were States over which the rest of the international community had little hold. It is doubtful whether a parallel can be drawn between their support for Rhodesia and Britain's and the United States' continuing economic involvement in South Africa. The two Western States would not want to appear as international law breakers if sanctions ever became mandatory. The Catch 22 is that these two countries prevent the mandatory application of Article 41.

In addition to South Africa and Portugal, other prominent sanction breakers during the Rhodesian crisis were the multinational corporations. These proved to be the most difficult to prevent because of their diverse locations and their economic and political power. Multinationals are mainly based in the West and so it is natural that they should be the responsibility of those members which have a share in them. In particular, supervision should be co-ordinated by the three Western permanent members of the Council.[124]

Another main sanction breaker during the Rhodesian situation was the United States, which in 1970 defied the Security Council by passing the Byrd Amendment,[125] enabling it to trade with Southern Rhodesia in strategic materials. The Council, with the United States merely abstaining, censored the United States in resolution 320[126] in which it was 'deeply concerned by the report of the United States of America that it has authorised the importation of chrome ore and other minerals from Southern Rhodesia'. The Rhodesian economy could not but benefit from such illegal activities, evidenced by its economic growth in conjunction with the reported number of sanction violations. By 1968 there had been thirteen violations; this had increased to seventy-three by 1970 and 346 by 1976. The United States had committed forty-six violations by 1978.[127] The United States had ignored a mandatory decision of the Security Council and had therefore abrogated its treaty obligations and breached Charter law. The lead given by the United States led to the initial vigilance of other States being relaxed, with the result that the mandatory measures were then treated like voluntary measures – as a token gesture to be ignored with impunity.

It is possible that the United Kingdom and the United States would also be lax as regards any mandatory sanctions against South Africa, although it remains to be seen whether they would positively encourage their breach. However, it would be wrong to assert that economic sanctions are inherently ineffective; it would be correct to say that it is the attitude of certain members which causes them to be ineffective.

It is also argued that because a possible target nation is industrially and militarily strong, sanctions would serve no useful purpose and so should not be imposed. This argument is applicable to South Africa. The import of this pragmatic argument is that sanctions should only be applied selectively against States which the Council has decided are a threat to the peace or have breached the peace and are weak economically. The extreme of this would be the industrialised nations combining to sanction a poor Third World country. Surely, sanctions should be applied irrespective of the strength of the target State if the situation so warrants. However, arguments in favour of the Council adopting an objective and normative approach are subject to the geopolitical factors which govern the work of that body.

Rhodesia was internally strong. It was self-sufficient in agriculture, had abundant minerals, including gold, and a strong industrial base, but it still needed trade and investment. This is why the Council should have implemented a total embargo against the country, for, as Pokalas points out, 'had the embargo been properly implemented by States' legislation, strictly enforced by States' administration and judicial sectors, and diligently coordinated by the Committee, the Rhodesian economy would have floundered and ultimately collapsed'.[128]

The only effective method of ensuring that the weaknesses of the target State's economy are exposed is to impose a comprehensive embargo. Limited embargos are insufficient because even if they are aimed at those areas of weakness the other unsanctioned areas of the economy will develop to compensate. An arms embargo, such as that imposed against South Africa, is a folly because South Africa's strong economy and natural resources supply have enabled it to produce its own weapons.

Other non-violent means

Article 41 lists non-violent measures other than economic sanctions which might be utilised in a situation of a threat to or breach of the peace. These constitute mainly token gestures of international concern and censure. In 1946, the Security Council failed to adopt mandatory diplomatic sanctions in the form of a severance of diplomatic relations with the Franco regime in Spain after a committee failed to find a threat to the peace. The thwarted aim was to pressure the Spanish government into a less dictatorial rule.

Similarly, in relation to South Africa, a voluntary boycott 'in the field of sporting and cultural relations' has been requested by the Security Council.[129] The United Kingdom does not strictly implement these calls, relying instead on sporting associations and pressure groups to ensure the boycott. This is indicative of the seriousness with which voluntary measures are taken. Such measures, even if they are mandatory, add little to the Security Council's armoury and do not appear to induce the target States to make any radical reforms.

Military measures

The Organisation's role in the maintenance of international peace was premised, in 1945, on the ability of its primary organ, the Security Council, ultimately to use military measures to enforce the peace. The Council's ultimate weapon and deterrent was contained in Article 42: 'Should the Security Council consider that measures provided for in Article 41 would be inadequate or have proved to be inadequate, it may take such action by air, sea, or land forces as may be necessary to maintain or restore international peace and security.'

It is generally agreed that the use of such military measures would require a 'decision' of the Council, which would be binding on members by means of the military agreements envisaged in Article 43.[130] Since the agreements in Article 43 were not arrived at because of an East-West rift, it is argued that Article 42 is defunct. The only method by which a military enforcement action could be taken by the Council is by recommendation under Article 39, which, itself, expressly states that actions taken under Articles 41 and 42 are only authorised by decisions.

However, we have seen that the development of a power to recommend measures under Article 41 could be attributed to a reinterpretation of that Article to allow recommendations as well as decisions. It has been suggested that Article 39 is the true base for such recommendatory measures, but this appears incorrect without a finding of a threat to or breach of the peace.

Wherever one places its power to recommend sanctions, it is clear that the Council has such a power. Similarly, it has the power to recommend military measures, as evidenced by its actions in Korea and by its authorisation of the Beira patrol.

On 9 April 1966, the Council adopted resolution 221 which, *inter alia*, authorised Britain 'to prevent, by the use of force if necessary, the arrival at Beira of vessels reasonably believed to be carrying oil for Southern Rhodesia', after determining that the arrival of oil at Beira destined for Rhodesia was a threat to the peace. In the absence of any Article 42 agreement between Britain and the United Nations, this resolution can only be regarded as a recommendation to Britain, presumably under Article 39, to take enforcement action.

The Beira patrol was maintained successfully by Britain until 1975. Resolution 221 was itself a result of a threatened breach of the voluntary oil embargo imposed against Rhodesia by two Greek-registered tankers.[131] The 'Joanna V' was already in Beira, but as a result of resolution 221, which also empowered the United Kingdom to arrest the ship upon her departure if she discharged her oil, it left with a full load. The 'Manuela' was stopped by a British warship before entering the port, with the result that the captain changed the tanker's course away from Beira.[132]

The case of Korea was a 'historical aberration' which will probably never be repeated again.[133] United Nations' enforcement action was only made possible by the absence of the Soviet Union, which enabled the United States to use the Security Council to confer legitimacy on its policy of containing communism wherever it threatened to expand. Although other countries contributed to the United Nations' force, and although the force used the United Nations' flag, the action was essentially dictated by United States' foreign policy, under the command of a United States' general – MacArthur – who took his orders from Washington, not the United Nations.

In the absence of the Soviet Union, the Council adopted resolution 82[134] which found a 'breach of the peace' and called for a cessation of hostilities and a withdrawal of North Korean forces to the 38th parallel. Non-compliance with resolution 82 caused the Council to adopt resolution 83 on 27 June 1950, which recommended that members furnish armed assistance to South Korea; this in turn was followed by resolution 84[135] which recommended that member States providing forces make them 'available to a unified command under the United States of America'.

Although the call in resolution 82 was probably an example of a mandatory provisional measure called for with Article 40 in mind after an implied finding under Article 39,[136] the call for military assistance was only recommendatory and therefore was probably adopted with Article 39 in mind rather than Article 42.[137] The resolution did not purport to bind members to supply military assistance, a move which in the absence of agreements under Article 43 is practically impossible.

The action in Korea represented the only clear use by the United Nations of military measures so as to amount to an engagement in a conflict. It was also relatively successful in that it did prevent the North Koreans from gaining territorially by the use of force by eventually pushing them back to the 38th parallel. However, it involved the manipulation of the Council and the Assembly by the West, particularly the United States, who would have been quite happy to 'liberate' North Korea if it had not been for the intervention of Communist China after the UN force had pushed over the 38th parallel. Although the General Assembly had tacitly authorised this, such actions went beyond the requirements of enforcing the peace between North and South Korea, to amount to an attempted United Nations' conquest of a country and the enforcment of a settlement upon it. These objectives were those of the United States, using its superiority in the United Nations at the time to continue the Cold War. As it happens, the United States had to settle for a continuing division of Korea at the 38th parallel which has been made permanent by the failure of any process of settlement to unify the country. It could be said that the result of the Korean war, whether it was a United Nations' action or not, was to freeze the conflict and maintain the *status quo*, which is a normal 'half' successful result of a United Nations' action. However, the division of Korea is a product of ideology, a result of a conflict of power. In such a case it is defensible to have a limited objective of freezing the dispute rather than to attempt to settle it because any such attempt may lead to escalation as evidenced by Chinese intervention after the United Nations' force had crossed the 38th parallel in an attempt to settle the problem once and for all.

Conclusion

In this chapter we have examined the powers of the Security Council in an order which could loosely be described as representing a gradual scale of severity. Unfortunately, the top of the scale − military measures and economic sanctions (Articles 41 and 42) − is severely limited in effectiveness by geopolitical considerations, although it is arguable whether economic measures could be successful if freed from these limitations. The lower one goes down the scale − the lowest point possibly being a call on the parties to a dispute to settle it by peaceful means − the fewer geopolitical limitations there are. This is exemplified by the Council's willingness in Central America and, until recently, the Gulf war to call for settlement but to venture very little further up the scale.

Nevertheless, at each point on the scale geopolitical limitations play a part − consensus dictates that generally the Council resolution produced is indicating to the parties the furthest point on the scale that the Council is willing to reach. It is very unlikely that the Council will go beyond that point − witness the refusal of Western members to allow the imposition of mandatory sanctions against South Africa; and even if it does (possibly because of a change in the governments of those members), and goes to the furthest practical point along its scale – the imposition of economic sanctions – the sanctioned State has had ample time to prepare.

There is little possibility of improving the substantive content of Security Council resolutions and action, until the national interests of the members, particularly the permanent members, is less important than the collective responsibility of the United Nations. This is unlikely, except if the permanent members can arrive at a gentlemen's agreement whereby they define their national interests more narrowly, and by this method more areas of the world might be open to collective action by the Security Council.

One possible procedural method which could help to limit perceived national interests is the reform already mentioned whereby an independent investigation process would force the Council to examine every conflict or potential conflict, in whatever area of the world it occurred. Such a method might induce the permanent members to explain, in the many cases in which they are involved, why the Council should not be allowed to act. In their own spheres of influence, at the moment, the superpowers not only prevent constructive Council action, but any kind of criticism. Independent investigation could embarrass them into redefining their national interests more narrowly.

Another procedural reform would be aimed at making the Security Council more able to take preventative action, in preference to its present method of crisis management which makes it ineffective in many cases because it is faced with *faits accomplis*. Recently, the Security Council has become, in effect, 'an off-season General Assembly',[138] by the vast increase in the number of invited speakers who are not representing the members of the Council nor, in many cases, the parties to the dispute or conflict. In a sample number of years the average number of speakers per meeting reached eight in 1985 when previously (in the years sampled) it was no higher than six, and the proportion of invited speakers representing States not parties to the dispute or involved in a situation has (in the years sampled) risen from 0% in 1955 to 15% in 1965, to 25% in 1975, and to a staggering 50% in 1985.[139] These facts combined with the increasing representation of various organisations and groupings at Council meeting must mean that the Council's ability to act to a given dangerous situation or threat to or breach of the peace is severely hindered.

A procedural reform would bring practice back into line with the Charter, which states in Article 31 that the Council may invite non-members whenever it 'considers that the interests of that member are specially affected'. At the moment any State and most non-State organisations can express their views because the invited speakers are allowed into the forum unless there is an objection.[140]

However, our two procedural reforms are not going to radically increase the effectiveness of the Council. Only a change of perspective from national to collective security will facilitate a significant increase in success rate.

Notes

1 J.P. Cot and A. Pellet, *La Charte des Nations Unies*, 627.
2 R.B. Russell and J.E. Muther, *A History of the United Nations Charter*, 657 (1958).
3 What is now Chapter VII of the UN Charter.
4 Chapter VIIA, para.1 of the proposals.
5 Article 36(1) of the Charter.
6 Article 34 of the Charter.
7 Article 37(2) of the Charter.
8 L.M. Goodrich, E. Hambro and P.S. Simons, *The Charter of the United Nations*, 258, 2nd ed. (1969).
9 This interpretation is supported by the French text for Article 33(2): 'Le Conseil de Sécurité, s'il le juge nécessaire, invite les parties à régler leur différend par de tels moyens.'
10 See UN doc. S/14942 (1982).
11 SC 2345 mtg, 37 UN S/PV 33 (1982).
12 SC 2349 mtg, 37 UN S/PV (1982).
13 SC Res. 502, 37 UN SCOR Resolutions 15 (1982).
14 SC 2430 mtg, 38 UN S/PV (1983).
15 UN doc. S/15649 (1983).
16 SC Res. 530, 38 UN SCOR Resolutions 10 (1983).
17 UN doc. S/14941 (1982).
18 See also SC Res. 562, 40 UN SCOR 5 (1985).
19 *Nicaragua* case, I.C.J. *Rep.* 1986, 14.
20 SC Res. 479, 35 UN SCOR Resolutions 23 (1980).
21 See for example SC Res. 582, 41 UN SCOR Resolutions 13 (1986).
22 Goodrich, Hambro and Simons, *The Charter*, 161.
23 A.C. Arend, 'The Obligation to Persue Peaceful Settlement in International Disputes during Hostilities', 24 *Virginia Journal of International Law* (1983), 97.
24 See the Manila Declaration on the Peaceful Settlement of International Disputes; GA Res. 37/10, 37 UN GAOR Supp (No. 51) 261 (1982).
25 SC Res. 15, 1 UN SCOR Resolutions 6 (1946).
26 UN doc. S/360/REV 1 (1947).
27 SC 136 mtg, 2 UN SCOR (1947).
28 UN doc. S/3232 (1954).
29 See SC 675 mtg, 9 UN SCOR (1954).
30 SC 2802 mtg, 43 UN S/PV (1988).
31 SC Res. 289, 25 UN SCOR Resolutions 13 (1970) re Guinea; SC Res. 294, 26 UN SCOR Resolutions 2 (1971) re Senegal. See also SC Res. 568, 40 UN SCOR Resolutions 20 (1985) re South African attacks on Botswana; and SC Res. 57, 40 UN SCOR Resolutions 16 (1985) re South African incursions into Angola.
32 SC Res. 290, 25 UN SCOR Resolutions 13 (1970). But see SC Res. 302, 26 UN SCOR Resolutions 3 (1971) re Senegal.
33 Report of the Security Council's Special Mission, 32 UN SCOR Special Supp. (No. 3) (1977).
34 SC Res. 419, 32 UN SCOR Resolutions 18 (1977).
35 For other bodies established *strictu sensu* under Article 34 see: SC Res. 496, 36 UN SCOR Resolutions 11 (1981) to investigate mercenary aggression against the

Seychelles; SC Res. 189, 19 UN SCOR Resolutions 11 (1964) to investigate alleged aggression against Cambodia.

36 UN doc. S/11863 (1975).
37 See SC Res. 379 and 380, 30 UN SCOR Resolutions 8–9 (1975).
38 SC 2826 mtg, 43 UN S/PV (1988). SC Res. 621, 43 UN S/PV (1988).
39 SC Res. 39, 3 UN SCOR Resolutions 2 (1948).
40 SC Res. 47, 3 UN SCOR Resolutions 3 (1948).
41 T.M. Franck, *Nation against Nation*, 52 (1985).
42 UN doc. S/649/REV 1 (1947).
43 SC Res. 27, 2 UN SCOR Resolutions 6 (1947).
44 SC Res. 30, 2 UN SCOR Resolutions 6 (1947).
45 See 18 *Dept of State Bulletin* (1948), 325–27.
46 SC Res. 36, 2 UN SCOR Resolutions 9 (1947).
47 UN doc. S/537 (1947).
48 SC Res. 593, 41 UN SCOR Resolutions 16 (1986).
49 See UN doc. S/16519 (1984). SC 2607 mtg, 40 UN S/PV (1985).
50 R. Higgins. 'The Place of International Law in the Settlement of Disputes by the UN Security Council', 63 *A.J.I.L.* (1970), 1, at 4.
51 *Ibid.* See also O. Schacter, 'The Quasi-judicial Role of the Security Council and the General Assembly', 58 *A.J.I.L.* (1964), 960.
52 UN docs. S/20093, S/20242, S/20442 (1988).
53 G. Perry, 'Security Council Resolution 242: The Withdrawal Clause', 31 *Middle East Journal* (1977), 413 at 432.
54 UN doc. S/10453/REV 1 (1971).
55 See SC 389 mtg, 3 UN SCOR (1948).
56 SC 417 mtg, 4 UN SCOR (1949).
57 UN doc. S/1274 (1949).
58 SC Res. 269, 24 UN SCOR Resolutions 2 (1969).
59 UN doc. S/12857 (1978).
60 *The Independent*, 17 April 1989, 14.
61 The stopping of new investments, the prohibition on the sale of krugerands, and sporting and cultural restrictions; SC Res. 566, 40 UN SCOR Resolutions 11 (1985).
62 UN doc. S/17633 (1985).
63 Contained in UN doc. S/12636 (1978).
64 SC Res. 554, 39 UN SCOR Resolutions 3 (1984).
65 SC Res. 581, 41 UN SCOR Resolutions 9 (1986).
66 SC 2662 mtg, 41 UN SCOR 38 (1986).
67 J. Kirkpatrick, 'Peaceful Dispute Resolution through the United Nations', 37 *Arbitration Journal* (1982), 3 at 6.
68 Keesing's *Contemporary Archives* (1985), 33762. See also *Keesing* (1987), 35020.
69 SC Res. 22, 2 UN SCOR Resolutions 3 (1947).
70 *Corfu Channel* case, I.C.J. *Rep.* 1949, 15 at 31–2.
71 UN doc. S/12167 (1978).
72 See *The Aegean Sea Continental Shelf* case, I.C.J. *Rep.* 1978, 3.
73 Cot and Pellet, *La Charte*, 616–17.
74 SC Res. 42, 43, 46, 3 UN SCOR Resolutions 14–15 (1948).
75 See I.S. Pogany, *The Security Council and the Arab-Israeli Conflict*, 41 (1984).
76 See for example SC Res. 49, 3 UN SCOR Resolutions 19 (1948).
77 UN doc. S/7906 (1967).
78 See SC 1341–46 mtgs, 22 UN SCOR (1967).
79 SC Res. 233, 22 UN SCOR Resolutions 2 (1967).

80 SC Res. 235, 22 UN SCOR Resolutions 3 (1967).
81 SC Res. 242, 22 UN SCOR Resolutions 8 (1967).
82 SC Res. 508, 37 UN SCOR Resolutions 5 (1982).
83 SC Res. 509, 37 UN SCOR Resolutions 6 (1982).
84 SC Res. 164, 16 UN SCOR Resolutions 9 (1961).
85 For example SC Res. 588, 41 UN SCOR Resolutions 13 (1986).
86 SC 2823 mtg, 43 UN S/PV (1988).
87 UN doc. S/19551 (1988), Iraq. UN doc. S/20094 (1988), Iran.
88 SC Res. 307, 26 UN SCOR Resolutions 11 (1971).
89 SC Res. 53, 3 UN SCOR Resolutions 21 (1948).
90 SC 293, 306 mtgs, 3 UN SCOR (1948).
91 SC Res. 54, 3 UN SCOR Resolutions 22 (1948).
92 SC Res. 61, 3 UN SCOR Resolutions 28 (1948).
93 SC Res. 62, 3 UN SCOR Resolutions 29 (1948).
94 See Pogany, *The Security Council and the Arab-Israeli Conflict*, 47.
95 SC Res. 66, 3 UN SCOR Resolutions 30 (1948).
96 SC 1779 mtg, 29 UN SCOR (1974).
97 SC Res. 353, 29 UN SCOR Resolutions 7 (1974).
98 SC Res. 354, 29 UN SCOR Resolutions 7 (1974).
99 SC Res. 355, 29 UN SCOR Resolutions 8 (1974).
100 SC Res. 502, 37 UN SCOR Resolutions 15 (1982).
101 SC Res. 505, 37 UN SCOR Resolutions 17 (1982).
102 SC Res. 82, 5 UN SCOR Resolutions 4 (1950).
103 SC Res. 217, 20 UN SCOR Resolutions 8 (1965).
104 SC 1265 mtg, 20 UN SCOR 15 (US) 16 (UK) 6 (Ivory Coast) (1965).
105 SC Res. 232, 21 UN SCOR Resolutions 7 (1966).
106 SC Res. 253, 23 UN SCOR Resolutions 8 (1968).
107 SC Res. 181, 18 UN SCOR Resolutions 7 (1963).
108 SC Res. 418, 32 UN SCOR Resolutions 5 (1977).
109 UN doc. S/18785 (1987), vetoed at SC 2747 mtg, 42 UN S/PV (1987). SC Res. 569, 40 UN SCOR Resolutions 8 (1985), calling for wide-ranging voluntary measures.
110 SC Res. 460, 34 UN SCOR Resolutions 15 (1979).
111 See UN doc. S/18474 (1986). SC Res. 591, 41 UN SCOR Resolutions 17 (1986).
112 See generally J. C. Nkala, *The United Nations, International Law, and the Rhodesian Independence Crisis* (1985); H. R. Strack, *Sanctions: The Case of Rhodesia* (1978); L. Kapunga, *The United Nations and Economic Sanctions in Rhodesia* (1973); J. Pokalas, 'Economic Sanctions: An Effective Alternative to Military Coercion?', 4 *Brooklyn Journal of International Law* (1980), 289.
113 See UN doc. S/12265 (1975).
114 J. A. Sigmon, 'Dispute Resolution in the United Nations: An Inefficient Forum?', 10 *Brooklyn Journal of International Law* (1984) 437, at 450.
115 See J. Hanlon and R. Omond, *The Sanctions Handbook*, 73 (1987).
116 Established by the Commonwealth. See *Mission to South Africa* (1986).
117 Hanlon and Omond, *The Sanctions Handbook*, 74.
118 Pokalas, 4 *Brooklyn Journal of International Law* (1980), 312.
119 See GA Res. 1747, 17 UN GAOR Supp. (No. 17A) 3 (1962).
120 Pokalas, 4 *Brooklyn Journal of International Law* (1980), 312.
121 Sigmon, 10 *Brooklyn Journal of International Law* (1984), 442.
122 Hanlon and Omond, *The Sanctions Handbook*, 135.
123 SC Res. 333, 28 UN SCOR Resolutions 14 (1973).

124 See Nkala, *The Rhodesian Independence Crisis*, 81.
125 See Strack, *Sanctions*, 162–4.
126 SC Res. 320, 27 UN SCOR Resolutions 9 (1972).
127 Pokalas, 4 *Brooklyn Journal of International Law* (1980), 314.
128 *Ibid.*, 306.
129 SC Res. 569, 40 UN SCOR Resolutions 8 (1985).
130 See Cot and Pellet, *La Charte*, 709–11.
131 SC 1276 mtg, 21 UN SCOR 5 (1966), UK.
132 See UN doc. S/7249 (1966).
133 J.F. Murphy, *The United Nations and the Control of International Violence*, 124 (1985).
134 SC Res. 82, 5 UN SCOR Resolutions 4 (1950).
135 SC Res. 84, 5 UN SCOR Resolutions 5 (1950).
136 But see Article 2(6). Goodrich, Hambro and Simons, *The Charter*, 58–60.
137 SC 477 mtg, 5 UN SCOR 3 (1950), UK.
138 SC 2662 mtg, 41 UN S/PV 33 (1986), UK. SC 2608 mtg, 40 UN S/PV 73 (1985), France. Also M.C. Smouts, 'Reflexions sur les Methods de Travail du Conseil de Sécurité', 28 *Annuaire Francais de Droite International* (1982), 601.
139 In the years sampled the following figures were obtained for the average number of speakers per meeting: 1950, three; 1955, five; 1960, six; 1965, four; 1970, six; 1975, five; 1985, eight. The proportion of invited speakers who were not parties to the dispute in the years sampled were as follows: 1950, 0%; 1955, 0%; 1960, 7%; 1965, 15%; 1970, 13%; 1975, 25%; 1985, 50%.
140 See S.D. Bailey, *The Procedure of the United Nations Security Council*, 123–39, 2nd ed. (1988).

PART 2

The General Assembly's Role in the Maintenance of Peace

INTRODUCTION

Whereas the Security Council's position as the primary body responsible for the maintenance of international peace and security is reasonably well established and defined,[1] the General Assembly's role is nebulous and ill-defined.[2] The drafting of the provisions relating to the General Assembly's functions and powers was a source of contention between the smaller States represented at San Francisco and the sponsoring powers. The four power Dumbarton Oaks proposals gave the Assembly no real power. At San Francisco, the smaller States insisted that all the power should not be in the hands of the Council or, more specifically, in the hands of the veto-wielding powers. As a result Chapter IV, which indicates the powers of the General Assembly, became a compromise between the provisions granting generous powers to the Assembly to placate the smaller nations, namely Articles 10 and 14, and provisions attempting to restrict the powers and competence of the Assembly, that is Articles 11 and 12.

The result is an example of political compromise − a confusing set of provisions which have been interpreted advantageously by and for the benefit of whichever group or groups of States is dominating the Assembly at a particular time. In the early years of the Organisation the body was Western dominated. With the advent of rapid decolonisation in the late 1950s and during the 1960s the whole complexion of the Organisation changed with the Non Aligned movement seizing virtual control of the Assembly.

During the early years the Soviets protected their interests by the use of the veto in the Security Council and were fiercely critical of any attempt to give the Western dominated Assembly more than subsidiary powers in the field of international peace, basing their objections on a narrow interpretation of the relevant Charter provisions. Nevertheless, the West used its dominant position to introduce procedures and bodies to circumvent the paralysis in the Council brought on by the Soviet veto, using a liberal interpretation of the Charter.

In 1945 the membership of the United Nations numbered fifty-one, whereas this has now increased to 159. The bulk of this increase consists of the 100 or so members of the Non Aligned, dramatically altering the balance of power in the Assembly. The Socialist States have cleverly adopted similar stances to the Non Aligned on such issues as colonialism and self-determination, which understandably are of considerable concern to the Non Aligned. Paradoxically, the West, whom one would expect to dominate questions of freedom and self-determination (though not in colonial situations), has not been able to align itself on these issues with the newly independent States. Thus, it is the erstwhile colonial powers and their allies (namely the 'West') which are now, in the majority of discussions and votes, in the minority in the Assembly. Consequently, the West has withdrawn its liberal interpretation of the Charter which it used so successfully in the early years, and now argues on a narrow constitutional basis that the Security Council is the primary body, where, predictably, the number of Western vetoes in protection of Western interests has increased dramatically.

Relatively, the number of Western and Socialist bloc countries has remained constant; the variable factor is the group of newly independent States which does not have a permanent member, from within its ranks, on the Security Council protecting its interests. Consequently, there is an increasing divergence on similar issues between the views of the Assembly, where a majority of two-thirds can adopt a resolution on 'important questions'[3] such as those concerning international peace, and those of the Council, where the overriding consideration is one of compromise in order to avoid the veto. In the early years the West dominated both bodies and so used the Assembly as a means of dealing with issues on which the Soviet Union was sensitive. Nevertheless, there was still a link between the Assembly and the Council during the Cold War period. The Cold War indeed continued during the 1950s and 1960s,[4] but the introduction of a third factor — the newly independent States — meant that the link between the Assembly and the Council became increasingly tenuous. The Assembly began to take initiatives and become antagonistic towards the Council.

The new majority viewed the Council as a private club protecting the interests of the superpowers and their allies[5] — a view highlighted by the decreasing representation in the Security Council of the membership of the Organisation. In 1945 the ratio of members of the Security Council to members of the Organisation was 11:51 (21.6%). In 1985 this percentage had decreased to 9.4% (15:159). It would take a Security Council of thirty-three members to reproduce the original ratio, and a non-permanent member could hope for election to the club once every sixteen years.[6] These figures emphasise the decreasing ties between the Council and the Assembly, with the latter acting with increasing independence in the field of international peace and security.

Luard accurately summarises the implications and importance to the

Non Aligned of its power in the General Assembly in his work on the period of Western domination (1945−55):

If the West had been tempted to use its votes to force through its own views with little thought of negotiations to impose the tyranny of the majority, how much more would the third world when it came to power, be tempted to do so? The West at least had possessed alternative means of securing the ends it cherished, overwhelming military power, widespread diplomatic opportunities, huge economic strength, unrivalled political leverage. The third world had none of these assets. It had no military power, little diplomatic experience, negligible economic strength, and insignificant political leverage. For these countries, it appeared, the one weapon at their disposal was the UN, which not long after [the period of Western domination] they knew to be permanently at their disposal. It is scarcely surprising that, armed with this weapon, and inspired by the example presented by their predecessors, they proceeded, over the coming decades, to exploit, to the best of their ability, the one asset at their disposal.[7]

It will be illustrated that the Non Aligned and Socialist majority has used its voting power to adopt resolutions on virtually anything concerning international relations. This is not a revolutionary concept, for at San Francisco the smaller States had made such proposals, to authorise the Assembly to consider, for example, 'any matter within the sphere of international relations' or 'affecting international relations'.[8] However, at the time, such provisions were not included.

Before analysing the provisions of the Charter, it must be noted that the division outlined above, where the Assembly consists of three blocs − Western, Non-Aligned and Socialist − is perhaps too simplistic a view. The General Assembly consists of many sub-divisions based loosely on regions such as the Group of Western States, League of Arab States, Group of African States, Group of Asian States, Group of Latin American States, and Group of Eastern European States. Sometimes these become more definitive and take the form of regional organisations from which one member is chosen from each to represent its views in the Assembly. The European Community, the Organisation of African Unity, the Organisation of American States, the Organisation of the Islamic Conference, and the Association of South East Asian States are examples of regional bodies which are represented in the General Assembly, each with a different degree of cohesiveness.

However, the Assembly is not like a political party system as found in a democratic society.[9] Nevertheless, in the course of examining and voting upon problems involving the use of force in international relations, the Assembly very regularly divides into the three blocs discussed above. East− West relations have always been of great significance in the maintenance of peace through the United Nations, and the Non Aligned has united on this issue on so many occasions because its militarily weak members are so often the victims of the use of force in which a superpower is involved. Thus, the Non Aligned is not only a significant coalition as regards self-determination, but also has become a united advocate of the non-use of force in international relations.[10]

Notes

1 See Article 24(1), Chapters VI and VII of the Charter.

2 See Articles 10–14 of the Charter.

3 See Article 18(2) of the Charter.

4 See generally C. Bown and P. J. Mooney, *Cold War to Detente*, 2nd ed. (1986).

5 GA Res. 1991 18 UN GAOR Supp. (No. 15) 21 (1963), established the composition of the Council as follows: five permanent members, five from Afro-Asian States, one from Eastern Europe, two from Latin America, two from Western European and other States.

6 See D. Nicol, *The United Nations Security Council: Towards Greater Effectiveness*, 4 (1982).

7 E. Luard, *A History of the United Nations: Vol. 1 The Years of Western Domination (1945–1955)*, 383 (1982).

8 New Zealand and Australia, UNCIO, vol. 9, 272, 266.

9 S. D. Bailey, *The General Assembly*, 23 (1960).

10 See generally M. J. Peterson, *The General Assembly in World Politics*, (1986).

CHAPTER 4

The powers of the General Assembly under the Charter

The notion that Articles 10, 11, 12, and 14 of the UN Charter can be subject to varying interpretations has already been raised in the introductory section to this Part where it was stated that the Western governments have changed from favouring a wide interpretation of these provisions, giving the Assembly wide powers in the field of international peace, to a more narrow constitutional position in later years.

The powers contained in Articles 10, 11 and 14

Proponents of a wide view of the competence of the General Assembly would point to Article 10 of the Charter:

The General Assembly may discuss any questions or any matters within the scope of the present Charter or relating to the powers or functions of any organs provided for in the present Charter, and, except as provided for in Article 12, may make recommendations to the Members of the United Nations or to the Security Council or to both on any such questions or matters.

Article 10 establishes a general competence for the Assembly to discuss any matter within the jurisdiction of the United Nations as determined by the Charter.[1] This power indeed makes the Assembly the 'town meeting place of the world', 'the open conscience of humanity', as intended.[2] Its power to make recommendations on any such matter must also cover the same area as the more concrete recommendatory powers of the Security Council under Chapters VI and VII as regards the maintenance of international peace and security. Hence, Article 10 is subject to Article 12 which attempts to delineate between the functions of the Assembly and those of the Security Council.

Once it is established that Article 10 creates the widest possible sphere of competence for the Assembly subject to Article 12, then the other provisions defining the powers of the Assembly are to some extent unnecessary unless they detract from the powers contained in Article 10. Article 11 deals more specifically and in a more limited fashion with the Assembly's role in the maintenance of international peace, but is subject to paragraph (4) which states that 'the powers of the General Assembly set forth in this Article shall not limit the general scope of Article 10'.

As if Article 10 is not enough, Article 14 re-emphasises the Assembly's potentially wide jurisdiction, with specific reference to international security:

Subject to the provisions of Article 12, the General Assembly may recommend measures for the peaceful adjustment of any situation, regardless of origin, which it deems likely to impair the general welfare or friendly relations among nations including situations resulting from a violation of the present Charter setting forth the purposes and principles of the United Nations.

Article 14, with its jurisdictional threshold of a situation deemed 'likely to impair the general welfare or friendly relations among nations', appears to give the Assembly access to a much wider range of situations in the field of international peace and security than the Security Council which technically requires a danger to international peace,[3] a threat to or breach of the peace, or an act of aggression to act under Chapter VI or VII. The test under Article 14 covers the whole spectrum of situations which might impair peace, whereas the provisions contained in Articles 34 and 39 deal with the more important, global and potentially explosive situations. The Assembly can, under Articles 10 and 14, discuss situations contained in Articles 34 and 39, but to prevent any clash between the work of the Security Council, which is primarily concerned with such situations, and the General Assembly, both Article 14 and Article 10 are subject to the limitation contained in Article 12.

Despite the fact that Article 14 is rarely cited or quoted in Assembly resolutions,[4] it, along with Article 10, is the basis of most resolutions directed towards the maintenance of international peace and security, enabling the Assembly to suggest measures or sanctions against States and to by-pass the domestic jurisdiction limitation contained in Article 2(7).[5]

Goodrich, Hambro and Simons agree that Article 14 has formed the basis of Assembly resolutions dealing with fundamental human rights and self-determination 'in the face of arguments that the questions being dealt with are matters of domestic jurisdiction'.[6] The above authors cite the report of the Special Commission set up by the Assembly in 1953 to study the apartheid policies of South Africa. The Commission interpreted the scope of Article 14 as covering cases which 'were likely to bring interests into conflict with one another'.[7] This epitomises a rather more relaxed approach to Article 2(7) in the General Assembly compared to the Security Council, where the situation must usually be a threat to the peace or of international concern before intervention takes place.

The reference in Article 14 to the purposes and principles of the United Nations indicates that perhaps one of the major roles of the General Assembly is to deal with the right to self-determination contained in Article 1(2). Also, Articles 1(3) and 13(1)(b) contain references to 'human rights and fundamental freedoms'. These provisions, combined with the Assembly's role as regards the maintenance of international peace and security contained in Articles 10, 14, and indeed Article 11, suggest that the General Assembly has a major, if not primary, role in situations concerning either human rights or the question of self-determination, or both, even when the situation also concerns the maintenance of international peace.

Whether one could say that the proper division of functions between the Security Council and the General Assembly as regards the maintenance of international peace and security depends on whether the situation is predominantly one of human rights and self-determination (in which case the General Assembly is perhaps the organ jurisdictionally competent to deal with it) will be examined later. For the moment it is sufficient to say that this view is practice based.[8]

Given that Articles 10 and 14 empower the General Assembly to discuss matters which may be a danger to international peace within Article 34, Chapter VI, or a threat to or breach of the peace within Article 39, Chapter VII, subject to Article 12, Article 11, in paragraphs 2 and 3, explains the relationship between the Assembly and the Security Council as regards questions which come within Chapter VII or situations under Chapter VI. Nevertheless, by paragraph 4 of Article 11, Article 10 is stated not to be subject to the restrictions contained in Article 11. This confusing situation may be explained by the compromise that brought these provisions about between the smaller States advocating wide powers and the sponsoring States attempting to limit these powers. Article 11(2) and (3) attempts to refine the wide area of overlap between the two organs created by Articles 10 and 14.

Article 11(3) deals specifically with a situation which comes within Chapter VI, as defined by Article 34: 'The General Assembly may call the attention of the Security Council to situations which are likely to endanger international peace.' Article 11(3) seems to envisage the possibility of concurrent jurisdiction between the two organs in that it does not place an obligation on the Assembly to refer any such situation to the Council. However, if the Council is exercising its functions as regards the situation, Article 12 operates to prevent the Assembly recommending measures though not from deliberating on the situation.

Article 24(2) refers to Chapter VI as containing 'specific powers granted to the Security Council' for the discharge of its primary responsibility, and all the Articles, except Article 35, seem to envisage exclusivity of operation to the Security Council. Nevertheless, Articles 10 and 14 empower the Assembly to make recommendations for specific settlement similar to those contained in Chapter VI. Article 11(3) operates as a safety valve in that the Security Council is the body designed to deal with such situations. Article 11(3) does perform this function to a certain extent, as evidenced by the fact that it is one of the rare Charter provisions actually cited in Assembly resolutions – for example on the situation in South Africa.[9]

Article 24(2) also states that Chapter VII contains the specific powers of the Security Council, and, indeed, its power conferring provisions (Articles 39 to 42) do not mention the Assembly nor seem to envisage the Assembly entering into Chapter VII. Article 11(2) provides an answer to the conundrum of whether the Assembly can utilise Chapter VII:

The General Assembly may discuss any questions relating to the maintenance of international peace and security brought before it and, except as provided in Article 12, may make recommendations with regard to any such questions to the States concerned or to the Security Council, or to both. Any such question on which action is necessary shall be referred to the Security Council either before or after discussion.

Article 11(2) enables the General Assembly to find a 'threat to the peace', a 'breach of the peace' or an 'act of aggression' and to make recommendations thereon to restore international peace – a power concurrent with that of the Security Council under Article 39. It is a recommendatory power only, any coercive measures under Chapter VII requiring a mandatory decision can only be adopted by the Security Council.[10] This interpretation of Article 11(2) is supported by the International Court in the *Expenses* case:

The Court considers that the kind of action referred to in Article 11, paragraph 2, is coercive or enforcement action. The word 'action' must mean such action as is solely within the province of the Security Council. It cannot refer to recommendations which the Security Council might make, as for instance under Article 38 [or Article 39], because the General Assembly under Article 11 has a comparable power. If the word 'action' in Article 11, paragraph 2, was interpreted to mean that the General Assembly could make recommendations only of a general character affecting peace and security in the abstract, and not in relation to specific cases, the paragraph would not have provided that the General Assembly may make recommendations on questions brought before it by States or by the Security Council.[11]

The tenor of this judgement suggests that the General Assembly can go so far as to recommend action by the Security Council, or to suggest voluntary sanctions, or to recommend military measures under the Uniting for Peace procedure. Kelsen thought that the limitation in Article 11(2) precluded the recommendation of enforcement action, but considered that in any case Article 10 could be used.[12] Indeed, on the assumption that Article 10 contains the *lex generalis* and Article 11, and to a certain extent Article 14, the *lex specialis*, the provisions of Article 11 are to a certain extent unnecessary under the principle that the extent of the Assembly's powers are defined by the general, and in this case wider, rather than the specific, and in this case narrower, provisions.

Effectively, therefore, the General Assembly is subject to two central limiting factors (apart from its lack of power to undertake coercive action on more than a recommendatory basis), namely the limitations contained in Articles 12 and 2(7).

The limitation imposed by Article 12

Articles 10, 11(2) and 14 comprise the recommendatory powers of the General Assembly as far as the maintenance of international peace and security is concerned. All are subject to the limitation contained in Article 12(1): 'While the Security Council is exercising in respect of any dispute or situation the functions assigned to it in the present Charter, the General Assembly shall not make any recommendations with regard to that dispute or situation unless the Security Council so requests.'

Article 12 is probably the most difficult provision, in constitutional terms, to reconcile with the practice of the General Assembly. As we have seen, the other provisions can be interpreted to enable the Assembly to pass resolutions on any matter concerning the maintenance of peace as long as they do not purport to be mandatory. However, as shall be illustrated in chapter 5, the Assembly often adopts resolutions on a matter at the same time at which the Security Council is considering the question. Two arguments to escape Article 12 could be employed in this situation − that the Security Council, although considering the question and perhaps even adopting resolutions on it, is not actually performing the 'functions assigned to it in the Charter', or that the resolution adopted by the General Assembly is not actually a recommendation.

It seems to have become established practice to equate items on the Security Council's agenda with that body exercising its functions in relation to the matter. The theory behind the list of matters which the Secretary General submits to the General Assembly is that it tells the Assembly which issues it is not allowed to discuss because they are receiving attention in the Security Council.[13] In effect, this amounts to defining 'functions' in Article 12(1) with reference to Article 12(2).

The Secretary General with the consent of the Security Council, shall notify the General Assembly at each session of any matters relative to the maintenance of international peace and security which are being dealt with by the Security Council and shall similarly notify the General Assembly, or the Members of the United Nations if the General Assembly is not in session, immediately the Security Council ceases to deal with such matters.

Some subscribe to the view that Article 12(2) defines whether the Council is functioning or not. However, they recognise the artificiality of the process and concede that in practice the Assembly is not limited by the list nor would it be reasonable to expect it to be. Even when the Council adopts a resolution, the Assembly will sometimes adopt its own on the same question, the justification, according to this approach, being not one of legal interpretation 'but of necessity for the Assembly to promote the aims of the Charter when the Security Council cannot or will not do so'.[14]

The question of whether a recommendation adopted in the face of Article 12 with the requisite two-thirds majority with or without minority objections is *ultra vires* will be examined later. Suffice to say for the moment that the procedure in which the list of matters seized by the Security Council is also those matters in relation to which it is exercising the functions assigned to it may still be formally accepted, but in practice it has all but been disregarded.

Nevertheless, in the early years, this procedural rule was applied with some regularity. One of these cases was the Greek question (1947–48), which is worth examining in some detail because it is illustrative of how Western domination of the Organisation enabled it to manipulate the procedure to its own advantage.

The United States had committed itself by the Truman Doctrine[15] to the economic and military support of Greece and Turkey. It was therefore interested in the prevention of a Communist takeover in Greece. In the Security Council it managed to establish a Commission to examine the situation.[16] In May 1947 the majority of the Commission reported that Yugoslavia, Bulgaria and Albania had supported guerrilla warfare in Greece.[17] The United States proposed that the Council endorse the Commission's recommendation to send a permanent body to Greece to observe her borders.[18] This was seen by the Communist countries as a Cold War move by a Council and a Commission dominated by Western countries. The proposal was vetoed by the Soviet Union.[19]

The United States simply waited for the regular session of the General Assembly in the autumn of 1947 to propose a similar resolution[20] condemning Albania, Bulgaria and Yugoslavia, and establishing a permanent Committee, UNSCOB, to help observe the borders. Thus, the United States had successfully used its overwhelming support in the United Nations to pass resolutions to reinforce its sphere of influence in the Balkans and to prevent the encroachment of communism.

Technically, however, the United States and its supporters managed to keep within the provisions of the Charter, in that after the Soviets had vetoed its last draft resolution in the Council, it proposed that the item be removed from the agenda[21] to signify to the Assembly that it had ceased to deal with the matter, allowing the Assembly to make recommendations thereon. It was simply because the West dominated both organs that it could switch from Council to Assembly within the accepted constitutional procedure. It could easily win a procedural vote in the Council.

The Non Aligned group, nowadays, is not guaranteed, even with Socialist support, to win a procedural vote in the Council, and so in practice it tends to ignore the legal technicalities. In view of the importance of the United Nations to the Non Aligned, it is not surprising that they take the attitude that their disregard of a technical procedure adopted during a period of Western domination is no more reprehensible than the cynical manipulation by the West of the same procedure during the earlier period.[22] If one looks at the matters formally seized by the Security Council, one can see that it still contains matters first considered over forty years ago. For example, the Palestine question was first put on the Council agenda in 1947, the India-Pakistan question in 1948, South Africa in 1960, Namibia in 1968, and Western Sahara in 1975, and have not been removed since.[23] If a comparison is made between these and the examples of Assembly resolutions contained in the sections below, it is clear that the procedural construction of Article 12 has been breached on many occasions.

An examination of the meaning of the term 'recommendation' in Article 12 has important implications because the provisions granting powers to the General Assembly as regards international peace (Articles 10, 11 and 14) envisage Assembly resolutions only in the form of recommendations. The question remains whether the Assembly can pass resolutions which are not technically recommendations and so escape the limitation contained in Article 12. The International Court answered this question in the affirmative in the *Expenses* case:

While it is the Security Council which, exclusively, may order coercive action, the functions and powers conferred on the General Assembly are not confined to discussion, consideration, the initiation of studies and the making of recommendations, they are not merely hortatory. Article 18 deals with 'decisions' of the General Assembly on 'important questions'. These 'decisions' do indeed include certain recommendations, but others have dispositive force and effect. Among these latter decisions, Article 18 includes suspension of rights and privileges of membership, expulsion of Members, 'and budgetary questions'.[24]

The Court's judgement confers recognition on non-recommendatory type resolutions, which on a literal interpretation would not be subject to the limitation contained in Article 12. Chapter 6, which examines the concrete forms that General Assembly resolutions take, will illustrate that the Assembly often condemns, decides (in a hortatory, non-mandatory sense), demands or declares, thus leading to an argument that these types of resolution are not included in Article 12.

Nevertheless, it is very difficult to maintain that all but a few General Assembly resolutions are compatible with this analysis. Often the resolution may demand or decide in one part and recommend in another, particularly with the increased length of resolutions passed regularly on subjects such as the Middle East, Palestine, South Africa and Namibia. Also those resolutions which appear to confirm Security Council resolutions do often go beyond them and implicitly or even explicitly make further recommendations than their Council counterparts.

The limitation imposed by Article 2(7)

Article 2(7) prohibits the United Nations from intervening 'essentially within the domestic jurisdiction of any State'. It has already received examination when discussing the Security Council, when it was stated that Article 2(7) does not apply not only in those cases requiring enforcement measures under

Chapter VII as catered for by Article 2(7) itself, but also in cases of a threat
to the peace without such measures, or, indeed, of international concern
requiring only pacification under Chapter VI.

The General Assembly, however, has not developed a similar jurisprudence
or, indeed, any discernable principles governing the applicability of Article
2(7).[25] It is submitted that an agreed interpretation is not possible because the
equilibrium between national and international interests sought by the drafters
of Article 2(7) is not constant.[26]

As will be shown below, the denial of the right to self-determination was
originally within the domestic jurisdiction of a State and so outside the purview
of the United Nations, but now it is of international concern and so subject
to review. In the Security Council it takes only one permanent member to use
Article 2(7) as a basis for its veto and so that body has a more substantial
jurisprudence on the meaning of the domestic jurisdiction limitation. Nevertheless, it is possible to chart the involvement of the General Assembly in what
might superficially appear to be internal matters as developed in over forty
years of practice.[27]

The first clear interference in domestic internal affairs involved the
Assembly examining the regime of a State. In December 1946, the Assembly
passed a resolution which recommended the banning of Spain from the United
Nations and its specialised agencies and requested that all member States
should recall their ambassadors from Spain. It also stated that if a democratic
Spanish government was not established within a reasonable time, the Security
Council should consider adequate measures to remedy the situation.[28]

Rajan uses the example of the Hungarian crisis in 1956 to illustrate further
the questioning by the Assembly of the nature of a government.[29] However,
this is not altogether a good example, for it involved armed intervention by
an outside power – the USSR – in contravention of Article 2(4) which
effectively internationalised the situation. Nevertheless, the Assembly resolutions adopted at the Second Emergency Special Session did pass comment
on the regime in Hungary, despite Soviet objections based on Article 2(7).[30]
For example, the Assembly 'affirmed the right of the Hungarian people to
a government responsive to its national aspirations and dedicated to its
independence and well-being' as well as calling on the Soviet Union to
withdraw.[31]

The next area developed by General Assembly practice which effectively
puts it outside the limitation contained in Article 2(7) concerns Non Self-
Governing Territories. Rajan cites many cases which will be discussed
elsewhere – Tunisia, Algeria, the Portuguese Territories, Namibia and
Southern Rhodesia – to conclude that 'after all these actions ... there is no
shred of evidence to sustain the view that non self-governing territories fall
under the domestic jurisdiction of their respective metropolitan powers',[32]
despite objections by the colonial powers.[33] These objections are apt to be

ephemeral, for example the United Kingdom initially relied on Article 2(7) to deny vehemently the United Nations' jurisdiction as regards Southern Rhodesia,[34] but after UDI it was Britain which requested the Organisation's involvement.[35]

The Assembly's disregard of Article 2(7) on issues of human rights and fundamental freedoms can be traced back to the era of Western domination when that body was used to criticise the Eastern bloc. At its third annual session in 1949, the Assembly adopted a resolution expressing concern at the 'grave accusations made against the governments of Bulgaria and Hungary regarding the suppression of human right and fundamental freedoms'.[36] At the same session the Assembly criticised the Soviet Union, declaring that the measures preventing the wives of foreign nationals from leaving their own country to join their husbands were 'not in conformity with the Charter, and that if the wives were persons belonging to foreign diplomatic missions, such measures were contrary to diplomatic practice and likely to impair friendly relations between States'. The resolution therefore called on the Soviet Union to withdraw the measures.[37]

The use of Article 14 language in the latter case is illustrative of how that provision is used to empower the Assembly to discuss relatively trivial matters, for the practice criticised was hardly likely to even remotely endanger peace. It is not surprising, therefore, that with such a relatively minor matter escaping the provisions of Article 2(7), the Non Aligned/Socialist majority established since the 1950s has not paid much heed to its limitations.

The United Nations' involvement in the South African problem cannot be classified as a trivial concern, but it is a good illustration of how the Assembly has now elevated the denial of human rights and fundamental freedoms to one of international concern. Only the South African government has persistently based its objections on Article 2(7).[38] Although it was initially supported by some Western States,[39] it now stands alone.

An extension from Rajan's categories of non self-governing territories and cases concerning human rights and fundamental freedoms, is that of cases concerning the denial of the right to self-determination. It will be a constant theme throughout this Part that one of the Assembly's major purposes is the furtherance of the right to self-determination. It has virtually established that the denial of that right is a matter of international concern and so no longer within the sovereign domain of a State.[40]

The above categories all involve primary consideration of matters such as human rights and self-determination which result in considerations of international peace. It must be noted, however, that in cases primarily concerned with international peace and security, arguments based on domestic jurisdiction are used. Cases such as the Lebanon and Jordan (1958), Bangladesh (1971), Afghanistan (1980), and Kampuchea (1979), all involved arguments that the situation was internal and so covered by Article 2(7), but only usually by one party or power bloc involved in the dispute. Unlike the Security Council, however, these subjective arguments did not prevent the General Assembly from adopting resolutions.

Arguments of ultra vires

States objecting to the General Assembly adopting resolutions often argue that the resolution is *ultra vires*. For example, the argument is usually based on Article 12 or Article 2(7). The Assembly's continued consideration of the apartheid policies of the South African government has produced many objections based on Article 2(7). The South African ambassador has consistently asserted that his government must regard 'any resolution emanating from a discussion on or the consideration of the present item as *ultra vires* and, therefore, null and void'.[41] One can find many examples of objections based on Article 2(7).[42] However, if they are in the minority they do not appear to have any effect on the jurisdiction of the Assembly. It appears, to the observer, that the Assembly's jurisdiction is determined by that body and not necessarily by the Charter.

An example of a resolution being introduced despite objections based on Article 12 is the Uniting for Peace resolution.[43] Briefly, the resolution proposed to give competence to the Assembly, including the power to recommend enforcement measures, when the Security Council was paralysed by the veto. The Soviet Union and other Socialist States, being in the minority bloc at the time, objected to the resolution on the grounds that it was unconstitutional in that the 'functions' of the Security Council within the meaning of Article 12 included cases where the veto was used, since the veto was an integral part of the constitution of the Security Council. The Soviet representative thus asserted that the proposed procedure would amend the Charter without going through the amendment procedure envisaged by Article 109.[44] Nevertheless, the majority proceeded and adopted the resolution, the procedure of which the Soviets have boycotted ever since, even though they now often form part of the majority.

From a legal point of view the Charter of the United Nations 'is the primary source of its jurisdiction'.[45] Admittedly, as far as the provisions conferring powers on the General Assembly are concerned, there is considerable confusion as to the limits of its jurisdiction. Nevertheless, Articles 12 and 2(7) represent relatively clear limitations on its competence. Could clear breaches of these provisions be justified on the basis of the Assembly having implied powers to enable it to do so? A negative answer is furnished by the International Court in the *Reparations* case: 'Under international law, the Organisation must be deemed to have those powers which though not expressly provided in the Charter are conferred upon it by necessary implication as being essential to the performance of its duties.'[46] The Court does not allow the Organisation to imply powers which go against its Charter. Indeed, Ciobanu ties implied powers very securely to express provisions: 'Powers not expressed cannot freely be implied; implied powers flow from the grant of express powers, and are limited to those that are necessary to the exercise of powers expressly granted.'[47]

Even if one takes a much more liberal approach to implied or inherent powers than Ciobanu, there is no possibility of accommodating a clear breach of an express provision within their framework. Inherent powers have been defined very widely to allow international organisations to 'perform in principle every sovereign activity or take every action under international law, if they are really in a position to accomplish such purposes, provided their constitutions do not preclude such an activity'.[48] This definition of implied powers seems to go beyond the *dictum* of the International Court in the *Reparations* case in that it gives the Assembly virtual *carte blanche* to determine its own competence, as long as it does not do so in contradiction to the express terms.

However, there are many factors militating against even what appears to be a clear breach of the Charter being null and void. Firstly, there is a World Court judgement which, as part of a teleological interpretation, favoured a presumption against *ultra vires* where the action taken 'was appropriate for the fulfilment of one of the stated purposes of the United Nations'.[49] The presumption against *ultra vires* is a practical approach to the problem, recognising that a resolution adopted according to the voting provisions of the Charter has to be presumed to be valid, otherwise the Assembly's resolutions would remain in a state of limbo until the unlikely event of their challenge before the International Court. It is the lack of procedure for the challenge of resolutions that leads to this presumption. Judge Morelli made this clear in a separate judgement: 'The failure of an organ to conform to the rules concerning competence has no influence on the validity of the act, which amounts to saying that each organ of the United Nations is the judge of its own competence.'[50]

The same arguments apply to decisions of the Security Council, except that the Council is less likely than the Assembly to pass resolutions which are apparently in contravention of the Charter. One of the permanent members would probably prevent this by using its veto to protect its, or its bloc, interests. To this extent, the veto operates as a safeguard against the adoption of *ultra vires* resolutions. Also, the Council has a much greater competence in the field of international peace than the Assembly, which is much more likely to contravene the provisions (such as Article 12) which attempt to limit its competence and keep it the subsidiary body.

The approach that recognises the theory of 'la compétence de la compétence' – that the Council and Assembly act as judges of their own competence[51] – was not without recognition at San Francisco, where the relevant Committee stated that 'it is inevitable that each organ will interpret such parts of the Charter as are applicable to its particular functions. This process is inherent in the functioning of any body which operates under an instrument defining its functions and powers.'[52]

In addition to legal recognition of the Assembly's (and Council's) ability to act as its own judge, one must not forget the inherent difficulty in making an *ultra vires* objection count — a difficulty made worse by the practice of the Assembly of not citing the source of its authority in its resolutions. If there is no clear basis as to the resolution it is indeed difficult to challenge it, for the challenge itself must be based on an interpretation of the provision.

The principle of subsequent practice

A related question to that discussed in the above section is whether the Assembly has re-interpreted the Charter by its subsequent practice.

The principle of subsequent practice as regards treaty interpretation is reasonably clear and is accepted as affording legitimate evidence as to its correct interpretation. A common, consistent practice by the vast majority of parties to a multilateral treaty such as the Charter of the United Nations 'must come near to being conclusive on how the treaty should be interpreted'. Indeed, this amounts to 'not so much the meaning of an existing text, as a revision of it, but a revision brought about by practice or conduct, rather than affected by and recorded in writing'. Further, 'conduct usually forms a more reliable guide to intention or purpose than anything to be found for instance in the preparatory work of the treaty simply because it has taken concrete and active, and not merely paper or verbal, form'.[53]

So if the Assembly has consistently adopted resolutions on matters subject to Article 2(7) and Article 12 by a sufficiently large majority throughout its forty years of practice, it might be possible to state that this amounts to a revision of those provisions. On the presumption that a consistent two-thirds majority, present and voting (which is required for important questions), is sufficient, it is submitted that such a revision has taken place. The revision amounts to a severe restriction on the domestic jurisdiction limitation contained in Article 2(7); a virtual disregard of the division of competence between the Assembly and the Council contained in Article 12; and, in effect, an interpretation of the vague powers contained in Articles 10, 11 and 14 to give the Assembly competence and powers with regard to any matter in international relations, with the exception of the ability to take mandatory measures.

The following two chapters will attempt to rationalise and categorise the practice of the Assembly, first in the matter of competence, particularly as regards the Security Council, and, secondly, as regards the concrete forms the powers of the Assembly, derived from its competence, take.

Notes

1 H. Kelsen, *The Law of the United Nations*, 198 (1951).
2 See the *Yearbook of the United Nations* (1946–47), 51.
3 But see Article 35.
4 See for example GA Res. 721, 8 UN GAOR Supp. (No. 17) 6 (1953).
5 J.P. Cot and A. Pellet, *La Charte des Nations Unies*, 337–40 (1985).
6 L.M. Goodrich, E. Hambro and P.S. Simons, *The Charter of the United Nations*, 143, 2nd ed. (1969).
7 8 UN GAOR Supp. (No. 16) para. 114.
8 Repertory of the United Nations Practice, Supp. (No. 1) 173, at para. 16.
9 See for example GA Res. 1663, 16 UN GAOR Supp. (No. 17) 10 (1961).
10 See Cot and Pellet, *La Charte*, 288–9.
11 *Certain Expenses of the United Nations* case, I.C.J. *Rep.* 1962, 151, at 164–65.
12 Kelsen, *Law of the UN*, 205.
13 For example UN doc. S/16880 (1985).
14 D.W. Bowett, *Law of International Institutions*, 48–9, 4th ed. (1982).
15 See L.B. Sohn, *Cases on United Nations Law*, 347–8 (1967).
16 SC Res. 15, 1 UN SCOR Resolutions 6 (1946).
17 UN doc. S/360/REV 1 (1947).
18 UN doc. S/391 (1947).
19 See SC 170 mtg, 2 UN SCOR (1947).
20 GA Res. 109, 2 UN GAOR Resolutions 12 (1947).
21 SC 170 mtg, 2 UN SCOR (1947).
22 But see also Poland during the Council's discussion of the Spanish Question; SC 48 mtg, 1 UN SCOR 392 (1946).
23 UN doc. S/16680 (1985).
24 I.C.J. *Rep.* 1962, 163.
25 Cot and Pellet, *La Charte*, 159.
26 See *Nationality Decrees in Tunis and Morocco* case [1923] *P.C.I.J.* ser B, No. 4, at 24.
27 See M.S. Rajan, *The Expanding Jurisdiction of the United Nations*, (1982).
28 GA Res. 39. 1 UN GAOR Resolutions 12 (1946).
29 Rajan, *The Expanding Jurisdiction*, 17–25.
30 SC 746 mtg, 11 UN SCOR (1956).
31 GA Res. 1004, 2 UN GAOR ESS Supp. (No. 1) 2 (1956).
32 Rajan, *The Expanding Jurisdiction*, 84.
33 For French objections see, for example, GA 996 plen. mtg, 3 UN GAOR SS (1961), re Tunisia; GA 956 plen. mtg, 15 UN GAOR (1960), re Algeria. For Portuguese objections see, for example, GA 1099 plen. mtg, 17 UN GAOR (1962).
34 See GA 1163 plen. mtg, 17 UN GAOR 656 (1962).
35 SC 276 mtg, 21 UN SCOR 5 (1966).
36 GA Res. 272, 3 UN GAOR Resolutions 17 (1949).
37 GA Res. 285, 3 UN GAOR Resolutions 34 (1949).
38 GA 401 plen. mtg, 7 UN GAOR 332 (1952).
39 *Ibid.*, 334–5 (UK and France).
40 See D. Ciobanu, *Preliminary Objections Related to the Jurisdiction of the United Nations Political Organs*, 40–2 (1975).
41 GA 401 plen. mtg, 17 UN GAOR 336 (1962).
42 On Afghanistan see GA 1 plen. mtg, 6 UN GAOR ESS para. 112 (1980), Poland. On Kampuchea see GA 64 plen. mtg, 34 UN GAOR 60–61, 120 (1979), GDR, Bulgaria and Czechoslovakia.

43 GA Res. 377, 5 UN GAOR Supp. (No. 20) 10 (1950).
44 GA 301 plen. mtg, 5 UN GAOR para. 138 (1950).
45 Ciobanu, *Preliminary Objections*, 67.
46 *Reparation for Injuries Suffered in the Service of the United Nations* case, I.C.J.
    Rep. 1949, 174, at 182.
47 Ciobanu, *Preliminary Objections*, 68.
48 A. Prandler, 'Competence of the Security Council and the General Assembly', 27
    Questions of International Law (1977), 153, at 167.
49 *Expenses* case, I.C.J. *Rep.* 1962, at 168.
50 *Ibid.*, 223–4.
51 Ciobanu, *Preliminary Objections*, 162–73.
52 UNCIO, vol. 13, 709.
53 G. Fitzmaurice, 'The Law and Procedure of the International Court of Justice',
    33 *B.Y.I.L.* (1957), 223–5. See also McNair, *Law of Treaties*, 424–31 (1961), and
    G. Haraszti, *Some Fundamental Problems of the Law of Treaties*, 138–45 (1973).

CHAPTER 5

The division of competence between the Security Council and the General Assembly in the maintenance of peace

Given that it has been established in chapter 4 that Article 11(2) only operated to prohibit the Assembly from taking mandatory, coercive action and that Article 12 had been revised by Assembly practice, it remains to be seen as to what form this revision has taken − in other words, to examine the evolution by practice of the division of competence between the Council and the Assembly in the field of international peace. Because the Assembly is technically only a subsidiary body in this field its competence and powers are determined by the division of the total UN powers and competence in the field of international peace between the two organs. Thus, by examining the Assembly's perception of its competence it will be possible to determine the extent of its powers in the field of international peace and security.

Five areas will be examined in which the Assembly has:

(i)   acted in a parallel manner to the Security Council. This basically means repeating the work of the Council without pre-empting it or complementing it;

(ii) pre-empted, prejudged or usurped the role or work of the Security Council. In other words, the Assembly has entered the Council's sphere of operation; for example by making a finding under Article 39. *Strictu sensu*, we have already seen in chapter 4 that there is nothing in the Charter, except for Article 12, to prevent the Assembly from adopting recommendatory measures under Chapter VII following a finding under Article 39. Nevertheless, the whole tenor of the Charter and the wording of Chapter VII suggests that the functions and powers contained in that Chapter are the sole reserve of the Security Council;

(iii) supplemented or complemented the role or work of the Council. This area involves the Assembly dealing with the same dispute as the Security Council but in a different manner - by concentrating on other areas of the dispute from the Security Council. It is neither repeating the work of the Council as in (i), or prejudicing it as in (ii);

(iv) performed the functions of the Security Council. In other words, it has taken over the role of the Council which has failed to fulfil its primary responsibilty for the maintenance of international peace and security under Article 24. The main example of this is the Uniting for Peace procedure. There is no question of the Assembly pre-empting the Council since the Council has usually already considered the question but is unable to act;

(v) acted within its own sphere of competence in which there is also a question of international peace. For example, if a conflict is dominated by questions of fundamental human rights or the problem of self-determination then, arguably, the General Assembly has the primary role as the body responsible for the protection of those rights, even though the situation also involves the maintenance of international peace. This category can be viewed as representing an alternative way of analysing the question of division of competence as a whole and thus can be contrasted with the four areas of analysis above.

Inevitably there are some grey areas where it might be argued that one cannot categorise the Assembly's competence as such. For example, it might successfully be argued that it cannot be said that the General Assembly has added nothing to the work of the Security Council in a situation even though its resolutions are basically the same (i.e. (i) above), since a repetition adds to the weight of international opinion and therefore supplements the work of the Council (i.e. (iii) above). This must be kept in mind when considering the areas below.

Cases where the General Assembly has acted in a manner parallel to that of the Security Council

Central America

Considering that the resolutions passed by the Security Council are inevitably weak because of the involvement of one of the permanent members, one might have expected the Assembly to fill the void. On the surface the Assembly's first resolution on the subject[1] appears much firmer, more comprehensive and jurisdictionally more explicit than the corresponding Council resolution.[2] The Council resolution puts emphasis on the efforts of the Contadora group and appears to be adopted under Article 33(2). The Assembly resolution, on the other hand, uses more explicit Charter language when it expresses deep concern 'at the worsening of tensions and conflicts in Central America and the increase in outside interference and acts of aggression against the countries of the region, which endanger international peace and security'. Although the resolution may be said to act as a jurisdictional complement to the Council resolution by indicating that the overall situation is of a type to be dealt with by the powers contained in Chapter VI, with the occasional act coming within Article 39, it merely makes more explicit what is the implicit basis of the Council resolution without adding significantly to the recommendations for specific settlement.[3]

During its forty-second session the Assembly adopted a resolution without vote expressing its 'firmest support' for the Guatemala Agreement.[4] This resolution is based on previous General Assembly resolutions and so to some extent still parallels the Council's resolution. However, by expressing support for a specific peace plan rather than just the Contadora process, it could be argued that the Assembly has gone beyond the Council's basic position, although it is doubtful whether the Western States, particularly the United States, would have given their support if the majority of members had put this interpretation on the resolution.

Iraqi nuclear reactor

The commentator in Cot and Pellet has designated the Assembly's resolutions on this subject as 'parallel' to that of the Council.[5] *Prima facie*, the Assembly does appear to have merely repeated the Council's resolution. However, on further examination the Assembly has gone further than the Council by attempting to bring this single act into the continuing problems of the Middle East.

The Assembly passed a resolution which recalled the Security Council resolution[6] and noted Israel's refusal to comply with it. The resolution virtually amounted to an attack on Israel and the United States. Like the Council resolution, the Assembly condemned Israel for its 'act of aggression' but went further by saying that it also 'constitutes a new and dangerous escalation in the threat to international peace and security'. The Assembly, by finding a continuing threat as well as a single act of aggression, is attempting to pave the way for the adoption of enforcement action by the Council. Indeed, the resolution contained a request to the Council 'to institute effective enforcement action to prevent Israel from further endangering international peace and security through its acts of aggression and continued policies of expansion, occupation and annexation'.

The Assembly's attempt at pre-empting the work of the Council was continued in 1982.[7] Although only Israel and the United States voted against the resolution, some members expressed the hope that the item would not become a permanent fixture on the Assembly's agenda, which according to the British representative would 'ritualise' and 'trivialise' the subject.[8]

The Dutch representative advanced the argument that by its resolution the Security Council was seized of the issue and an annual debate on the subject would not be respecting the Council's primary responsibilty.[9] Obviously over two-thirds of the Assembly are not influenced in their voting by such a strict interpretation of competence under Article 12, for the Assembly has adopted

further resolutions on the topic, the most recent of which reiterated its call
to the Security Council to take 'urgent and effective measures to ensure that
Israel complies without further delay with the provisions of resolution 487
(1981)'.[10]

The Gulf war

On this topic the General Assembly does nothing more than to parallel the
Security Council. The Assembly has passed one resolution on the conflict
which was to all intents and purposes a reaffirmation of previous Council
resolutions.[11] The only value of the resolution is that of repetition, for it even
recognised, when calling for a cease-fire, that 'the Security Council has already
called for an immediate cease-fire and end to all military operations'. It
reflected the Council's jurisdictional findings when it deemed that the conflict
endangered international peace and security. One would have thought that
the provisions of Article 12 would have played some role in the discussions.
However, the members apparently did not see the resolution as treading on
the toes of the Council. The representative of Jamaica made it plain that
nothing in the resolution 'proposes the removal of the issue from the purview'
of the Council and was not 'an attempt to circumvent the fundamental role
of the Security Council'.[12]

Some of the members thought that the Assembly should have gone further
and found a 'breach of the peace'.[13] Such a finding might have forced the
Security Council to consider earlier action under Chapter VII which, in the
case of the Gulf war, which lasted eight years, might have been a good idea,
for the Council's attempts at pacification were a failure, until the acceptance
in August 1988 of Council resolution 598 and the establishment of an effective
cease-fire.[14]

Cyprus 1974 – present

Sometimes, in the case of disputes which are never off the Security Council's
agenda, it appears as if the General Assembly, in its annual session of three
to four months, is taking part of the burden off the Council by adopting
resolutions on the conflict. In some cases the Assembly seizes this opportuni-
ty either to complement the Council's resolutions or to pre-empt them. In the
case of Cyprus, however, the Assembly has added little to the work of the
Council, except perhaps an increased weight of international opinion.

After the Greek-backed coup against Makarios and the Turkish invasion
of the northern part of Cyprus in 1974, the General Assembly virtually repeated
earlier Council resolutions[15] in its resolution passed at its twenty-ninth session
which expressed grave concern 'about the continuation of the Cyprus crisis,
which constitutes a threat to international peace and security', and urged the
withdrawal of foreign forces and the cessation of all 'foreign interference in
its affairs'.[16]

By the time the Assembly passed this resolution the Turkish intervention had become a *fait accompli*. This partly explains why the Assembly and the Council share the responsibilty of dealing with the Cyprus situation, for once the Council had acted promptly in accordance with Article 28(1) during the initial crisis in 1974 and the situation had become on-going, there was no practical reason why both organs should not share the burden, even though the situation is primarily one of international peace and in theory Article 12 should apply.

The Assembly has passed a long line of resolutions on the Cyprus situation. In its 1983 resolution[17] the Assembly made it clear that it was acting together with the Security Council when it demanded the implementation of the relevant resolutions adopted by both organs on the subject. During the discussions in the plenary meetings of the General Assembly there was very little said about any conflict between the two organs; indeed, most suggestions were about a harnessed effort or, more correctly, a channel of support for the Secretary General's efforts.[18] Nevertheless, the resolution induced five negative votes and twenty abstentions, mainly from Western nations who objected to a paragraph in the resolution which recommended that

the Security Council should examine the question of implementation, within a specific time frame, of its relevant resolutions and consider and adopt thereafter, if necessary, all appropriate and practical measures under the Charter for ensuring the speedy and effective implementation of the resolutions of the United Nations on Cyprus.

Those abstaining and those casting negative votes explained that they thought the recommendation to the Security Council was 'inappropriate' for it was the Council's prerogative to decide upon further measures.[19]

Throughout this chapter it will become apparent that, since the end of their period of dominance in the mid 1950s, the Western States rely on legal objections based on Charter provisions in order to attempt to prevent the Assembly encroaching on the work of the Council, whereas the Socialist and Non Aligned countries skip over such objections. This more constitutional approach covers the self-interest of the Western States who would like to see the Security Council remain the primary body in which they have a triple veto to protect their vital interests rather than allow the Assembly to have greater power with its overwhelming Non Aligned and Socialist majority. The Socialist and Non Aligned countries are apt to interpret Articles 10, 11 and 14 very widely, and ignore Article 12, assuming, of course, that they have them in mind since they very rarely refer to them.

The Congo
As well as acting under the Uniting for Peace procedure at its fourth emergency special session in 1960 at the request of the Security Council, the General Assembly also passed resolutions paralleling those of the Security Council at

its fifteenth annual session.[20] Like the Council, the Assembly saw the
presence of Belgian troops as the 'central factor' in the 'grave situation'
and called for their withdrawal. Like its Council counterpart, it found
a 'threat to the peace' but was more conciliatory in trying to obtain the
Congolese authorities' co-operation with the United Nations. In this respect
the Assembly supplemented the Council's resolution, for, as the representative
of the Ivory Coast pointed out, the decision taken by the Council created
an 'atmosphere of tension' which the Assembly was attempting to diffuse.[21]

Certain members had attempted to introduce a proposal that the Assembly
should 'decide' that Belgium should withdraw all personnel within twenty-
one days. This was not adopted because of objections by moderate States.
The representative of Ireland explained these objections clearly.

[the General Assembly] has the useful functions of making recommendations and of registering
world opinion on various issues. In the exercise of these functions it has proved able, in
certain circumstances, to save the United Nations from the consequences of a paralysis brought
on by Security Council deadlocks; but from that to making the General Assembly a primary
decision making body seems to us a long step of doubtful legality and of even more doubtful
use.[22]

Indeed, the Charter provisions examined above contain only the power
of recommendation, with binding decisions remaining within the exclusive
power of the Security Council.[23] Perhaps the division of duties between
the two bodies is based on this – the General Assembly having a recommendatory register of world opinion function, whereas the Council makes
the primary decisions. If this is the case then Article 12 has no application
– both bodies could consider the same problem at the same time for they
are exercising different functions. This is too simplistic a dichotomy, for
the Security Council often adopts purely recommendatory resolutions under
Chapter VI.

Cases where the General Assembly has pre-empted or prejudged the role of the Security Council

Portuguese Territories
With a vast increase in newly independent States joining the United Nations
there arose a significant gap between the resolutions of the General Assembly
and those of the Security Council as regards colonial or neo-colonial situations
(South Africa, Southern Rhodesia and Namibia) which involved considerations of international peace. As early as 1962 the General Assembly found
'that the policy and acts of the Portuguese Government with regard to the
territories under its administration have constituted a serious threat to international peace and security'. This finding under Article 39 suggests that the
situation required 'action' by the Security Council, which should have had

the question referred to it under Article 11(2). The resolution appeared to recognise this in that it requested the Security Council to take steps to 'secure the compliance of Portugal with its obligations as a Member State'.[24]

The Assembly expanded its finding under Article 39 not only to include 'the attitude of Portugal towards the African populations of its colonies', but also towards 'neighbouring States' which also constituted a 'threat to international peace and security'. On this occasion it suggested voluntary measures of its own while requesting that the Council take action.[25]

The resolutions in this case illustrate how the Non Aligned became increasingly exasperated with the Security Council. As we have seen, a finding of a threat to the peace by the Assembly is not prohibited by the Charter but it often represents the beginning of a course of action leading to the Assembly taking the primary role in international peace, evidenced in this case by the recommendation of measures. Admittedly, neither is the adoption of voluntary measures against the letter of the Charter, but it is against the basic division of responsibilities in the Charter which designates the Council as the primary body. Besides, on a strict interpretation of Article 12, the Assembly, in adopting the second of the resolutions referred to above, was acting in an unconstitutional way since the question of the Portuguese Territories had been on the Security Council agenda since 1963[26] and has never been removed.

The majority saw it as their duty, despite what the Charter might suggest, to cajole the Council, in particular the Western States, into adopting more forceful measures. In this they failed, for whereas the Assembly found the situation a threat to the peace in 1962, the Council only found a danger to international peace in 1972.[27]

Southern Rhodesia
In the case of Southern Rhodesia the Assembly found the situation a threat to the peace several years before the Security Council.[28] A finding of a threat to the peace is mainly a political decision and so one might expect a difference in the timing of such a finding in two organs with different voting procedures. Nevertheless, once the situation came to a head with UDI one might have expected the Security Council to take the lead. Not so, for the General Assembly was first to condemn UDI and referred the matter to the Security Council.[29] It even urged the Security Council to adopt enforcement measures under Chapter VII[30] before the Council had even agreed to condemn.

The Assembly, throughout the problems in Southern Rhodesia, seemed to be pushing the Council, reaching decisions which the Council often reluctantly followed, and above all acting as the conscience of the Security Council. There were objections. The Dutch representative pointed out that the Security Council had been seized of the problem since 1963 and so, by virtue of Article 12, the Assembly could not make recommendations unless the Council so requested.[31]

The Dutch ambassador also stated that the situation was not a threat to the peace with the consequence that no enforcement measures could be taken. His and other objections were ignored as the Council adopted mandatory economic measures against the minority Smith regime.[32] Nevertheless, the Assembly did not stop pushing to have the embargo made more effective. It called on the Council to take the next logical and legal step within the meaning of Articles 2(5), 4 and 5 of taking mandatory sanctions against the sanction breakers – principally South Africa and Portugal.[33] This call was repeated (but never followed) in 1973 in a resolution which contained an appeal to those vetoing permanent members (the United States, Britain and France) to stop preventing the Council from performing its duty.[34] It may be stepping on the toes of the Council, but the Assembly has taken it upon itself to act as the conscience of the Council, particularly the permanent members.

South Africa
During the early years of its consideration of the South African problem the Assembly was contented with finding that the continuance of the policies of the South African government 'seriously endangers international peace and security', while calling on the Security Council to consider the question under Article 11(3).[35]

However, four years later, in 1965, the Socialist/Non Aligned majority's patience ran out when it adopted a resolution which drew the Council's attention to the fact that the 'situation in South Africa constitutes a threat to international peace and security; that action under Chapter VII of the Charter is essential to solve the problem of apartheid and that universally applied economic sanctions are the only means of achieving a peaceful solution'.[36]

De facto, the General Assembly had pre-empted the Security Council's prerogative of making a finding under Article 39. The majority ignored the problem of division of powers. The representative of Norway, however, expressed the minority view that it was 'the Security Council and the Security Council alone, which has the authority to stipulate if a situation or crisis is of such a nature that sanctions should be imposed'. He stated that although the 'General Assembly can and should exert its influence on the Security Council', in his opinion, the resolution went too far in finding a threat to the peace.[37] A riposte to this argument would be to say that such a finding is necessary for the Organisation as a whole to get involved in a domestic situation, and if the Security Council is unable to make such a finding (despite overwhelming international opinion) it is for the General Assembly to make one.

A majority of members see the Assembly's role as that of removing the block put up by Western States in the Council to the adoption of mandatory economic sanctions by repeating its finding of a threat, urging mandatory sanctions (and strongly recommending voluntary ones of its own), and by persistently criticising those States deemed 'guilty' of 'colluding' with the 'illegitimate', 'racist' regime.

In 1976 the Assembly adopted a resolution calling on the governments of France, the United Kingdom and the United States 'to desist from misusing their veto power in the Security Council to protect the racist regime of South Africa'; 'to enable the Security Council to determine the existence of a threat to the peace'; and 'to facilitate the adoption' of mandatory measures under Chapter VII.[38]

Such an approach does seem to encroach on the powers of the Council by criticising permanent members, but the Assembly does have support for its finding of a threat to the peace from various bodies it has set up to investigate the situation. The grounds for such a finding are: South African attacks on frontline States; until recently its illegal occupation of Namibia; and, above all, the nature of apartheid itself.[39] The overwhelming weight of world opinion appears to be behind such a finding and the imposition of mandatory sanctions, and so the Assembly sees it as its duty to goad the recalcitrant permanent members into supporting such action. Such an approach seems to be a liberal interpretation of the proviso in Article 11(2), which requires the Assembly to refer any question on which action is necessary to the Security Council in that it attempts to virtually direct the Council into taking mandatory action after attempting to force the Council's hand by making a finding under Article 39. The majority of members seem to view the Council's acts so far as not constituting a performance of its functions, so that Article 12 does not preclude the General Assembly from discussing a matter which has remained on the Council's agenda for many years.

The annual resolutions on South Africa have become increasingly reflective of the ideological dominance of the Non Aligned and Socialist blocs in the Assembly, as that majority continues with its policy of condemnation rather than negotiation with the apartheid regime. This attitude is understandable to a certain extent in that the Pretoria government has consistently refuted attempts at what it sees as interference in its internal affairs – a policy which is not conducive to settlement. The only viable alternative left to the UN is to try to bring an end to apartheid by external pressure, hence the call by the Assembly for mandatory action, and the increasingly anti-Western content of its resolutions, as the Western permanent members, in particular Britain and the United States, continue to block any such move in the Council.

In order to fulfil its aims the Assembly has to use the term 'threat to the peace' to cover not only the 'policies and actions of the apartheid regime', but also the 'escalating acts of aggression and subversion of that regime against independent African States'[40] and 'collaboration with the racist regime and apartheid institutions' by countries such as the United Kingdom, the United States, West Germany, Japan and Belgium.[41] However, an overuse of the

term 'threat to the peace' not only devalues its impact, but is also unlikely
to facilitate the achievement of the Assembly's goals, for the Council has yet
to make such a finding as regards the situation in South Africa and, if it is
to do so, it must have the agreement of the Western members who are unlikely
to agree as long as they are included in that threat. In the Rhodesian situation
the Assembly legitimately called for imposition of sanctions against the
sanction breakers. South Africa and Portugal had breached a mandatory
decision of the Security Council in that case. In the case of South Africa, the
Western States have broken no such decision and therefore do not auto-
matically represent a threat to the peace. Nevertheless, the Assembly has used
its wide discretion to find that they do.

Convinced that the method of ending apartheid should be coercive and not
pacific, the Assembly adopts annual resolutions calling for the imposition of
mandatory economic sanctions by the Council under Chapter VII, while
recommending a wide range of voluntary measures itself. Indeed, a recent
resolution lumps together the whole range of findings under Article 39, while
calling on Western States to abandon 'constructive engagement' and support
the Council in imposing mandatory economic sanctions.[42]

South West Africa/Namibia

During the early stages of the South West Africa dispute, it was not considered
that there was a problem concerning the maintenance of international peace
and security and so the General Assembly dealt with it as a problem involving
trusteeship. Although it passed its first resolution on the subject in 1946,[43]
it did not reach a jurisdictional finding until 1960, when it considered 'with
grave concern that the present situation in South West Africa constitutes a
serious threat to international peace and security'.[44] Nevertheless, it did not
request, under Article 11(2) or (3), that the Security Council meet, even though
by making a finding of a 'threat to the peace' it brought the situation within
the ambit of the Council's primary responsibility. Instead it invited the
Committee on South West Africa to propose 'conditions for restoring a climate
of peace and security'. This culminated in an appeal to members close to the
government of South Africa to bring pressure to bear.[45]

Neither the report of the Fourth Committee which led to the 1960 resolution[46] nor the report of the Committee on South West Africa,[47] nor the
meetings of the Assembly[48] discussed in any great detail why the situation was
a threat to the peace. It seems to be a politically expedient move by the members
to galvanise world opinion and prepare the Security Council to take action
to help in ending South African occupation. The Western countries opposed
such a finding but had to admit that the situation concerned international peace
and security when Liberia proposed that a simple majority be required to adopt
resolutions on the question of Namibia. The Western States argued that under
Article 18 a two-thirds majority was required for recommendations regarding

international peace and security, and since the resolution in question[49] found a 'threat to the peace' a two-thirds majority was required.[50]

The General Assembly's recommendations as regards Namibia parallel its resolutions on South Africa, in that in the early years, although it pre-empted the Council by making a finding under Article 39, it was content to make a request to the Security Council 'to keep watch over the critical situation in South West Africa'. It then widened its use of Article 39 language in order to present the Council with all the opportunities it could for imposing sanctions against South Africa. In 1976 it found, in addition to a 'threat to the peace', that the illegal occupation constituted an 'act of aggression against the Namibian people'.[51] In 1977 it expressed deep concern at 'the increasing militarisation of Namibia and the continuing acts of aggression against neighbouring African countries including the most recent acts of aggression against Angola and Zambia'.[52] However, since then the resolutions have become ritual and repetitive with an increase in anti-Western bias.

In 1981, the Assembly named France, the United States and the United Kingdom as being

in collusion with the South African racists as manifested in their triple vetoes in the Security Council where the majority of the world body demonstrated its determination to adopt concrete political and economic measures aimed at isolating terrorist South Africa in order to compel it to vacate Namibia.[53]

A recent ritual condemnation of South Africa and Western States occurred at the Assembly's fortieth session in which it expressed 'its dismay at the failure to date of the Security Council to discharge effectively its responsibilities for the maintenance of peace and security in southern Africa, owing to the opposition of its Western permanent members' and called for mandatory economic sanctions.[54] Despite its condemnation of the linkage of South African withdrawal from Namibia with Cuban withdrawal from Angola, it is to be expected that the Assembly will support the peace plan agreed between Angola, Cuba and South Africa in December 1988, too late for consideration at the Assembly's forty-third session.[55]

One would expect Western States to object, and to use Articles 11(2) and 12 as a legal basis. In fact, the relevant parts of neither of the above resolutions were voted against, with Western nations being content to abstain. The representative of Canada explained the West's position: 'The authority of the General Assembly is recommendatory in character; moreover, the General Assembly cannot arrogate to itself powers it does not have by using language appropriate only to the Security Council. Nothing in this text, therefore, gives rise to a legal obligation'.[56]

The Western States realise that they cannot stop the resolutions from being adopted because they are heavily outnumbered. Since the resolutions are validly adopted, arguments based on Articles 11 and 12 would be futile, so the thrust of the West's arguments (when it bothers to state one) is that the resolutions of the Assembly are of paper value only, mere recommendations – the real power of decision-making lies in the Security Council. The Western States attempt to confine the Assembly to a forum where the majority of members let off steam.

The Middle East

It will be shown that initially, after the failure of the Assembly's partition plan for Palestine, that body went about complementing the decisions of the Security Council until the 1970s when it started to encroach on the Security Council's primary role when passing its annual resolutions on the Middle East conflict and the problem of Palestine.

In its resolutions on the Middle East question the Assembly has shown the same propensity for entering the Council's area of competence while isolating the generally pro-Israeli Western countries, even though it may appear as if the Assembly is supporting the relevant Council resolution. For example, in 1971 the Assembly adopted a resolution which appeared to accord with the Council's actions in that it stated 'that the Security Council resolution 242 (1967) should be implemented in all its parts in order to achieve a just and lasting peace in the Middle East'. However, the resolution went further and found a 'threat to the peace', which the Council had not, and suggested the Council take steps for the implementation of resolution 242. The West's main objections, however, were with the alterations of the balance of the Council's resolution, such as the Assembly's expression of grave concern at Israel's 'continued occupation', rather than with the introduction of the term 'threat to the peace' which, in Assembly terms, unlike those of the Council, cannot make the resolution mandatory.[57] The Dutch also felt 'as a conscientious Member of the United Nations, that Article 12 of the Charter should be scrupulously observed'.[58]

Nevertheless, more than two-thirds of the Assembly are not so 'conscientious', and in 1975 it adopted a resolution which, in addition to a finding of a threat to the peace, provided an example of a comprehensive, pre-emptive request to the Council to take measures 'to ensure complete Israeli withdrawal from all the occupied Arab territories as well as a full recognition of the inalienable national rights of the Palestinian people and the attainment of those rights'.[59]

The resolutions have become increasingly antagonistic; naming the United States as aiding Israeli 'aggression' against the Palestinian people;[60] calling for voluntary measures against Israel and demanding that it comply with Article 25 as regards Council resolutions;[61] condemning Israel's links with South Africa; and criticising the United States for vetoing a draft resolution in the Security Council which prevented that body from taking Chapter VII action against Israel for its invasion of the Lebanon.[62] In effect, the

Assembly has arrogated to itself a virtually limitless competence as far as recommendatory resolutions are concerned.

The United States representative was forced to respond to a recent resolution by rejecting 'pernicious charges' which 'purport to engage the Assembly in matters which, under the United Nations' Charter, are expressly and necessarily reserved to the Security Council'.[63] One might argue as to on what provisions of the Charter he bases this assertion. Indeed, the relevant Articles tend to suggest a sacrosanct sphere of competence for the primary body, but it is possible to point to other provisions which confer on the Assembly a generous sphere of operation. Perhaps a better approach was taken by the representative of New Zealand who stated a willingness to support any resolution which furthered the principles contained in Security Council resolutions.[64]

This approach would not unduly restrict the competence of the Assembly as long as it acted in accord with the Council's resolutions and did not attempt any new initiative. In fact, New Zealand was unable to support the resolution because it was too antagonistic towards the Council and Israel.

Cyprus 1964

Whereas in 1974 the Assembly appeared to act in a parallel fashion to the Security Council, in 1964 there were objections that it was attempting to go beyond the relevant resolutions of the Security Council when it merely called upon 'all States to refrain from any intervention directed against' the Republic of Cyprus.[65] This seems a minor transgression as compared to those above, but it was deemed by those voting against it or abstaining to be anti-Turkish. According to the representative of the United States, the Assembly should not have gone 'beyond the basic resolution of the Security Council' or showed favouritism to one of the parties to the dispute.[66]

Perhaps this was an early example of the new majority of recently independent States along with Socialist countries flexing their collective muscle (very slightly) to the consternation of the West. Twenty years on that resolution and its encroachment on the competence of the Security Council would probably pass by without comment.

The Assembly appears to have interpreted the term 'functions' in Article 12 not only to allow it to deal with situations already on the Council's agenda, but also to permit it to act when the Council is deliberating and passing resolutions on the matter. Indeed, the Assembly seems to have developed a power to determine whether the Council is functioning, even if it is deliberating and resolving. The Assembly not only appears to have the competence to determine its own competence, but in so doing it has arrogated to itself the competence to determine whether the Council is functioning. It has thus gone beyond the theory of 'la compétence de la compétence' for it has most probably entered into the jurisdiction of the Security Council. It is debatable whether such a revision would survive a challenge of *ultra vires* before the International Court.

Cases in which the General Assembly has supplemented or complemented the work of the Security Council

East Timor

Although the General Assembly produced a resolution which was remarkably similar to its Council counterpart,[67] it could not be accused of merely repeating or paralleling the Council for it seized the issue and adopted its resolution before the Council. Indonesia had moved its troops into East Timor on 7 December, the General Assembly adopted its resolution on 12 December, whereas the Council could virtually only repeat the Assembly's call on 22 December.

The Assembly did not really pre-empt the Council, for the resolution contained no findings under Article 39 but did contain a request to the Council 'in conformity with' Article 11(3) to consider the situation. The Assembly was not performing the Council's role, for the Council did act eventually, except more slowly. It was a case of the Assembly aiding the Council, the machinery of which, on this occasion, lacked the necessary alacrity.

Subsequently the Assembly dealt with the situation on an regular basis until the early 1980s. Although it repeated its own, and later the Council's, call for Indonesian withdrawal, in later years it concentrated more on humanitarian issues,[68] possibly in the forlorn hope that the Security Council would take up the issue again. Nevertheless, the Assembly restricted itself to a call under Article 11(3) rather than crying out for Chapter VII measures. Unlike in the cases in area (ii) above, the Non Aligned States were unwilling to suggest enforcement action against one of their own. This was reflected in the relatively measured but weak Assembly resolutions.

Tunisia

After the Security Council had failed to adopt a resolution which dealt more than temporarily with the Tunisian conflict,[69] the General Assembly held its Third Special Session in August 1961 under Article 20.

The representative of Tunisia stated that the General Assembly should act because of the inability of the Council to end French aggression and to secure the withdrawal of French troops who were in Tunisia 'against the will of the people'.[70] Nevertheless, the Assembly did not adopt a resolution condemning French aggression; instead it adopted one calling for negotiations and French withdrawal. The resolution classified the situation as a 'source of international friction' and a danger to international peace and security.[71]

Although the resolution did not favour the French, it built upon rather than detracted from the work of the Council. The Council was able to act with some immediacy and call for a cease-fire but, as on so many occasions, was unable to go that step further and recommend a basis for settlement. Instead, the Assembly performed this task making explicit what was implicit in the Council resolution – that the situation was of a kind that should be subject to pacific settlement. The Assembly did not upset the work of the Council by finding a 'breach of the peace' or an 'act of aggression' which would not induce any settlement. On this occasion the Assembly did constitute a 'compelling summons to the conscience of the world'.[72]

Namibia

In 1966 the General Assembly terminated South Africa's mandate over Namibia[73] and called 'the attention of the Security Council to the present resolution'. This represented quite a good example of the dovetailing of the Assembly and the Council; a fact recognised by the International Court.

By resolution 2145 the General Assembly terminated the Mandate. However, lacking the necessary powers to ensure the withdrawal of South Africa from the Territory, it enlisted the help of the Security Council by calling the latter's attention to the resolution, thus acting in accordance with Article 11, paragraph 2 of the Charter.[74]

The Council went on to adopt resolutions for this purpose.[75] However, the Assembly then became increasingly exasperated with the Council's inability to end South Africa's presence and started to prejudge issues that should be considered by the Council, finding that the situation was a threat to the peace and an act of aggression against the Namibian people. This also reflected the Non Aligned's view that Assembly resolutions should represent the ideal standard which should then be used to embarrass the Council, which has at best a pragmatic approach to disputes.[76] On the other hand, the Dutch representative reminded the Assembly that it was veering away from co-operation with the Council to being antagonistic towards it by making such findings which 'prejudge a definite opinion which only the Security Council is entitled to express', making the Assembly resolutions 'constitutionally impermissible, factually incorrect and politically inappropriate'.[77]

Palestine

The Assembly's actions over Palestine also reflect upon the fact that in the early years, when there was a Western majority in both organs, the Assembly acted as a complement to the Council, whereas after the mid-1950s, with the increase in newly independent, Non Aligned countries, the Assembly's resolutions became increasingly extreme and divorced from those of the Council.

After the failure of its partition plan for Palestine, the Assembly set about complementing the Council in its efforts to restore peace and stability to the region. For example, it passed a resolution in 1948[78] which strongly affirmed the General Assembly's 'support for the efforts of the Security Council to secure a truce in Palestine'. To further the Council's efforts, the Assembly appointed a mediator to 'promote a peaceful adjustment of the future situation in Palestine' and to 'co-operate with the Truce Commission for Palestine appointed by the Security Council on 23 April 1948'.

From this relatively harmonious position the Assembly and Council have become increasingly divorced in their dealings with the Palestinian problem. Annual resolutions on the Palestine situation have been adopted since the mid-1970s, based on the reports of the Committee on the Exercise of the Inalienable Rights of the Palestinian people – a heavily biased Committee on which the West refuses to serve.

These annual resolutions go beyond, criticise and undermine those of the Council. A good example of this is the resolution adopted in 1980, which expressed the view that Security Council resolution 242 did not provide an adequate basis for settlement because it did not guarantee the inalienable rights of the Palestinian people.[79]

It reflects badly on the UN's ability to settle disputes when the supposedly subsidiary body is constantly undermining and questioning the decisions of the primary organ, a fact that did not escape the attention of the Soviet Union. The Soviet representative stated that despite the adoption of the 1980 resolution, 'the fundamental decisions of the Security Council in connection with the settlement of the situation in the Middle East maintain their full force'.[80] Although the Soviet Union and its allies are able to align themselves with the majority on most issues, it has to protect the primacy of the Security Council on those issues in which it is in the minority.

Cases where the General Assembly has performed the functions of the Security Council

There are three methods by which the General Assembly has become the primary organ as regards a situation concerning international peace – by means of the Interim Committee or little Assembly, by the Uniting for Peace procedure in Emergency Special Session, or by Special Session under Article 20. Only the last of these is specifically authorised by the Charter. The former two methods were both created in the period of Western domination in an attempt to give the Assembly power when the Security Council was paralysed by the Soviet veto.

The Interim Committee of the General Assembly

The first method the pro-Western majority employed in an attempt to give more primacy in affairs of peace and security to the Assembly when the Council was blocked concentrated on increasing the effective length of the

Assembly's session beyond its four monthly regular session. The Assembly adopted a proposal by the United States[81] creating a little Assembly consisting of all the members which could be convened all year round. What was intended was to give the Assembly competence in the area of international peace when not in regular session – an 'all year' Assembly.

Its responsibilities included the study of problems relating to international peace and reporting to the Assembly at its regular session. Thus, the power of recommendation still remained with the Assembly proper and so the little Assembly did not represent a serious revision of the Charter to extend the Assembly's period of competence. In practice it represented even less of a threat to the Council's primacy, for although it did submit reports to the General Assembly during the United Nations' first decade, it was severely paralysed by the Soviet boycott and was eclipsed by another Western sponsored idea – the Uniting for Peace resolution.

The creators of the Interim Committee saw it as a subsidiary organ of the General Assembly under Article 22. Prandler argues that it was created unconstitutionally, for theoretically its powers in the field of international peace undermined those of the Security Council and it is doubtful whether subsidiary bodies can have an independent scope of duties.[82] One would have thought that the little Assembly's powers came under the Assembly's umbrella of powers – either Articles 10, 11 or 14, and so it had no duties independent of the Assembly, and undermined the Security Council's competence only in that it attempted to extend the Assembly's period of session.

The Uniting for Peace procedure
The immediate reason for the adoption of the Uniting for Peace resolution[83] was the return, in August 1950, of the Soviet Union to the Security Council, leading to the discontinuation of the Council as the body dealing with the United Nations' involvement in Korea. In fact, the Assembly adopted a resolution on Korea after the Soviets had returned to the Security Council but before the Uniting for Peace resolution was adopted.[84] However, the Western influenced majority in the General Assembly was also of the view that the frequent use of the Soviet veto during the period 1946–50 was an abuse of that right and that the ideal of Great Power unanimity at San Francisco was no longer attainable.

The method proposed by the United States, Canada, France, the Philippines, the United Kingdom, Turkey and Uruguay by which paralysis of the Security Council would be circumvented was the Uniting for Peace resolution, the salient part of which stated,

that if the Security Council because of lack of unanimity of the permanent members, fails to exercise its primary responsibility for the maintenance of international peace and security in any case where there appears to be a threat to the peace, breach of the peace, or act of aggression, the General Assembly shall consider the matter immediately with a view to making the appropriate recommendations to Members for collective measures, including in cases of a breach of the peace or act of aggression the use of armed force when necessary, to maintain or restore international peace and security. If not in session at the time, the General Assembly may meet in emergency special session within 24 hours of the request therefor. Such emergency special session shall be called if requested by the Security Council on a vote of any seven [now nine] members, or by a majority of the Members of the United Nations.[85]

The resolution was introduced at the height of the Cold War and predictably led to an East-West dichotomy in the discussions leading up to it. Since it was the time of Western domination, the Socialist countries argued against its adoption on the basis that Articles 10 to 14 of the Charter indicate that the Security Council and the General Assembly 'cannot be substituted for one another, they merely complement each other'.[86] The pro-Western States argued, *inter alia*, that the resolution was valid on a wide interpretation of Article 12 – for when the Council was paralysed by the veto it was not functioning in the sense of that provision.[87] To this the representative of the Soviet Union replied that the operation of the veto was an integral function of the Security Council. He also objected that the proposed resolution would require only a procedural vote to transfer the matter from the Security Council to the Assembly, whilst Special Sessions called under Article 20 needed a substantive vote. Finally the Soviet Union argued that the proposed resolution was unconstitutional because, by Article 11(2), coercive action was within the sole ambit of the Council.[88]

The World Court has stated that 'action' in Article 11(2) refers to coercive action, but it failed to state whether this excluded the Assembly from recommending coercive measures. At some points the Court suggested that 'action' is restricted to mandatory, coercive action 'ordered' by the Security Council. In other words, the Assembly may not be barred from recommending enforcement action as part of its significant responsibility for the maintenance of peace as recognised by the Court.[89]

It is this writer's opinion that the ambiguous statements of the Court, in addition to the presumption against *ultra vires*, signify that the Uniting for Peace resolution is not unconstitutional. It represents an interpretation of Articles 11(2) and 12 that has been accepted and acted upon by the members of the United Nations. To cast doubts on the legal validity of the resolution would mean that any action taken under the resolution would be suspect until the World Court is asked to decide on the issue. This would jeopardise a not insignificant segment of Assembly resolutions.

Nevertheless, in over forty years of practice there have been only nine emergency special sessions called using the Uniting for Peace procedure[90] – this cannot be regarded as making the procedure a major factor in the extension of the competence of the General Assembly. As has been pointed out, at the time of the resolution's adoption there was a significant link between both organs – they were dominated by a Western majority. The West tried to strengthen the link in terms of the transfer of problems from one organ to the other by means of the Uniting for Peace resolution. With the new majority in the Assembly the Uniting for Peace procedure has no such use, for the Security Council is not controlled by that majority but by the permanent members, in particular the superpowers. Thus, in later years, the procedure has become a vehicle either for condemnation of *fait accomplis* in which one of the superpowers is involved or for the reinforcement of the Assembly's previous recommendations on the topic in question. To emphasise the change in significance of the Uniting for Peace procedure the examination below is divided into the early period and the later period.

The early years. Before the adoption of the Uniting for Peace resolution, President Truman spoke before the General Assembly and indicated that he envisaged the procedure being used in situations such as Korea.[91] In fact the Assembly had already made a substantial contribution to UN action in Korea by passing a resolution which allowed the UN force to continue its operations to establish 'a unified, independent and democratic government of Korea' after the Security Council had been deadlocked by the return of the Soviet representative.[92] This resolution impliedly authorised General MacArthur to cross the 38th parallel and so could be classified as authorising enforcement action. President Truman probably had this in mind when he and Secretary of State Acheson introduced the Uniting for Peace resolution.

The early successes of the procedure lay in the peacekeeping function – the establishment of UNEF in 1956, and the facility to take over the running of ONUC in 1960 when the Security Council was paralysed by the Soviet veto. However, the peacekeeping function has gradually gravitated towards the Security Council – evidenced by the failure of the General Assembly to produce any constructive resolution on the Middle East in its Fifth Emergency Special Session after the Six Day War in 1967. The resolution adopted merely passed the records of the session to the Security Council[93] because after four weeks of discussion the Assembly itself could not agree on a compromise.

Without a role in the peacekeeping function and with situations like Korea being unlikely to arise again, it was becoming clear that the Uniting for Peace resolution was not going to result in the primacy of the General Assembly in matters of international peace. Gradually its function was to evolve into one where the Assembly is to be used to condemn cases of direct superpower intervention which will obviously result in a paralysed Security Council. The signs were there as early as the Second Emergency Special Session on Hungary in 1956, in which the Assembly adopted a resolution which virtually paralleled the draft resolution vetoed in the Security Council in that it condemned the Soviet attack without classifying it as a breach of the peace or an act of aggression, as would seem to be required by the terms of the Uniting for Peace resolution.[94] Again, in 1958 when American and British troops were invited into Lebanon and Jordan respectively, the Assembly could merely adopt a nondescript resolution which called for mutual respect for and non-interference between Arab countries.[95]

However, on one occasion the General Assembly managed to act in a manner which suggested that it could take on the role of the Council. During the Bangladesh crisis in 1971 the Security Council was hopelessly deadlocked and so sought the help of the Assembly which was in its twenty-sixth session at the time. The Council resolution cited the Uniting for Peace procedure, although the Assembly did not meet in emergency special session.[96] The Assembly responded with commendable alacrity by adopting a resolution which found that the 'hostilities between India and Pakistan constitute an immediate threat to international peace and security' and called for a cease-fire and withdrawal.[97] Admittedly there was no recommendation of enforcement action (which was highly unlikely anyway); nevertheless, the Assembly made a finding of a threat and made the recommendations which the Council, at the minimum, should have made much earlier in the conflict. The Assembly was in fact performing the role of the Council.

The later years. Since Bangladesh the Uniting for Peace procedure has become indistinguishable in its impact from Assembly actions taken in ordinary or special sessions. The Sixth Emergency Special Session on Afghanistan adopted a resolution which was a mirror image of the draft resolution defeated in the Security Council by the Soviet veto. It deplored the 'recent armed intervention' after expressing grave concern 'at the recent developments in Afghanistan and their implications for international peace and security'.[98] Its call for withdrawal was subsequently repeated annually until 1988. The Assembly's repeated condemnation may have contributed to the Soviet withdrawal in 1989 by adding to the weight of world opinion against its intervention,[99] an argument that can be used to support most Assembly resolutions on a particular conflict. The advent of the Geneva Accords on Afghanistan in April 1988 led to the Assembly, at its forty-third session, supporting the implementation of the Accords but also urging a comprehensive internal settlement.[100] It may be that if the conflict continues the Assembly might start to condemn the indirect intervention of the United States, the Soviet Union and Pakistan in the internal struggle − intervention which is contrary to the Accords.

The problem is that, when dealing with superpower interventions, no matter how quickly the General Assembly is convened, whether by the Security Council or by a majority of its Members, it is still generally dealing with a *fait accompli*. In these cases the Uniting for Peace procedure is superfluous, and often the Assembly waits until its annual session. After the United States intervened in Grenada the Assembly was already in its regular session so that it produced a resolution relatively quickly, which again mirrored the draft vetoed by the United States in the Council, deploring the 'armed intervention' and calling for withdrawal.[101] However, in the case of the Vietnamese intervention in Kampuchea, the Assembly waited many months before expressing deep regret at the 'armed intervention by outside forces' and calling for withdrawal.[102] Again, after the air raids by the United States against Libya on 15 April 1986, the Assembly waited until its forty-first annual session to condemn the attacks as a violation of international law and as a serious threat to peace and security in the Mediterranean region.[103]

In these situations of superpower intervention the Uniting for Peace procedure is not necessary. The speed of condemnation is not too important. What is required is for the Assembly to have regard to the purpose of the Uniting for Peace resolution – that it should act in the manner in which the Council was designed to act. In this respect, the latest Kampuchean resolutions have taken a step forward by finding a 'threat to the peace'.[104] The Council was unable to make such a jurisdictional finding because of the Soviet veto, but there is no such reason why the Assembly should not make a finding of a threat to the peace which could lead to the possible recommendation of measures by that body, whereas the mere condemnation of armed intervention has no such potential. Further action by the Assembly may be unlikely but there is no reason why it should not leave itself the possibility.

In other situations the Uniting for Peace resolution has become an additional tool in the hands of the majority of the members, who, for example, in 1981 called the Eighth Emergency Special Session of the Assembly to discuss the Namibian situation. The resolution produced added nothing to the plethora of Assembly resolutions passed at its annual sessions. It blamed the three Western permanent members for vetoing drafts aimed at introducing mandatory economic sanctions and called on the Council to respond to the 'overwhelming demand of the international community' to impose mandatory sanctions in the 'light of the serious threat to the peace'.[105]

In this respect they are little different from the special sessions which can be called by a majority of members under Article 20.

Special Sessions
Article 20 of the Charter provides that 'the General Assembly shall meet in regular annual sessions and in such special session as occasion may require. Special sessions shall be invoked by the Secretary General at the request of the Security Council or of a majority of the Members of the United Nations.'

The procedure envisaged by the Charter for convoking a special session does not appear significantly different from that established under the Uniting for Peace resolution. The difference is that the resolution specifically grants the Assembly the power to recommend collective measures and establishes the machinery to enable it to carry out these measures. We have already seen that Article 10 in itself grants the power to the Assembly to recommend voluntary measures, so that whether in normal or special session it has the same powers as those purportedly granted by the Uniting for Peace resolution.

Subsequent practice also has shown that the Assembly has the power to recommend voluntary measures, which means in effect that Article 20 and the Uniting for Peace resolution are conterminous - their only impact is to extend the Assembly's powers of consideration and recommendation beyond the annual regular session. What seems to have confused the sponsors of the Uniting for Peace resolution is doubts over whether the Assembly could recommend enforcement measures. They failed to take account of the perfectly valid argument in favour of the Assembly having this power, a power it had already utilised in the Korean situation and to be recognised as legitimate by subsequent practice. The Uniting for Peace resolution thus remains an unnecessary monument to the era of Western domination.

Up until 1988 there were fifteen Special Sessions of the General Assembly, which, disarmament apart, differed little from the Emergency Special Sessions of that body.[106] For example, the Eighth Emergency Special Session on Namibia discussed in the section above was a parallel of the Ninth Special Session which again produced nothing different from the annual Namibian debate.[107] Both procedures are used by the majority in an attempt to assert the independence of the Assembly from the Security Council on matters relating to international peace. However, the resolutions produced reflect the Assembly's main jealousy − that neither under Article 20 nor under the Uniting for Peace resolution (as well as in its regular sessions) can it introduce mandatory, enforcement measures.

Cases in which the General Assembly has acted within its own area of competence even though they also concern international peace and security

It has been suggested in chapter 4 that the expansive jurisdiction of the General Assembly can be explained partly by its desire to further and protect the right of self-determination and the protection of human rights. These principles are enshrined in the Charter but no specific organ is entrusted with their protection. It is therefore natural that the Assembly − embodying the United Nations − should adopt itself as the defender of these principles. Often issues of self-determination and human rights involve questions of peace and security, and thus we frequently have both the Security Council and the General Assembly involved. Strictly, on this analysis, the Assembly should concentrate on the self-determination aspect only, without considering the security situation, but, as shall be illustrated below, this is often impossible in situations where the denial of self-determination is in itself seen as a threat to the peace.

Algeria
The problem of the colonial situation in Algeria was never brought before the Security Council, although the Assembly passed a resolution[108] which found not only that the Algerian people had a 'right to self-determination and

independence', but also that 'the present situation in Algeria constitutes a threat to international peace and security'. It can be argued that in internal situations a finding of a 'threat to the peace' can only be based on a denial of self-determination or an abuse of human rights. Therefore, in many cases both the Assembly and the Council have legitimate claims to competence, although, as evidenced here, the Assembly is much more willing to find a threat to the peace in internal situations.

Western Sahara
A good illustation of the correct division of duties is found in the cases of the Falklands, the Comoros and Western Sahara. With regard to Western Sahara, before the conflict in 1975, the Assembly was solely concerned with the territory because it involved decolonisation. In 1974 it did consider 'that the persistence of a colonial situation in Western Sahara jeopardises stability and harmony in north-west Africa',[109] but it was mainly concerned with obtaining an advisory opinion of the International Court as to the legal status of the territory so that it could make recommendations as to decolonisation.

When trouble erupted with the Green March, the Security Council became involved as the emphasis became one of restoring international peace,[110] with the Assembly, at a later date, addressing the issue of self-determination.[111] The General Assembly has since adopted annual resolutions on the subject. A recent resolution[112] reaffirmed that the 'question of Western Sahara is a question of decolonisation which remains to be completed on the basis of the exercise by the people of Western Sahara of their inalienable right to self-determination and independence'. The question of self-determination is the Assembly's area, but to achieve this aim it must make recommendations in the area of securing international peace − in this case by calling for a cease-fire between Polisario and Morocco. Thus a confusion arises, but if one concentrates on the main import of the resolution − the protection of the right to self-determination − it can be seen that we are in the Assembly's sphere of competence, with the cease-fire being a necessary pre-condition to the establishment of self-determination.

The Falklands
The Assembly had adopted resolutions before the conflict in 1982 relating to the decolonisation of the islands.[113] When the conflict arose the Security Council became solely concerned with the issue. Once the conflict was over the Assembly again returned to the question of decolonisation by urging negotiations towards pacific settlement, while reminding the States involved of the principles of the non-use of force.[114]

The Comoros

A rather less straightforward division of powers between the Council and the Assembly can be seen over the question of the continuing French colonisation of the Comoran island of Mayotte.

The problem was raised in the Council where France had to veto a draft resolution which would have criticised the holding of a referendum on the island by the French.[115] The French ambassador scoffed at the idea that the situation was one which concerned international peace,[116] and indeed it appeared to be a simple question of decolonisation and self-determination better left to the General Assembly. Indeed, at its thirty-first session the Assembly adopted a resolution[117] which condemned the referendum and the French presence on the island. It urged France to enter into negotiations with the Comoran government.

The problem has become one of ritual debate and resolution in the Assembly and, as with the situations below, once it becomes ritualised the Assembly seems to forget its jurisdictional competence and allows the resolution to stray into the realm of international peace. The 1985 resolution on the Comoros revealed this tendency, which arises out of frustration of its resolutions not being heeded, in that it was premised on the principle 'that a speedy resolution of the problem is essential for the preservation of the peace and security of the region'.[118]

Southern Africa and the Middle East

These situations have been grouped together for they are illustrative of how, in long-running situations, the Assembly will stray from its true sphere of competence. This is usually due to a majority of members equating a denial of self-determination with a threat to the peace. The General Assembly then sees its function as trying to bring the Security Council into line with this finding and urging it to take proper measures based thereon. These areas have been discussed above in the section on the pre-emption of the Council. This section is an alternative way of looking at the problem. The section on prejudging can perhaps be seen as an example of how by ritualising the topics the Assembly loses sight of its purpose – the protection of fundamental human rights and the right of self-determination – and concentrates on the question of peace based on its finding of a threat, which, generally speaking, should be dealt with by the Security Council.

In the Southern Rhodesian situation the Assembly was primarily concerned with the implementation of the 1960 Declaration on the Granting of Independence to Colonial Countries and Peoples and not with problems of international peace and security as such.[119] However, this culminated in the merging of the two areas in 1963 when the Assembly decided that the failure to accord 'basic political rights' to the 'vast majority of the African population' and the 'entrenchment of the minority regime in power' created an 'explosive situation' which constituted a 'threat to international peace and security'.[120] The equation of a denial of human rights and self-determination with a threat to the peace[121] shifted the emphasis towards the Council. One could argue that after the Council had made a similar finding in 1966 the Assembly should have left the situation to the Council. Nevertheless, the Assembly kept prejudging the work of the Council until the settlement of the situation in 1980.

The situation in the Portuguese Territories parallels that of Southern Rhodesia. For example, in 1962, the Assembly found 'that the continued refusal of Portugal to recognise the legitimate aspirations of the Angolan people to self-determination' constituted a threat to international peace and security.[122]

The Socialist and Non Aligned majority in the Assembly seem to favour the view that a denial of self-determination can constitute a threat to the peace.[123] Thus, the Assembly is often in disagreement with the Council where the Western vetoes deny such findings. With the Assembly and Council out of step the Assembly finds itself constantly urging the Council to align itself with the majority, resulting in resolutions which pre-empt and prejudge the work of the Council.

Again in the case of South Africa, the Assembly began by concentrating on the denial of self-determination and of human rights. In 1952 the Assembly established a Commission of Three to examine the question of race conflict in South Africa.[124] The Commission's report concluded that the racial policies of the government of South Africa were contrary to the Charter and the Universal Declaration of Human Rights and that the continuance of these policies would endanger friendly relations among States.[125] The Assembly established the basis of its examination of the South Africa problem in 1953 when it found that

enduring peace will not be secured solely by collective arrangements against breaches of international peace, but that a genuine and lasting peace depends upon the observance of all the Purposes and Principles established in the Charter intended to achieve the maintenance of international peace and security, and especially upon respect for and observance of human rights and fundamental freedoms for all.[126]

This inevitably led the Assembly to find a threat to the peace and then to urge the Council to step in line. The problem is that with Western States believing that there is no question of finding a threat to the peace based solely on a denial of human rights, there is bound to be antagonism between the Council and the Assembly. The Western States believe that findings of a threat to the peace must be made by the Council alone, which suggests that there must be something more than a denial of human rights.[127]

As long as the West takes this view the two organs will not be in accord. The Assembly will continue to attack the problem from the angle of a denial of human rights and self-determination, whereas a minority in the Council will continue to look for some sign of a danger to international peace arising from something more than the internal situation. What this decision-blocking minority seem to forget is that the constant South African attacks against neighbouring States are sufficient manifestations of the threat to enable it to find a 'threat to the peace', which would constitute a finding not based solely on the internal situation.

As we have seen, the General Assembly's consideration of the Palestinian problem has been expanded into a consideration of the whole Middle Eastern problem which is essentially one of securing international peace. Nevertheless, the basis of the Assembly's involvement is centred around the self-determination of the Palestinian people. Its resolution of 1974 is a typical example, containing an expression of deep concern 'that the problem of Palestine continues to endanger international peace and security'. Article 11(3) would tend to suggest that the Security Council should be called on to deal with the situation. However, the rest of the resolution is concerned with a reaffirmation of the Palestinians' right to self-determination, independence and sovereignty, and recognises the 'right of the Palestinian people to regain its rights by all means in accordance with the purposes and principles of the Charter of the United Nations'.[128] For the Assembly the issues of self-determination and the maintenance of peace are inextricably linked.

The difficulty is that since the resolutions are pro-Palestinian, and thus anti-Israeli, Israel's supporters on the Security Council are unlikely to take up the Assembly's resolutions. This leads the majority of the Assembly to adopt resolutions which increasingly impinge on the area of competence of the Security Council. Indeed, the Assembly now adopts annual resolutions not only on the Middle East and Palestine, but also on the Occupied Territories. The latter are concerned mainly with human rights abuses, but also contain demands for Israeli withdrawal.[129]

Conclusion

The above examination of the practice of the Assembly suggests that as a central basis for its involvement the Assembly focuses upon the question of self-determination and the abuse of human rights (area (v) above). It is from this base that it expands its competence into the realms of international security where it often antagonises the Council and usurps its role (area (ii) and perhaps area (iv) above), rather than complementing it (area (iii) above) or paralleling it (area (i) above). The expansion of competence has led to Article 12 being reinterpreted, so that in effect the Assembly purports to determine whether the Council is functioning or not, not only in the sense that it considers situations and conflicts with which the Council is dealing conterminously, but also in the sense that it is prepared to criticise the Council or to make determinations and to take measures (apart from mandatory ones) which the

Council is not prepared to do. In other words, if the Council is not dealing with the situation to the Assembly's satisfaction, the Assembly believes that the Council is not functioning within the meaning of Article 12, so leaving the Assembly free to take steps.

Notes

1 GA Res. 38/10, 38 UN GAOR Supp. (No. 47) 21 (1983).
2 SC Res. 530, 38 UN SCOR Resolutions 10 (1983).
3 GA 47–52 plen. mtgs, 38 UN A/PV (1983). But see GA Res. 41/31, 41 UN GAOR Supp. (No. 53) 23 (1986) re ICJ's judgement on Nicaragua.
4 GA Res. 42/1, 42 UN A/PV (1987).
5 J. P. Cot and A. Pellet, *La Charte des Nations Unies*, 304 (1985).
6 GA Res. 36/27, 36 UN GAOR Supp. (No. 51) 27 (1981).
7 GA Res. 37/18, 37 UN GAOR Supp. (No. 51) 22 (1982).
8 GA 70 plen. mtg, 37 UN A/PV Denmark 58, FRG 58, Belgium 61, Canada 63, UK 59 (1982).
9 *Ibid.*, at 57.
10 GA Res. 40/6, 40 UN GAOR Supp. (No. 53) 37 (1985).
11 GA Res. 37/3, 37 UN GAOR Supp. (No. 51) 14 (1983).
12 GA 41 plen. mtg, 37 UN A/PV 33–5 (1982).
13 *Ibid.*, at 28 (Mexico) and at 34 (Bhutan).
14 SC Res. 598, 42 UN SCOR Resolutions 5 (1987).
15 See for example SC Res. 353, 29 UN SCOR Resolutions 7 (1974).
16 GA Res. 3312, 29 UN GAOR Supp. (No. 31) 3 (1974).
17 GA Res 37/253, 37 UN GAOR Supp. (No. 51) 48 (1983).
18 See for example USSR, GA 118 plen. mtg, 37 UN A/PV 26 (1983); Laos, GA 119 plen. mtg, 27.
19 See for example UK, France and Austria, GA 121 plen. mtg, 37 UN A/PV 51 (1983).
20 GA Res. 1599, 1600, 15 UN GAOR Supp. (No. 16A) 17 (1961).
21 GA 982 plen. mtg, 19 UN GAOR 279 (1964).
22 GA 983 plen. mtg, 19 UN GAOR 290 (1964).
23 But see Cot and Pellet, *La Charte*, 340.
24 GA Res. 1807, 17 UN GAOR Supp. (No. 17) 39 (1962).
25 GA Res. 2107, 20 UN GAOR Supp. (No. 14) 62 (1965).
26 UN doc. S/16880 (1985).
27 SC Res. 312, 27 UN SCOR Resolutions 10 (1972).
28 Compare GA Res 1889, 18 UN GAOR Supp. (No. 15) 46 (1963), with SC Res. 221, 21 UN SCOR Resolutions 5 (1966).
29 GA Res. 2024, 20 UN GAOR Supp. (No. 14) 55 (1965). Compare SC Res. 217, 20 UN SCOR Resolutions 8 (1965).
30 GA Res. 2151, 20 UN GAOR Supp. (No. 16) 68 (1966).
31 GA 1468 plen. mtg, 21 UN GAOR 4 (1966).
32 SC Res. 232, 21 UN SCOR Resolutions 7 (1966). SC Res. 253, 23 UN SCOR Resolutions 5 (1968).
33 GA Res. 2652, 25 UN GAOR Supp. (No. 28) 89 (1970).
34 GA Res. 3116, 28 UN GAOR Supp. (No. 30) 99 (1973).
35 GA Res. 1663, 16 UN GAOR Supp. (No. 17) 10 (1961).
36 GA Res. 2054, 20 UN GAOR Supp. (No. 14) 52 (1965).
37 GA 1395 plen. mtg, 20 UN GAOR 12 (1965).

38 GA Res. 31/6, 31 UN GAOR Supp. (No. 39) 52 (1976).
39 Report of the Special Committee Against Apartheid, UN doc. A/34/22 (1979).
40 GA Res. 35/206, 35 UN GAOR Supp. (No. 48) 29 (1980).
41 GA Res. 34/93, 34 UN GAOR Supp. (No. 46) 29 (1979).
42 GA Res. 40/64, 40 UN GAOR Supp. (No. 53) 32 (1985).
43 GA Res. 65, 1 UN GAOR Resolutions 123 (1946).
44 GA Res. 1568, 15 UN GAOR Supp. (No. 16) 33 (1960).
45 GA Res. 1593, 15 UN GAOR Supp. (No. 16A) 7 (1961).
46 UN doc. A/4643 (1960).
47 UN doc. A/4464 (1960).
48 GA 954 plen. mtg, 15 UN GAOR (1960).
49 Referring to GA Res. 2074, 20 UN GAOR Supp. (No. 14) 60 (1965).
50 Liberia, GA 1399 mtg, 20 UN GAOR 1, Ireland 2, UK 2, US 4–5 (1965).
51 GA Res. 31/146, 31 UN GAOR Supp. (No. 39) 130 (1976).
52 GA Res. 34/92, 34 UN GAOR Supp. (No. 46) 22 (1979).
53 GA Res. 36/121, 36 UN GAOR Supp. (No. 51) 29 (1981).
54 GA Res. 40/97, 40 UN GAOR Supp. (No. 53) 44 (1985).
55 GA Res. 43/26, 43 UN A/PV (1988).
56 GA 8 plen. mtg, 8 UN GAOR ESS 197 (1981).
57 GA 2016 plen. mtg, 26 UN GAOR 25 (1971), US.
58 GA 2009 plen. mtg, 26 UN GAOR 8 (1971).
59 GA Res. 3414, 30 UN GAOR Supp. (No. 34) 6 (1975). Contrast SC Res. 242, 22
    UN SCOR Resolutions 8 (1967).
60 GA Res. 36/226, 36 UN GAOR Supp. (No. 51) 47 (1981).
61 GA Res. 37/123, 37 UN GAOR Supp. (No. 51) 36 (1982).
62 GA Res. 40/168, 40 UN GAOR Supp. (No. 53) 57 (1985).
63 GA 118 plen. mtg, 40 UN A/PV 63 (1985).
64 *Ibid.*
65 GA Res 2077, 20 UN GAOR Supp. (No. 14) 9 (1965). See SC Res 186, 19 UN SCOR
    Resolutions 2 (1964).
66 GA 1402 plen. mtg, 20 UN GAOR 7 (1965).
67 GA Res. 3485, 30 UN GAOR Supp. (No. 34) 118 (1975). Compare SC Res. 384,
    30 UN SCOR Resolutions 10 (1975).
68 See for example GA Res. 37/30, 37 UN GAOR Supp. (No. 51) 227 (1982).
69 See SC Res. 164, 16 UN SCOR Resolutions 9 (1961).
70 GA 966 plen. mtg, 3 UN GAOR SS 3 (1961).
71 GA Res. 1622, 3 UN GAOR SS Resolutions 2 (1961).
72 US at GA 998 plen mtg, 3 UN GAOR SS 39–40 (1961), US.
73 GA Res. 2145, 21 UN GAOR Supp. (No. 16) 2 (1966).
74 *Namibia* case, I.C.J. *Rep.* 1971, 16, at para. 106.
75 SC Res. 264 and 269, 24 UN SCOR Resolutions 1–2 (1969).
76 GA 1454 plen. mtg, 21 UN GAOR 19 (1966), Sudan; GA 1661 plen. mtg, 22 UN
    GAOR 7 (1968), Yemen; GA 1663 mtg, 22 UN GAOR 2 (1968), Nigeria; GA 1664
    plen. mtg, 22 UN GAOR 3 (1968), Malawi.
77 GA 1671 plen. mtg, 22 UN GAOR 2 (1968).
78 GA Res. 186, 2 UN GAOR SS Resolutions 5 (1948).
79 GA Res. 35/169, 35 UN GAOR Supp. (No. 48) 26 (1980).
80 GA 95 plen. mtg, 35 UN GAOR 1683 (1980).
81 GA Res. 111, 2 UN GAOR Resolutions 15 (1947).
82 Prandler, 27 *Questions of International Law* (1977), 154.
83 GA Res. 377, 5 UN GAOR Resolutions 10 (1950).

84 GA Res. 376, 5 UN GAOR Resolutions 9 (1950).
85 The resolution also established a Peace Observation Commission and a Collective Measures Committee.
86 GA 299 plen. mtg, 5 UN GAOR 305 (1950), Poland.
87 *Ibid.*, at 314, Bolivia.
88 GA 301 plen. mtg, 5 UN GAOR 332 (1950).
89 *Expenses* case, I.C.J. *Rep.* 1962, 162–5.
90 1st, 1956, UNEF; 2nd, 1956, Hungary; 3rd, 1958, Lebanon and Jordan; 4th, 1960, Congo; 5th, 1967, Middle East; 6th, 1980, Afghanistan; 7th, 1980 and 1982, Palestine; 8th, 1981, Namibia; 9th, 1982, Israeli Occupied Territories.
91 GA 295 plen. mtg, 5 UN GAOR (1950).
92 GA Res. 376 (1950).
93 GA Res. 2256, 5 UN GAOR ESS Supp. (No. 1) 1 (1967).
94 GA Res. 1004, 2 UN GAOR ESS Supp. (No. 1) 2 (1956). Compare UN doc. S/3760/REV 1 (1956).
95 GA Res. 1237, 3 UN GAOR ESS Supp. (No. 1) 1 (1958).
96 SC Res. 303, 26 UN SCOR Resolutions 10 (1971).
97 GA Res. 2793, 26 UN GAOR Supp. (No. 29) 3 (1971).
98 GA Res. ES-6/2, 6 UN GAOR ESS Supp. (No. 1) 2 (1980). Compare UN doc. S/13729 (1980).
99 GA 74 plen. mtg, 40 UN A/PV 7 (1985).
100 GA Res. 43/20, 43 UN A/PV (1988).
101 GA Res. 38/7, 38 UN GAOR Supp. (No. 47) 19 (1983). Compare UN doc. S/16077/REV 1 (1983).
102 GA Res. 34/22, 34 UN GAOR Supp. (No. 46) 16 (1979).
103 GA Res. 41/38, 41 UN GAOR Supp. (No. 53) 34 (1986).
104 GA Res. 39/5, 39 UN GAOR Supp. (No. 51) 16 (1984).
105 GA Res. ES-8/2, 8 UN GAOR ESS (1981).
106 Apart from Special Sessions on disarmament and economic problems there follows a summary of the other Special Sessions: 1st, 1947, Palestine; 2nd, 1948, Palestine; 3rd, 1961, Tunisia; 5th, 1967, S.W. Africa; 9th, 1978, Namibia; 14th, 1986, Namibia.
107 See GA Res. S-9/2, 9 UN GAOR SS Supp. (No. 2) 3 (1978).
108 GA Res. 1573, 15 UN GAOR Supp. (No. 16) 3 (1960).
109 GA Res. 3292, 29 UN GAOR Supp. (No. 31) 103 (1974).
110 SC Res. 377 and 379, 30 UN SCOR Resolutions 8 (1975).
111 GA Res. 3458, 30 UN GAOR Supp. (No. 34) 116 (1975).
112 GA Res. 42/78, 42 UN A/PV (1987).
113 See for example GA Res. 31/49, 31 UN GAOR Supp. (No. 39) 122 (1976).
114 GA Res. 43/25, 43 UN A/PV (1988).
115 UN doc. S/11967 (1976).
116 SC 1886 mtg, 31 UN SCOR 2 (1976).
117 GA Res. 31/4, 31 UN GAOR Supp. (No. 39) 10 (1976).
118 GA Res. 40/62, 40 UN GAOR Supp. (No. 53) 31 (1985).
119 See GA Res. 1747, 16 UN GAOR Supp. (No. 17A) 3 (1962).
120 GA Res. 1889, 18 UN GAOR Supp. (No. 15) 46 (1963).
121 See GA 1367 plen. mtg, 20 UN GAOR 11 (1965), where the Soviet Union makes this equation; contrast US and UK views at 8 and 14.
122 GA Res. 1742, 16 UN GAOR Supp. (No. 17) 67 (1962).
123 GA 1099 plen. mtg, 16 UN GAOR 1304 (1962), Yugoslavia re Portuguese Territories.

124 GA Res. 616, 7 UN GAOR Supp. (No. 20) 8 (1952).
125 UN doc. A/2505 (1953).
126 GA Res. 721, 8 UN GAOR Supp. (No. 17) 6 (1953).
127 GA 98 plen. mtg, 35 UN GAOR 1716 (1980), UK.
128 GA Res. 3236, 29 UN GAOR Supp. (No. 31) 4 (1974).
129 GA Res. 43/21, 43 UN A/PV (1988).

CHAPTER 6

The powers of the General Assembly in practice

Due to the poor drafting of Articles 10 to 14 of the Charter it has been possible to argue that the provisions can be interpreted to give the Assembly a wide range of recommendatory powers, equivalent to the Security Council's powers of recommendation under Chapters VI and VII. This chapter will contain an examination of how the practice of the Assembly has followed this path to such an extent that in certain areas of recommendation, for example on disarmament and on general principles of international peace, the General Assembly is undoubtedly the primary organ. Theoretically the Assembly's resolutions are non-mandatory, and in practice this remains so, although in certain instances the language of the resolutions reflect the present day majority's desire that perhaps they should be binding.

Disarmament

Article 11(1) of the Charter states:

The General Assembly may consider the general principles of co-operation in the maintenance of international peace and security, including the principles governing disarmament and the regulation of armaments, and may make recommendations with regard to such principles to the Members or to the Security Council or both.

It is generally recognised that this is the basis of disarmament resolutions adopted by the General Assembly, while resolutions concerning general principles come under Article 13(1)(a).[1] In fact the General Assembly has taken on the responsibilities of the United Nations as regards disarmament, for the Security Council has abstained from exercising its competence as regards disarmament given to it under Article 26.

In practice the Assembly has elevated disarmament from the relatively low-key treatment given to it under the Charter, to one of the most important areas of UN work.[2] The work on disarmament is not only done in the regular and special sessions of the Assembly,[3] but also by bodies set up or brought under the auspices of the United Nations – for example the Disarmament Commission and the Conference on Disarmament.[4]

The Assembly has interpreted its powers under Article 11(1) widely to go beyond the recommendation of mere principles to resolutions establishing bodies to study the problem and to provide the machinery for the negotiation of disarmament. Indeed, it is remarkable that during forty years of superpower arms build-up the discussions and agreements on disarmament, either inside or outside the United Nations, have continued. To this extent the General Assembly has proved an effective organ, not for achieving disarmament but for maintaining a dialogue over levels and the regulation of armament. To this end, a major success was achieved during the period of *détente* in the 1970s, resulting in the adoption in 1978 of a resolution at the Tenth Special Session by consensus. The resolution embodied the goals, principles, objectives and priorities for disarmament and new machinery for putting them into effect.[5]

The Committee on Disarmament which has been meeting in Geneva since 1962, having a membership of thirty-one States under the co-chairmanship of the Soviet Union and the United States, was brought under UN auspices by the 1978 resolution. The resolution opened the Committee up to all nuclear weapon States and thirty-two to thirty-five others to be chosen in consultation with the President of the General Assembly, with a personal representative of the Secretary General serving as Secretary to the Committee. It was also agreed to establish a Disarmament Commission made up of the entire UN membership to follow up the work of the special session, make recommendations on various disarmament problems, and consider the elements of a comprehensive disarmament programme.

The resolution begins with a statement that 'States for a long time have sought to maintain their security through possession of arms yet the accumulation of weapons today constitutes much more a threat than a protection for the future of mankind'. 'The time has come', it says, 'to abandon the use of force in international relations and to seek security in disarmament through a gradual but effective process beginning with a reduction in the present level of armaments'. The document expands on these principles by emphasising the importance of refraining from threats against the sovereignty and territorial integrity of any State or against peoples under a colonial or foreign domination. Non-intervention in internal affairs, the inviolability of frontiers, and the peaceful settlement of disputes are also stressed. From these premises, the resolution states that all nations have the right to participate in disarmament negotiations, that disarmament measures should be equitable and balanced to ensure security to each State, and that they should be accompanied by adequate verification.

From general principles the resolution moves on to a more practical approach by establishing a programme of action which sets forth objectives and priorities, immediate and short-term measures to halt and reverse the arms race. Special importance is given to efforts to curb nuclear and other mass destruction weapons. Negotiations for the reduction of conventional arms and armed forces are also called for. Emphasising the need to work towards the complete elimination of nuclear weapons, the programme favours such measures as an agreement on a comprehensive nuclear test ban, further Soviet-United States negotiations on strategic arms limitations and reductions, nuclear weapon free zones, and expanded non-proliferation agreements. Suggested as especially desirable measures are steps by the Security Council to 'prevent the frustration' of the objective of a denuclearised Africa, and consideration of steps to give effect to the proposal for a nuclear weapon free zone in the Middle East. Other provisions call for an expert study of the relationship between disarmament and development, and continuation of a study of the interrelationship between disarmament and international security.

The 1978 Special Session resolution has been analysed in some detail because it represents possibly the most important achievement of the United Nations as regards disarmament. Its adoption by consensus represented the crossing of ideological and political frontiers. It may appear, in some respects, naive − for example, expressing the hope that the Security Council would become involved in disarmament. However, it must be remembered that the period of *détente* had raised hopes of a Council less divided by East−West ideology. Undoubtedly, the resolution put the UN at the centre of the disarmament stage.

However, the next decade saw the return of the Cold War, which meant that disarmament talks, once again, were dominated by the spirit of confrontation.[6] The Twelfth and Fifteenth Special Sessions on disarmament in 1982 and 1988 produced no new concrete proposals or recommendations.[7] Again, we see the schism in the Assembly which so often puts the Western States in the minority. However, away from the United Nations, the recent thaw in the Cold War has evidenced itself strongly in the form of a 1987 treaty to eliminate all intermediate range nuclear weapons.[8] Unfortunately, this thaw has not yet spread to the Assembly's consideration of disarmament issues.

From a promising base in 1978, the Assembly, sponsored disarmament programme has faltered, and its Conference on Disarmament has become a place for rigid positions and oratorical exchanges.[9] The Assembly adopts numerous disarmament resolutions at its annual sessions, but these are only adopted by a majority (usually non-nuclear States), are repetitive, and create no new initiatives.

General principles

Article 13(1)(a) of the Charter allows the Assembly to initiate studies and make recommendations for the purpose of 'promoting international co-operation in the political field and encouraging the progressive development of international law and its codification', while sub-paragraph (b) gives the same power, *inter alia*, 'in the realisation of human rights and fundamental freedoms'.

It is out of sub-paragraph (a) that the power to pass resolutions enunciating general principles has developed. Nevertheless, sub-paragraph (b) is significant in that the general principles generally represent a compromise between the human rights lobby (and more recently the national liberation or self-determination lobby) and those States who want to emphasise the (greater) importance of sovereignty and territorial integrity. This aspect will be concentrated on, for it is illustrative of the influence of the various factions of the General Assembly – an influence which tends to result in an unsatisfactory compromise.

In 1949, a majority of States were still committed to the principle of the inviolability of the sovereignty of States which in 1945 was embodied in Article 2(4) of the Charter. The Draft Declaration on Rights and Duties of States was adopted unanimously in 1949[10] in accordance with Article 13. It represented an affirmation and clarification of the sovereignty principle. It stated that every State has complete jurisdiction in its own territory; the right of independence, including freedom to choose its own government; the duty not to intervene in another State or to foment civil strife therein; and the duty to treat all persons under its jurisdiction with respect for human rights and fundamental freedoms.

Although the balance of the resolution is clearly in favour of affirming the doctrine of absolute sovereignty, there are suggestions that perhaps this concept is subject to the principle of self-determination (right to choose a government) and respect for human rights. In 1949, it was the United States and its allies who supported these nascent principles, even advocating that all the contents of the draft resolution embodied international law, reflecting the Western majority's criticism of the form of government and abuse of rights in Eastern Europe. The Eastern bloc doubted that the principles contained in the declaration embodied international law.[11]

However, by 1960 the tables had turned, and it was the Soviet Union and the newly independent countries[12] advocating firm anti-colonial and hence pro self-determination resolutions. The Declaration on the Granting of Independence to Colonial Countries and Peoples[13] recognised the 'increasingly powerful trend towards freedom' in dependent territories and emphasised that colonialism was not only a denial of self-determination, but also of fundamental human rights and therefore was contrary to the Charter. This represents a move away from the sovereignty principle, at least insofar as metropolitan powers and their dominions were concerned.

The resolution was adopted by eighty-nine votes to nil. However, nine Western and pro-Western States abstained,[14] the United States abandoning their previous principled approach for more practical reasoning. The all or nothing approach (no stage between a colony and an independent State) of the resolution was criticised by the representative of the United States because it would lead to the political fragmentation of some States and would 'fly in the face of political and economic realities in many areas of the world'.[15] The United States' preference for an approach based on economic realities has increasingly alienated it from the majority of Assembly members who prefer a more abstract, principled approach.

The impact of the decolonised majority became increasingly apparent in 1965 with the unanimous adoption of the Declaration on the Inadmissibility of Intervention in the Domestic Affairs of States.[16] Although compromise was necessary to achieve unanimity, the influence of the national liberation lobby eroded even further the by then mainly Western support for non-intervention and sovereignty, and to this extent correlates with the demise of Article 2(7).

The resolution declares that no State has the right to intervene in the affairs of another. This includes indirect intervention, which is defined as helping or financing subversive activities against a State. So far the Declaration entirely supports the Western view. However, the resolution then contradicts itself. After reaffirming the principles of self-determination and respect for human rights and fundamental freedoms, it states that 'all States shall contribute to the complete elimination of racial discrimination and colonialism'. This suggests that indirect intervention is permissible if it aids self-determination in colonial or racial situations. The Western States voted for the resolution on the understanding that the word 'contribute' did not allow intervention in favour of self-determination.[17] Inevitably, the Soviets favoured the view that it did, and increased the Cold War rhetoric against the United States by accusing it of denying self-determination in Vietnam and the Dominican Republic,[18] whereas the United States accused the Soviet Union of intervention in violation of the sovereignty of Vietnam.[19]

Similarly, in 1970, the Declaration on Principles Concerning Friendly Relations and Cooperation among States in accordance with the United Nations' Charter[20] represented a compromise. Indirect intervention was declared illegal but, at the same time, the declaration expressed the right of people to take 'forcible action in pursuit of their right to self-determination' and that they were 'entitled to seek and receive support in accordance with the purposes and principles of the Charter'. Support for forcible action suggests that the support could be forcible as well. However, the reference to the Charter tends to suggest that it is support short of the use or threat of force, which after all would be contrary to Article 2(4), and, as the representative of Australia pointed out, a mere recommendatory Assembly resolution cannot amend the Charter.[21] Most Western States explicitly granted their vote on the understanding that the Declaration did not diminish the principle of the non-use of force.[22] The Socialist and Non Aligned nations did not express a view, probably in order not to invoke any negative Western votes, but it is interesting that they saw the Declaration as a crystallisation of international law.[23]

In the *Nicaragua* case, the International Court relied on the Declaration as evidence of *opinio juris* on the illegality of the United States' indirect armed intervention in Nicaragua.[24] It also said that if clear evidence could be adduced to show that Nicaragua was supplying arms to the rebels in El Salvador, this would be a breach of the principles of non-intervention and the non-use of force, despite any claims that the rebels were fighting to achieve self-determination. The Court did not find sufficient evidence of this, but stated that even if there was adequate proof the supply of arms did not constitute an intervention amounting to an 'armed attack' which would justify the United States' sponsored operation as self-defence. It also relied on the 1974 Definition of Aggression to conclude that the training and arming of the Contras by the United States amounted to an indirect use of force.[25] The Court was not convinced by ideological arguments of self-determination and so its judgement can be said to constitute a pro-Western interpretation of the 1970 Declaration and the 1974 Definition, despite the fact that on the substantive issues the Court found against the major Western power involved.

The unhappy compromise between Western powers and the national liberation lobby was continued when the Assembly finally adopted by consensus the definition of aggression[26] which has been discussed in chapter 2. The definition purportedly outlawed indirect as well as direct aggression, but made this subject to the right of peoples striving to achieve self-determination 'to struggle to that end and to seek and receive support'. Indeed, despite the World Court's judgement, which seized on those parts of the definition which strengthened the principle of the non-use of force whilst ignoring those parts detrimental to it on the ground of lack of *opinio juris*, the Assembly adopted a further resolution in 1988 which, while purporting to ban indirect intervention and aggression, still declared that peoples, 'particularly those under colonial and racist regimes', have the right 'to achieve self-determination and have the right to seek and receive support'.[27]

The power of the General Assembly to adopt resolutions on general principles has not led to 'the progressive development of international law' in the area of the non-use of force. Instead, the principle contained in Article 2(4) has been seriously weakened by these recommendations which suggest that the principle is subject to the use of allowable force in the pursuit of the right to self-determination or national liberation. This represents a serious undermining of the fundamental provision of the Charter. The compromise necessary for the adoption of these resolutions has resulted in a confusing set of principles with which one superpower could argue that it is supporting national liberation, while the other could justifiably accuse it of intervention. The modern war inevitably involves indirect force, usually with the substantial involvement of a superpower. Instead of adapting the principle on the non-use of force to cover this development, the Assembly has sown serious seeds of doubt on its applicability in certain situations involving indirect force.

Cease-fire and withdrawal

Whereas Assembly recommendations on disarmament and those enunciating general principles on the use of force are directly adopted under Articles 11(1) and 13(1) respectively, resolutions which call for a cease-fire, withdrawal or for voluntary measures, or which recommend a settlement, cannot be attributed to any particular Charter provision, but, instead, are concrete manifestations of the general powers of Articles 10, 11(2) and 14. As has already been stated in chapter 4, Article 10 can be interpreted to give the Assembly similar recommendatory powers to those granted to the Council in Chapters VI and VII, subject to the limitation in Article 12. To a large extent the powers examined below are similar to those recommendatory powers employed by the Security Council.

The Assembly makes relatively few cease-fire and withdrawal calls. The Security Council usually responds first and makes the necessary call. However, if the General Assembly is in its regular session it may be able to make the call more quickly than the Council — with speedier calls likely to have more impact, the quicker the call the more effective it is likely to be. The Assembly has made such calls in the case of the Indonesian invasion of East Timor in 1975[28] and in the case of the Turkish invasion of Cyprus in 1974.[29]

If the Council is deadlocked by a conflict of interests of the permanent members, the General Assembly sometimes takes up the role of the organ making the preliminary call for a cease-fire and withdrawal. This is done either immediately, under the Uniting for Peace procedure, or the Assembly waits until its regular session. If done in emergency special session the call has greater immediacy than if the regular session is waited for. However, the Council is likely to be paralysed because of superpower involvement and so any cease-fire call is seen as a gesture. In this respect it does not matter if the regular session is waited for.

In the case of the Soviet intervention in Hungary in 1956,[30] the Assembly met in emergency special session and called for a cease-fire and a withdrawal of Soviet troops.[31] The call was seen as a gesture by some members, or more optimistically by others as a warning or holding measure to prevent further Soviet interventions.[32] In the case of the Vietnamese intervention in Kampuchea, the Assembly waited eleven months before calling for a cease-fire.[33] This wait could hardly justify some of the members hailing the resolution as a valiant effort to save the 'dying' Kampuchean people.[34] Often the Assembly passes a resolution in order to save the Organisation's face when the primary body is racked by arguments and vetoes. For example, the Assembly's resolution[35] calling for a cease-fire in the Bangladesh situation was seen as essential in rescuing the UN from its 'darkest hour'.[36] In terms of effectiveness, therefore, the Assembly call has not directly brought about an immediate cease-fire or withdrawal, instead it adds to the weight of opinion against belligerents which eventually may lead to a cease-fire and more importantly a withdrawal.

In terms of withdrawal calls, the Assembly's most important ones were in the cases of Hungary, Bangladesh, Cyprus, East Timor, Kampuchea, Afghanistan, and Grenada.[37] In the cases of Bangladesh and Grenada, withdrawal was affected only after the intervening forces had achieved their objectives. However, in the case of Afghanistan, Soviet withdrawal occurred without the political objectives behind the intervention being achieved. This is probably mainly due to the fact that the Soviet Union found that it could not achieve its goals after nearly a decade of fighting. However, it may be that the weight of world opinion represented by the Assembly in its annual resolutions was a factor influencing the decision to withdraw. Similarly, the final withdrawal of Vietnamese troops from Kampuchea in September 1989 was a product of a combination of factors, both political and economic, including the consistent Assembly calls for Vietnamese withdrawal.

Voluntary measures

The most radical interpretation of the Assembly's powers involves its use of voluntary measures. We have seen in chapter 3 in the case of the Security Council that it can recommend military measures under Article 39, and has adopted the practice of suggesting economic measures under Article 41. Both these recommendatory powers used by the Security Council were not envisaged by the drafters of the Charter, and so represent an extension by subsequent practice. It has been argued that the General Assembly has similar recommendatory powers to the Council, and, by extension, it has the power to recommend military action and to recommend voluntary sanctions. The former power has been expressly granted by the Uniting for Peace resolution, although it can be argued that the Assembly has had such powers from the time that the Security Council claimed similar powers.

Nevertheless, the Assembly has very rarely used its power to recommend military action. The only clear instance, which occurred before the Uniting for Peace resolution was adopted, was in the case of Korea, when the Assembly recommended that a 'unified, independent and democratic' Korea be established and that UN forces remain in Korea for that purpose.[38] This impliedly authorised General MacArthur to cross the 38th parallel into North Korea. Paradoxically, although the Uniting for Peace resolution was adopted only a few days later, there has been no further clear instance of the Assembly recommending coercive measures in the form of military action.

Korea also involved one of the first instances of the Assembly recommending voluntary sanctions.[39] These were not only directed against North Korea, but also against Communist China which had entered the war when General MacArthur's forces threatened the Chinese border, and involved an embargo on military supplies and equipment.[40] The Soviet Union declared these sanctions invalid on the grounds that they constituted 'action' within the meaning of Article 11(2).[41]

Since Korea the Assembly has, in practice, firmly established the power to recommend voluntary sanctions. However, in contrast with the Korean precedent such sanctions have mainly been adopted on the instigation and affirmative votes of the Non Aligned and Socialist majority. Voluntary sanctions have been called for in the cases of South Africa,[42] the Portuguese Territories,[43] Southern Rhodesia,[44] and Namibia.[45] The Assembly's power to recommend voluntary measures has been confined, in practice, to colonial or racist situations (and then mainly in Africa), although by tying zionism to racism it has been able to justify imposing, or more correctly recommending, voluntary measures against Israel.[46]

Calls for voluntary measures by the Assembly are unlikely to be effective. Blanket calls for economic measures against a country rely solely on the members to impose them for they are inherently difficult to supervise. Resolutions calling for more specific measures will not be observed by those members voting against them, nor in many cases by those voting for them, because of their non-mandatory nature. Thus, as with withdrawal calls, voluntary measures are often gestures of support for or condemnation of a State. Also they are often used to try and force the Security Council to adopt similar, mandatory measures combined with effective enforcement machinery.

Gestures of support, or what could be termed positive measures, sometimes take the form of encouragement for and calls of support for national liberation movements, for example, those in Southern Rhodesia before independence,[47] those in South Africa,[48] Namibia,[49] and the Palestinian people.[50] In effect, the Assembly has virtually legitimised the use of force by 'freedom fighters' struggling for self-determination in colonial or neo-colonial situations. This is evident in some of the general principle resolutions examined above as well as those adopted in specific situations. Although these fighters are regarded as criminals in the country in which they are fighting or rebelling, for the majority of the international community they are 'legitimate' fighters.[51] Röling has suggested that this development is partly due to the lack of collective enforcement machinery available to the UN to deal with such situations itself, resulting instead in moral support for those fighting for 'justice'. He states that the UN has developed the concept of 'justice' to allow it to prevail, in certain situations involving the denial of human rights or self-determination, over the ban on the use of force.

Political settlement

Political settlement of a dispute or problem requires some degree of consent or a (greater) degree of coercion of the parties to the dispute. Whereas the Council has the option of using mandatory coercion, the Assembly only has the powers of recommendation and therefore, in general (apart from the recommendation of measures), if it is to succeed it must try to attain some degree of co-operation from the parties. However, throughout its history the Assembly has shown a greater concern for votes than for concrete successes.

The partition of Palestine is a good example of a case where the Assembly sought to impose a solution on the area and the parties through the inadequate means of a non-binding recommendation. Palestine was the subject of the First Special Session of the Assembly in May 1947. The session was requested by the mandatory power, Britain, because it was dissatisfied with its position due to increasing antagonism between Jews and Arabs and the conflicting purposes of achieving a homeland for the Jews and independence for an Arab dominated Palestine. The session established a Special Committee on Palestine[52] which submitted a report to the Second Annual Session of the Assembly. The report of the majority recommended partition of Palestine as a means of reconciling the above conflicting principles, whereas the minority believed a federated State could achieve this.[53]

The Assembly established an *ad hoc* committee consisting of every member to consider the report. The *ad hoc* committee did not use the report as a basis for negotiation between the parties, instead it supported the majority's proposals and recommended partition with economic union;[54] a proposal which favoured the Jews and which was supported by both the Soviet Union and the United States.[55] The solution recommended was an ideal one aimed at solving the problem of the mandate and the age old problem of a Jewish homeland all at one stroke.[56] It was bound to fail because at no stage were the parties involved in the plan – a plan which was particularly unfavourable to one of the parties to the dispute, the Palestinians.

Only the representative of Colombia questioned the recommendation for partition in any great detail. First he criticised the theory behind the majority report, stating that 'the legal competence of the General Assembly to set up two independent States in Palestine, without regard to the principle of self-determination has not been established to our satisfaction'.[57] He then proposed a resolution to improve the practical chances of the Assembly successfully helping to end the Palestinian problem,[58] by authorising the *ad hoc* committee to 'take all steps necessary to try to bring about an agreement between the representatives of the Arab and Jewish populations of Palestine as to the future government and political constitution of that country'.

Instead the majority continued on its course, which was bound to alienate one of the parties and its supporters – the Arabs represented by the Arab Higher Committee. The United States proposed that two sub-committees be set up, one to examine the majority report of the Special Committee and one to consider the minority report. States supporting the Jewish cause polarised around the first sub-committee, while mainly Arab States were represented in the second sub-committee. The result was modified versions of both reports which were more extreme – for example, the minority report abandoned the federated State ideal and recommended independence for Palestine based on self-determination.[59] The Assembly was, in effect, driving the two parties further apart. The *ad hoc* committee voted for the partition plan contained in the first sub-committee's report,[60] and finally the Assembly adopted the partition plan.[61] The resolution took the form of a recommendation but was obviously based on the premise that the Council would enforce it if it was ignored. This too was unrealistic, but at the time, the relative impotence of the Council was not clear.

Fighting between the two communities despite truce calls by the Council led to the Second Special Session of the Assembly in April and May 1948 one month before the end of the mandate. The idealistic approach of the First Session was replaced by disillusionment and the whole session was without effect. The Assembly failed to pass a resolution on the state of its rapidly disintegrating partition plan. The United States reversed its support for partition and suggested UN trusteeship.[62] The Assembly did not take up this option. In effect, the Assembly abandoned Palestine to a military solution, with the first Arab-Israeli war breaking out on 14 May as the mandate ended. The Assembly was guilty of deciding the fate of Palestine by a majority of only vaguely interested States. It was concerned with voting victories rather than any practical attempt at reconciliation and negotiation between the parties mainly concerned.

The modern Assembly is overwhelmingly pro-Palestinian in its approach to the Middle East crisis. Thus, although the position as to the parties of the Assembly has altered, its basic approach has not changed. Its resolutions are pro-Arab and so are not conducive for encouraging Israel to negotiate.

Security Council resolution 242, adopted in 1967 and designed to induce all the parties to negotiate, is a good example of how the requirements of compromise necessary in the Council produce a more balanced approach. The Assembly, however, imposes the will of the majority, and in so doing has undermined the Council's work which necessarily has to accommodate the views of the minority pro-Israeli members. The Assembly has consistently adopted resolutions which, while purportedly supporting Council resolution 242, destroy its balance in a variety of ways. For example, a recent Assembly resolution purports to lay down the guidelines for a proposed International Conference on the Middle East.[63]

Another example of the majority of the Assembly attempting to decide the fate of a country occurred at about the same time as the initial Assembly action on Palestine. Basically, the Assembly accepted the United States' proposal[64] for the settlement of the Korean problem in 1947. The Assembly recommended elections to be held by 31 March 1948 in the American and Soviet occupied zones under UN supervision to establish a single national assembly and a government.[65] This was done despite Soviet objections that the basis of a solution to the Korean problem had been laid down in the Moscow Agreement.[66] The Assembly had effectively ignored the Soviets, who, through the North Koreans, were hardly likely to agree to the Western inspired plan. The majority still seemed to believe in sweeping political change without negotiation or initial investigation.[67] Without the consent of the Soviet Union and the North Korean authorities the plan was bound for failure.

The case of South West Africa (Namibia) was slightly different in that South Africa had breached international law by continuing to administer the territory. Thus, the UN was in a difficult position, for it would reflect badly on the Organisation's prestige to negotiate with an illegal occupier of a mandated territory.[68] In effect, the United Nations had become a party to a dispute with South Africa over Namibia. It will be illustrated below that the Assembly's attempts at achieving a solution in cases of colonial, neo-colonial or racist domination are often hampered by its vision of itself as the representative of colonial or repressed peoples, hence its one-sided resolutions.

In 1950, the International Court opined that South West Africa was still under a mandate which could only be modified by South Africa with the 'consent' of the United Nations.[69] The word 'consent' is important here, for it is required not only of the UN to achieve a solution but also of South Africa. Without South Africa's consent, and in the absence of effective mandatory measures by the Council, the problem of Namibia was unlikely to be resolved by the UN. However, as typical of a party to a dispute, the UN has ignored this fact, and has embarked on a unilateral approach to the problem by adopting resolutions on Namibia which although ideally and legally desirable, are, nevertheless, unattainable. The Assembly disavowed the mandate and established the necessary machinery for UN administration with a view to the exercise of the right of self-determination by the Namibian people.[70] Sympathies must lie with the United Nations, for although it was acting in a partisan manner, it was after all a party with international law on its side.

Other cases in which the Assembly adopts the position of the representative of peoples denied the right to self-determination include the Portuguese Territories, Southern Rhodesia, and South Africa itself. The denial of the right to self-determination is contrary to international law and has certainly been viewed as such by the majority of the Assembly for over two decades. However, although law is on its side, the majority of the Assembly, by acting as a protector of peoples without sufficient international personality to represent themselves, allows its vision to be clouded by its commitment to one side in the dispute - an attitude unlikely to result in settlement of the problem. It recommends that self-determination be achieved,[71] or even demands that it be allowed, without establishing any reasonable basis for achieving this. The Assembly does not seem to realise that having justice on its side is insufficient to achieve a settlement. A judgemental approach is likely to succeed only in making the other party intransigent unless the Assembly can enlist the help of the Council to enforce the judgement of the international community.

In other disputes, not involving colonial or racist domination, although still concerned with the denial of the right to self-determination, the Assembly adopts resolutions which have more objectivity about them and are more likely to result in the parties consenting to negotiation. Sometimes, however, this objectivity results in weak resolutions simply because the majority of members of the Assembly are not committed to finding a resolution to the dispute. A case in point is the Assembly's attempt at dealing with the dispute over Western Sahara. Although the Assembly had obtained an advisory opinion from the World Court favouring self-determination for the Western Saharans[72] (and so, as in the cases of colonial and racist domination, the Assembly had law on its side), the resultant Assembly resolution was reflective of the fact that the Non Aligned majority in the Assembly was unwilling to indict two of its members as neo-colonialists (Morocco and Mauritania). It virtually granted recognition to the Tripartite Agreement concluded in Madrid on 14 November 1975 between Spain, Morocco and Mauritania deciding the fate of the territory. The Assembly made a rather pathetic plea to the 'interim administration' established by the Agreement, 'to take all necessary steps to ensure that the Saharan populations originating in the Territory will be able to exercise their inalienable right of self-determination'.[73]

Nevertheless, the Assembly has shown greater signs of supporting the Polisario guerrillas against Morocco when, in 1980, it took account of the peace agreement between Polisario and Mauritania and urged Morocco to negotiate with Polisario. Morocco, however, had taken over the sector previously occupied by Mauritania.[74] The resolution effectively recognised Polisario as a party to the dispute, in contrast to the above cases where the Assembly becomes the party representing the people. This belated approach to the problem is probably a good balance between too great a commitment to self-determination and too little. This is illustrated by the fact that the Assembly has legitimised the use of force in one neo-colonial situation to which it was over committed (Namibia), whereas in a case of lesser commitment (Western Sahara) no such extreme measures have been attempted.

Ignoring for a moment the problem of self-determination, the Assembly does attempt to create a viable framework for the settlement of disputes in a few cases, and to this extent, often goes further than the Security Council. For example, in 1980, it passed a resolution on the Kampuchean problem[75] which called for an International Conference on Kampuchea and laid out the principles to be the basis of discussion – the negotiation of an agreement for Vietnamese withdrawal, observance of human rights, free elections, and non-interference. It did not purport to isolate Vietnam; its purpose was to give it a way out. In the same vein, the Assembly expressed its unanimous support for the Central American peace plan agreed upon in Guatemala on 7 August 1987.[76] Finally, its encouragement[77] of the Secretary General in his 'good offices' role, produced an agreement on Afghanistan, which, while not settling the internal conflict, did lead to a Soviet withdrawal and is a good example of the UN providing neutral facilities for belligerents to settle their differences in a diplomatic manner.

The Assembly's non-recommendatory powers

One method of escaping the limitation upon the Assembly's powers embodied in Article 12 is to adopt a resolution which is not a recommendation. Articles 10 to 14 seem to create only recommendatory powers for the Assembly, but, as we have seen in chapter 4, theoretically the Assembly can adopt non-recommendatory resolutions. However, there is no power to enable the Assembly to adopt mandatory resolutions, so, although the resolutions may 'demand', 'decide' or 'declare', they are not mandatory decisions in the sense of Article 25 and Chapter VII. Besides, the resolutions are almost always mixed – in that they contain both recommendations and decisions, declarations, or condemnations. In this form they must come within the limitation contained in Article 12.

The Assembly uses its declaratory or condemnatory power to strongly emphasise the United Nations' position as regards a particular dispute. In 1956, the Assembly declared 'that by using its armed force against the Hungarian people, the government of [the Soviet Union] is violating the political independence of Hungary',[78] as a follow up to the emergency special session on Hungary calling for withdrawal. The resolution also contained an 'objective', 'historical judgement' that the Soviet Union had breached Article 2(4).[79] In this respect the Assembly was acting like an international court in judging the Soviet Union guilty of a breach of the Charter. Although it has no power, like the International Court proper, to make a binding judgement, the verdict is important if the principle contained in Article 2(4) is not to be destroyed by constant breach. In 1986, the Assembly condemned the United States air raids on targets within Libya as 'a violation of the Charter and of International Law'.[80] Such resolutions offer evidence by way of State practice as to the status of Article 2(4) as a peremptory norm of international law.

Although the Assembly's declaration is not binding under the Charter, the fact is that it is based on a *jus cogens* which is binding on all States without exception. In the case of South West Africa, the Assembly based its declaration that the 'government of South Africa cannot avoid its international obligations by unilateral action'[81] on the advisory opinion of the International Court[82]. An advisory opinion is not binding; nevertheless, the Assembly's declaration has its basis in international law and so has considerable legal and moral suasion. Similarly, its resolution declaring that South Africa's mandate over Namibia had been disavowed,[83] although not technically binding, was given retroactive legal status by the World Court in 1971.[84] Although only an advisory opinion, the 1971 judgement on Namibia adds considerable weight to the Assembly's declaration.

Although the Assembly's declarations are often based on legal concepts, it could be argued that they are unlikely to aid a peaceful settlement of the dispute simply because they put one of the parties in the wrong and therefore make it unlikely that it will comply. The Assembly's declarations on South Africa are a case in point. In 1952 the Assembly declared:

that in a multi-racial society harmony and respect for human rights and freedoms and the peaceful development of a unified community are best assured when patterns of legislation and practice are directed towards ensuring equality before the law of all persons regardless of race, creed, or colour, and when economic, social and cultural and political participation of all racial groups is on the basis of equality.[85]

Even a pre-eminent Non Aligned State was compelled to abstain on the resolution because 'it expressed general sentiments which are fine and with which we are in complete agreement, but it does not adequately provide a solution for the problem with which the world is faced today'.[86]

Declaring that South Africa has breached the law of human rights is not going to gain that country's acquiescence in reform. Thus, the Assembly is reduced to calling on the Council to adopt mandatory enforcement measures, for its resolutions are insufficient to induce settlement. Nevertheless, the Assembly has continued its course of declarations and condemnations of Pretoria.[87] The aim is to reflect the feelings of the international community and to leave South Africa in 'no doubt' as to these sentiments[88]. However, without effective enforcement action to reinforce its calls, the Assembly can ill afford to antagonise the South Africans and to make them more intransigent. In the Southern Rhodesian situation the Assembly could afford to declare any attempt at independence based on minority rule[89] or any measures taken by the Smith regime[90] as illegal because the Council had adopted mandatory enforcement action.

Often declaratory or condemnatory resolutions are reflective of the frustration of the Assembly at the UN's inability to effect an outcome to a dispute or situation. In long-running cases this is inevitable, with the declarations being increasingly directed against the minority (the West) who are believed by the majority to be blocking any successful move to resolve the dispute. In 1985 it considered that strategic agreements between the United States and Israel, plus economic and military co-operation, had encouraged Israel in its 'aggression' and 'expansion'.[91] Such resolutions, although purportedly judgements of a legal nature, are no longer objective – they represent the majority laying down what it sees as the law to the minority.

The use of the term 'demands' often represents a hardening of the majority's attitude when a previous resolution has not been complied with. For example, after it had urged withdrawal of foreign troops from Cyprus in 1974,[92] the next year this became a 'demand'[93] as the first call had not been complied with. This is representative of Assembly practice in general, and of its general frustration at not having true mandatory powers such as those possessed, but rarely used, by the Council. Assembly resolutions which 'demand', 'decide', 'declare' or 'condemn' may, if repeated, represent a considerable depth of international feeling, but they are not, nor on the whole do they purport to be, binding.

Conclusion

The various factions which, in loose coalitions, have formed the majority in the General Assembly over its period of existence have seized on the vague powers conferred by the Charter to create a substantial body of recommendatory powers. In doing so the Assembly has interpreted Articles 12 and 2(7), which represent the only clear theoretical limitations on the Assembly's power and competence, in such a way that they do not represent practical barriers to the Assembly making recommendations on matters which may be classified either as ones in respect of which the Council is functioning, or as ones that may have been viewed as internal at some stage.

However, the Assembly has not used these powers effectively, either to induce the interested parties to negotiate or to establish a framework which, at a later stage, might induce them to come to the negotiating table. The majority in control of the Assembly seems to fail to recognise the inherent weakness in recommendatory powers – that they cannot force a recalcitrant State to comply. It follows that the Assembly's calls for cease-fire, withdrawal or for voluntary measures are not concrete, but token attempts to resolve the situation.[94] From this misperception of the import of Assembly resolutions there has arisen a desire on the part of some nations denied any degree of permanency on the Council that the Assembly should be able to make demands and decisions, resulting in recent resolutions purporting to do this. These are merely paper, hortatory resolutions which cannot bind. Unlike the interpretation of Articles 2(7) and 12 which has occurred consistently over forty years, a revision of the Charter to allow the Assembly to pass mandatory decisions would be of such a fundamental nature as to require either correct constitutional amendment, or more lengthy, consistent and overwhelming practice by the members than has occurred to date.

Its lack of mandatory powers and its failure to take account of minority views has meant that the Assembly has not become the primary organ in terms of international peace; its effectiveness would be improved if it ceased to act as if it were. This means adopting a more balanced approach to disputes. It should concentrate on the promotion of peaceful settlement rather than being concerned with voting victories. Nevertheless, one must not underestimate the value of the Assembly's fair and accurate condemnations of States in breach of international law as evidence of the majority of the world's support for the non-use of force and the promotion of peaceful settlement.

The recent trend in the Assembly by the Non Aligned to use its majority to isolate States not conforming to its views is only partly to blame for the ineffectiveness of the Assembly in maintaining international peace and security. Throughout the forty years of its life the Assembly, or more correctly the majority, has been more concerned with voting victories for political purposes sometimes entirely divorced from the subject of the vote − mainly to embarrass, isolate, or simply to criticise members deemed to be in opposition blocs or groups − than with any concrete attempt at creating viable conditions in which a solution could be achieved.

Notes

1 J. P. Cot and A. Pellet, *La Charte des Nations Unites*, 267 (1985); L. M. Goodrich, E. Hambro and P. S. Simons, *The Charter of the United Nations*, 117 2nd ed. (1969)
2 Cot and Pellet, *La Charte*, 268.
3 There have been three Special Sessions on disarmament, in 1978, 1982, and 1988.
4 For example see UN doc. A/40/27 (1985).
5 GA Res S-10/2, 10 UN GAOR SS Supp. (No. 4) 3 (1978).
6 Cot and Pellet, *La Charte*, 272.
7 See GA Res S-12/6, 12 UN GAOR SS Supp. (No. 6) 2 (1982). See also UN doc. A/S-15/6 (1988).
8 Keesing's *Contemporary Archives* (1987), 35601.
9 UN doc. A/39/1 (1984).
10 GA Res. 375, 4 UN GAOR Resolutions 66 (1949).
11 4 UN GAOR vol. (No. 2) Agenda Item 49 (1949).
12 GA 947 plen. mtg, 15 UN GAOR 1278−9 (1960).
13 GA Res. 1514, 15 UN GAOR Supp. (No. 16) 66 (1960).
14 Portugal, Spain, South Africa, United Kingdom, United States, Australia, Dominican Republic, France.
15 GA 947 plen. mtg, 15 UN GAOR 1283 (1960).
16 GA Res. 2131, 20 UN GAOR Supp. (No. 14) 10 (1965).
17 GA 1st Committee 1406 mtg, 19 UN GAOR para. 17 (1965).
18 *Ibid.*, 1404 mtg, 306.
19 *Ibid.*, 1406 mtg, para. 17.
20 GA Res. 2625, 25 UN GAOR Supp. (No. 28) 121 (1970).
21 GA, 6th Committee 1178 mtg, 25 UN GAOR 9 (1970).
22 GA, 6th Committee 1181 mtg, 25 UN GAOR 21 (1970), New Zealand; 1182 mtg, 27, Portugal.
23 *Ibid.*, 1178 mtg, 7, Poland; 1180 mtg 17, Senegal.

24 *Nicaragua* case, I.C.J. *Rep.*, 14, at paras. 187–201.

25 *Ibid.*, paras. 210–11.

26 GA Res. 3314, 29 UN GAOR Supp. (No. 31) 142 (1974).

27 Declaration on the Enhancement of the Effectiveness of the Principle of Refraining from the Threat or Use of Force in International Relations, GA Res. 42/22, 42 UN A/PV (1987).

28 GA Res. 3485, 30 UN GAOR Supp. (No. 34) 118 (1975).

29 GA Res. 3212, 29 UN GAOR Supp. (No. 31) 3 (1974).

30 See also the Assembly's cease-fire and withdrawal call regarding Suez in 1956, as a pre-condition to the imposition of its peacekeeping force.

31 GA Res. 1004, 2 UN GAOR ESS Supp. (No. 1) 2 (1956).

32 GA 564 plen. mtg, 2 UN GAOR ESS para. 187, 209 (1956), UK and New Zealand.

33 GA Res. 34/22, 34 UN GAOR Supp. (No. 46) 16 (1979).

34 GA 67 plen. mtg, 34 UN GAOR para. 127 (1979), France.

35 GA Res. 2793, 26 UN GAOR Supp. (No. 29) 3 (1971).

36 GA 2003 plen. mtg, 26 UN GAOR paras. 37, 194, 245 (1971), Ceylon, Nicaragua, and Tanzania.

37 GA Res. 1004 (1956); 2793 (1971); 3212 (1974); 3485 (1974); 34/22 (1979); GA Res. ES-6/2, 6 UN GAOR ESS Supp. (No. 1) 2 (1980); GA Res. 38/7, 38 UN GAOR Supp. (No. 47) 19 (1983); respectively.

38 GA Res. 367, 5 UN GAOR Resolutions 9 (1950). See GA 293 plen. mtg, 5 UN GAOR paras. 37, 70 (1950), France, USSR.

39 See also GA Res. 39, 1 UN GAOR Resolutions 63 (1946), re Spain.

40 GA Res. 500, 5 UN GAOR Supp. (No. 20A) 2 (1951).

41 GA 330 plen. mtg, 5 UN GAOR 739–40 (1951).

42 GA Res. 1663, 16 UN GAOR Supp. (No. 17) 10 (1961).

43 GA Res. 2107, 20 UN GAOR Supp. (No. 14) 62 (1965).

44 GA Res. 2151, 21 UN GAOR Supp. (No. 16) 68 (1966).

45 GA Res. 2372, 22 UN GAOR Supp. (No. 16A) 1 (1968).

46 See for example GA Res. 39/146, 39 UN GAOR Supp. (No. 51) 50 (1984).

47 GA Res. 2151 (1966).

48 GA Res. 2671, 25 UN GAOR Supp. (No. 28) 31 (1970).

49 GA Res. ES-8/2, 8 UN GAOR ESS Supp. (No. 1) 3 (1981).

50 GA Res. 3236, 29 UN GAOR Supp. (No. 31) 4 (1974).

51 B. V. A. Röling, 'The United Nations – A General Evaluation', in A. Cassese (ed.), *UN Law. Fundamental Rights*, 33 (1979).

52 GA Res. 106, 1 UN GAOR SS Resolutions 6 (1947).

53 2 UN GAOR Supp. (No. 11) (1947).

54 UN doc. A/364 (1947).

55 GA 124, 125 plen. mtgs, 2 UN GAOR 1324, 1359 (1947), US and USSR.

56 See E. Luard, *A History of the United Nations: vol. 1 The Years of Western Domination 1945–1955*, 169 (1982).

57 GA 127 plen. mtg, 2 UN GAOR 1398 (1947).

58 UN doc. A/518 (1947).

59 See GA 126 plen. mtg, 2 UN GAOR 1376 (1947).

60 See GA *Ad Hoc* Committee 32 mtg, 2 UN GAOR (1947).

61 GA Res. 181, 2 UN GAOR Resolutions 131 (1947).

62 UN doc. A/C.1/277–8 (1948).

63 GA Res. 38/58, 38 UN GAOR Supp. (No. 47) 46 (1983).

64 GA 111 plen. mtg, 2 UN GAOR 832 (1947).

65 GA Res. 112, 2 UN GAOR Resolutions 16 (1947).

66 See draft resolution UN doc. A/447, (1947).
67 See Luard, *A History of the UN: vol.*1, 233.
68 See GA Res. 65, 1 UN GAOR Resolutions 123 (1946).
69 *International Status of South West Africa case*, I.C.J. *Rep.* 1950, 128.
70 GA Res. 2145, 21 UN GAOR Supp. (No. 16) 2 (1966). See GA 1454 plen. mtg, 21 UN GAOR (1966), UK.
71 See GA Res. 1807, 17 UN GAOR Supp. (No. 17) 39 (1962), re Portuguese territories; GA Res. 1760, 17 UN GAOR Supp. (No. 17) 38 (1962), Southern Rhodesia; and GA Res. 3324, 29 UN GAOR Supp. (No. 31) 36 (1974), South Africa.
72 *Western Sahara case*, I.C.J. *Rep.* 1975, 12.
73 GA Res. 3458, 30 UN GAOR Supp. (No. 34) 116 (1975).
74 See GA Res. 35/19, 35 UN GAOR Supp. (No. 48) 213 (1980).
75 GA Res. 35/6, 35 UN GAOR Supp. (No. 48) 13 (1980).
76 See GA Res. 42/1, 42 UN A/PV (1987).
77 GA Res. 42/15, 42 UN A/PV (1987).
78 GA Res. 1131, 11 UN GAOR Supp. (No. 17) 64 (1956).
79 GA 618 plen. mtg, 11 UN GAOR para. 10 (1956), Peru.
80 GA Res. 41/38, 41 UN GAOR Supp. (No. 53) 34 (1986).
81 GA Res. 570, 6 UN GAOR Resolutions 63 (1952).
82 *SW Africa case*, I.C.J. *Rep.* 1950, 128.
83 GA Res. 2145, 21 UN GAOR Supp. (No. 16) 2 (1966).
84 See GA 1454 plen. mtg, 21 UN GAOR 26 (1966) on the 1950 judgement.
85 GA Res. 616, 7 UN GAOR Supp. (No. 20) 8 (1952).
86 GA 401 plen. mtg, 7 UN GAOR para.120 (1952), India.
87 For example, GA Res. 38/11, 38 UN GAOR Supp. (No. 47) 22 (1983).
88 GA 56 plen. mtg, 38 UN GAOR 8, 18, 23 (1983), Sierre Leone, India, China.
89 GA Res. 2012, 20 UN GAOR Supp. (No. 14) 53 (1965).
90 GA Res. 2652, 25 UN GAOR Supp. (No. 28) 89 (1970).
91 GA Res. 40/168, 40 UN GAOR Supp. (No. 53) 57 (1985). GA 118 plen. mtg, 40 UN GAOR 62−3 (1985).
92 GA Res. 3212, 29 UN GAOR Supp. (No. 31) 3 (1974).
93 GA Res. 3395, 30 UN GAOR Supp. (No. 34) 5 (1975).
94 Except when accompanied by effective peacekeeping measures; see for example Suez in 1956.

PART 3
Peacekeeping

INTRODUCTION

The development of a peacekeeping function is probably the most significant achievement of the United Nations in its attempt to maintain international peace and security. To the layman peacekeeping is a concrete manifestation of the United Nations, which offsets the common view that the Organisation produces only rhetoric and ideologically motivated resolutions. To the political scientist peacekeeping probably represents the most concerted effort the international community makes in regulating conflict. Other peaceful mechanisms are generally unsuccessful, as explained by Wiesman:

The tension and struggle between the forces for change and the forces for the maintenance of the *status quo* are constant and dynamic features of the international system. This struggle is manifested in the frequent occurrence of ferocious and intractable conflict. By contrast, but by no means as persistent and powerful as the systematic propensity to conflict, are the creation and utilisation of international structures, instruments, and procedures for the containment and resolution of these conflicts by political means. The attempts to superimpose peaceful regulatory systems upon the disordered world are extremely hazardous and difficult. The national political propensities to make war are far more powerful than the international processes to make peace. Nonetheless, the will, determination and imagination of peoples and States persist in the quest to make order out of chaos and prescribe peaceful measures for progressive social change.[1]

Peacekeeping is such a 'peaceful regulatory system'. Its success lies in the fact that it usually only has limited objectives, for example, in separating two protagonists. Other peaceful measures, such as resolving the conflict by negotiation, are not as successful for they involve far more ambitious objectives. The firm division between peacekeeping and peacemaking will be examined later.

To the international lawyer peacekeeping represents an intriguing puzzle, raising in particular such questions as the constitutional basis for such operations; whether nations hosting peacekeeping operations are surrendering their sovereignty; whether such forces can use force beyond that required for self-defence; and which political organ of the United Nations can authorise such forces? Consistent answers to such questions have proved difficult to arrive at given the *ad hoc* creation of such forces resulting in various mandates and sizes of forces. In this respect peacekeeping reflects the crisis management nature of most of the Organisation's work concerning international peace and security. Despite the establishment, in 1965, by the General Assembly of a Special Committee on Peacekeeping to try to formulate a more institutionalised basis for peacekeeping, forces are, in the main, only envisaged, created and assembled after a conflict has started, and then only if there is sufficient political consensus in the Security Council or the General Assembly.

Nevertheless, the United Nations has created eighteen peacekeeper or observer forces, so that it has now sufficient cumulative experience to gauge the requirements of a particular situation and create a force relatively quickly if so requested by the parties and agreed upon by the relevant political organ of the United Nations. Despite the creation of peacekeeping forces outside the United Nations, the Organisation's efforts still represent the most important in this field.

Chronological list of United Nations peacekeeping operations

1 UN Observers in Indonesia 1947–50.
2 UN Sub-Commission on the Balkans (UNSCOB) 1947–54.
3 UN Truce Supervision Organisation in Palestine (UNTSO) 1949– present.
4 UN Military Observer Group in India and Pakistan (UNMOGIP) 1949– present.
5 UN Emergency Force (UNEF I) 1956–67.
6 UN Observer Group in Lebanon (UNOGIL) 1958.
7 UN Operation in the Congo (ONUC) 1960–64.
8 UN Observers and Security Force in West Irian (UNSF) 1962–63.
9 UN Yemen Observation Mission (UNYOM) 1963–64.
10 UN Peacekeeping Force in Cyprus (UNFICYP) 1964– present.
11 UN India-Pakistan Observation Mission (UNIPOM) 1965–66.
12 UN Emergency Force (UNEF II) 1973–79.
13 UN Disengagement Observer Force (UNDOF) 1974– present.
14 UN Interim Force in Lebanon (UNIFIL) 1978– present.
15 UN Good Offices Mission in Afghanistan and Pakistan (UNGOMAP) 1988– present.
16 UN Iran-Iraq Military Observer Group (UNIIMOG) 1988– present.
17 UN Angola Verification Mission (UNAVEM) 1989– present.
18 UN Transition Assistance Group (UNTAG), 1989– present.

Franck gives a relatively narrow definition of peacekeeping as 'the peaceful interpositioning of UN personnel, in response to an invitation of the disputants, to oversee an agreed cease-fire'.[2] Such a definition is applicable only to inter-state peacekeeping – where a force is placed between two formerly hostile States which have agreed a cease-fire, whereas the United Nations has also undertaken intra-state peacekeeping, for example in the Congo, where a force is placed within one factionalised State. Franck's definition also ignores the technique of observation from which inter- and intra-state peacekeeping evolved. Observation has the limited function of reporting on the state of hostilities, whereas peacekeeping has the more intrusive function of separating the parties to the cease-fire without the force generally having the power to enforce the peace. However, the divisions between observation, peacekeeping and enforcement action are unclear — there are grey areas in which one function merges into another.

Wiseman has analysed United Nations' peacekeeping historically.[3] He labels the period 1946–56 as the 'nascent period' of peacekeeping with the creation of four observation teams which are the 'generic antecedents' of full peacekeeping forces which emerged in 1956 with the creation of UNEF I. This represented the beginning of what Wiseman calls the 'assertive period', which ended in 1967 with the withdrawal of UNEF I. During this period eight peacekeeping (including observation) forces were created. The withdrawal of UNEF I in 1967 with the ensuing Six Day War called into the question the effectiveness of United Nations' peacekeeping, so that between 1967 and 1973 it went through a 'dormant period' when no forces were created. Paradoxically, it took another conflict in the Middle East — the Yom Kippur War in 1973 — to spark off a 'resurgent period' in which three full peacekeeping forces were created. After the creation and emplacement of UNIFIL, and the authorisation without emplacement of UNTAG in 1978, the peacekeeping function of the United Nations was frozen for a decade due to a decline in East–West relations. However, the recent *rapprochement* between the superpowers has sparked off a revival, with four forces established between March 1988 and April 1989, culminating in the emplacemnt of UNTAG over ten years after it had initially been authorised.

The following analysis will be divided into three chapters which, in turn, are basically sub-divided into observation and peacekeeping. Chapter 7 will entail an analysis of the background to the creation of each force in order to put peacekeeping into a geopolitical context by looking at the question whether peacekeeping is limited to the intermediate areas of the world beyond the hemispheric or bloc influences of the superpowers. Chapter 8 will examine the constitutional basis of such forces. Unlike many works on peacekeeping such as Higgins'[4] and Bowett's,[5] the present study will examine the constitutional basis not only by reference to the enabling resolutions, but also by taking into account the functions and mandate of each force. The above writers tend to keep the questions of constitutional base, functions, mandate, and the problem of host State consent separate, whereas this writer considers that they are too interrelated for this type of treatment — the mandate of the force must correlate to the constitutional base, and the functions of the force must equate to the mandate. If there was no host State consent, then the force might be arguably one of enforcement. Chapter 9 will consider the question of the effectiveness of peacekeeping, which will not only involve an analysis of whether each force was successful in fulfilling its mandate, but also the wider question of whether peacekeeping performs a valuable role in the overall maintenance of international peace and security by the United Nations.

Notes

1 H. Wiseman, *Peacekeeping: Appraisals and Proposals*, 1 (1983).
2 T.M. Franck, *Nation against Nation*, 168 (1985).
3 Wiseman, *Peacekeeping*, ch. 2.
4 R. Higgins, *United Nations Peacekeeping: Documents and Commentary in 4 volumes: 1: Middle East 1946–1967*, (1969); *2: Asia 1946–1967*, (1970); *3: Africa 1946–1967* (1980); *4: Europe 1946–1979*, (1981).
5 D.W. Bowett, *United Nations Forces*, (1964).

CHAPTER 7

A geopolitical examination of peacekeeping by the United Nations

The main purpose of this chapter is to give a brief review of the creation of each force to try and analyse the historical and political circumstances under which they arose and to attempt to indicate in what circumstances peace-keeping forces are likely to be established. It may be that the circumstances are different for observation teams compared to peacekeeping forces.

United Nations' observation teams

The observation teams created in the nascent period (1946–56) all arose through the change that occurred in the international order following the Second World War. The first force to be created was the UN observation team in Indonesia in 1947, when a conflict arose involving the Dutch colonialists' attempt to maintain the old order against a rising tide of nationalism in Indonesia. The Security Council, with no direct permanent member involvement once the British withdrew their wartime forces, and with no member willing to stand in the way of decolonisation in this case, was able to authorise UN observers.

The need for such observers was apparent from the confused state of affairs in Indonesia, with various cease-fire lines, sporadic fighting and changing areas under the control of each side. Observers were needed to report the various stages achieved, with the help of quite vigorous Security Council resolutions, towards Indonesian independence.

Decolonisation was also the main cause of the conflict between the newly independent States of India and Pakistan over the disputed Indian state of Jammu and Kashmir which led to the Security Council establishing UNMOGIP in 1949. As with Indonesia, this again was a soft area of the world where none of the permanent members, particularly the superpowers, had sufficient interest in either side to protect them by the veto. As with all peacekeeping forces, UNMOGIP depended upon the co-operation of both parties. Thus, such forces are not usually created and emplaced until the fighting has come to an end and the belligerents are willing to accept a cease-fire. However, observation teams are not meant as buffer forces — they only observe the cease-fire and they are not usually large enough nor are they mandated to make the cease-fire effective as are peacekeeping forces proper. Thus, UNMOGIP observed throughout the outbreak of hostilities in 1965 and was present to observe the new cease-fire. In 1965, the fighting between India and Pakistan was on a wider front than in 1947, necessitating the emplacement of another team, for a limited period, beyond UNMOGIP's patrol. UNIPOM was in place from 1965–66, again under a Security Council mandate, illustrating that this area of the world was not considered part of a power bloc. UNIPOM was removed after a limited period but UNMOGIP remains because its area of patrol — Kashmir — continues to constitute a potential flashpoint where the United Nations needs a constant presence.

Along with UNMOGIP another observation team — UNTSO, created under Security Council auspices in 1949 — has lasted for nearly forty years in an even more troubled area of the world. Unlike UNEF, which was emplaced between Israel and Egypt for eleven years between 1956–67 and for a further six years between 1973–79, UNTSO has observed various cease-fires, truces and armistices between belligerents in the Middle East. The peculiar fact is that there is no Security Council resolution directly authorising UNTSO, nor, as with UNMOGIP, is there any periodic renewal of its mandate. It has a loose mandate which is best described as observing and reporting to the United Nations on the situation in the Middle East. Its longevity is probably a testimony to the fact that the Security Council, particularly the superpowers, need to keep in constant touch with the situation in an area where both the United States and the Soviet Union have interests, but in which neither is paramount, and UNTSO provides them with valuable, neutral information. UNTSO thus acts to some extent as an effective brake on the possibility of escalation based on a hasty, one-sided account of a conflict. During the period of UNEF'S interpositioning, UNTSO observers worked alongside the peacekeeping force; however, unlike UNEF, UNTSO observers were used after the Six Day War, as it was a political necessity for the United Nations to maintain some presence.

Observation is sufficiently flexible to be used equally successfully in intra-state conflicts such as Indonesia, as well as in inter-state conflicts such as the Gulf war, which after nearly a decade of fighting, stagnated sufficiently to allow a UN observer force (UNIIMOG) into the area in August 1988. It can also be of value where there is a combination of the two situations, evidenced by UNOGIL in the Lebanon in 1958 and by UNYOM in the Yemen in 1963. In both cases there arose the problem of outside military interference in a civil war. The countries involved, either directly or indirectly, were again situated in the intermediate areas of the world beyond the direct hemispheric influences of the superpowers, and of any of the other permanent members, thus allowing the Security Council to mandate both forces. Nevertheless, the fact that the Middle East was subject to superpower claims was evidenced by the United States' intervention in Lebanon, despite UNOGIL's report that the country was not being undermined by the United Arab Republic.

However, due to the Cold War, when the conflict in question is nearer both politically and geographically to the superpowers to amount to an East–West power struggle, there is less likelihood of an observation team being sent to the area by the Security Council. After the Second World War the world order changed dramatically to an East–West divide based on ideology, and nowhere was this better evidenced than in the Balkans where the pro-Western Greek government alleged military support for the communist insurgents from the surrounding communist countries of Bulgaria, Albania, and Yugoslavia. Although the Security Council was able to create a Commission of Investigation, it was left to the General Assembly, in 1947, to create a Sub-Committee which had observation functions. The Soviet Union objected to this. This situation is unlikely to happen again, for it was then only possible in the initial period of Western domination in the decade following the establishment of the United Nations. During this period the Organisation was used by the Western majority in the Cold War against the Soviet bloc. UNSCOB's effectiveness was limited because of its Cold War environment, evidenced by the refusal of the Socialist States to allow it on their territory.

Sometimes the United Nations has found it necessary to create a force which combines observation with other duties due to the circumstances of the situation. Although the main Indonesian question had been settled earlier, there were still disputes over several islands in the Indonesian archipelago. One such island was Irian where guerrilla warfare was being carried out by Indonesians parachuted into the jungle and Dutch armed forces in the western part of the island. The Netherlands and Indonesia came to an agreement on 15 August 1962[1] which provided for the administration of West Irian to be transferred by the Netherlands to a United Nations' Temporary Executive Authority (UNTEA) pending a transfer of the territory to Indonesia. A United Nations' Observer and Security Force (UNSF) was to observe the cease-fire which was to take place before authority was tranferred to UNTEA, and then to police the island until the transfer of sovereignty to Indonesia.

Thus, the force was really created by the parties, although it required the approval of the General Assembly – as the body which deals with questions of self-determination – rather than of the Security Council. Surprisingly, taking into account the large role given to the Secretary General in the control of UNTEA and UNSF, the Soviet Union voted for the creation of these bodies. At the time the continuing Congo question had brought Soviet objections as regards the amount of control the Secretary General had over ONUC and of the ability of the General Assembly to mandate such a force in the absence of Security Council consensus. Nevertheless, the Soviet Union was willing to vote in the Assembly for the creation of a force and an authority whose control amounted to virtual temporary sovereignty over the island.

The reasons for the Soviet Union's support are twofold. Again the crisis was relatively minor and did not involve questions of superpower influence – except to the extent of the Soviets' uneasy courtship with the Non Aligned of which Indonesia was a member. Also, the Soviet assent was due to the agreement of the parties which virtually created the United Nations' force.

Indeed, the recent spate of observer forces is the result of express or tacit agreement between the superpowers to allow observer forces into areas of global as well as regional confrontation. UNGOMAP, in Afghanistan at the moment, is a product of superpower accord as well as agreement between the regional States.[2] UNAVEM in Angola was a product of a regional agreement, but was also backed by the Soviet Union and the United States.[3] Both are primarily a result of the Soviet Union redefining its zones of influence. Thus, we can see that the warming in American–Soviet relations has allowed UN observer teams into what were formerly 'no-go' areas.

Indeed, all observer teams and peacekeeping forces depend on the co-operation of the parties; some arise directly from an agreement between the parties which the Security Council (or more rarely the Assembly, if the agreement calls for it) has the option of rubber-stamping.[4] Under the armistice agreement of 1949 between Israel on the one hand and Egypt, Syria, Jordan and Lebanon on the other,[5] UNTSO was given specific duties; UNYOM directly arose out of an agreement between Yemen, Saudi Arabia and the United Arab Republic negotiated by Secretary General U Thant;[6] UNMOGIP was a direct creation of the Karachi Agreement between India and Pakistan,[7] with which the Security Council had very little involvement; the Agreement on Disengagement between Syria and Israel called for the establishment of UNDOF.[8] Other forces are either requested by the States involved, such as ONUC or UNFICYP, or are consented to by the parties on the initiative of the United Nations – for example UNEF. To say that only in the latter situation does the initiative for the creation of a force come from the United Nations would be an exaggeration, ignoring the often significant contribution of the Secretary General.

United Nations' peacekeeping forces

Observation, supervision, and enforcement are the three possible stages of United Nations' military involvement in a conflict.[9] The first two are peacekeeping functions – observation has already been discussed, but it must be remembered that there is often a thin line between observation and full peacekeeping, as evidenced by the mandate and functions of UNSF in West Irian. Similarly, there is a grey area between peacekeeping and enforcement action, highlighted by the actions of ONUC in the Congo.

The nuances between the mandates of the various forces will be discussed in chapter 8.

For the purposes of this section, peacekeeping involves not only observation of the cease-fire, but also supervision, which on most occasions of inter-state conflict entails the creation of a buffer zone. Thus, a peacekeeping force acts as a buffer between the two belligerents – a function too large for, and requiring a different mandate than for, observation teams. Peacekeeping evolved from observation so as to give the United Nations a more active role after the cessation of hostilities. UNEF I was the first 'dramatically innovative venture'[10] into peacekeeping proper. It was created in 1956 by the General Assembly after a joint Anglo/French/Israeli plan to oppose, *inter alia*, Egyptian nationalisation of the Suez Canal. Permanent member involvement prevented the creation of such a force in the Security Council, so the question passed to the General Assembly where UNEF I was created with the substantial aid of the Secretary General.

It might be argued that the above procedure could be successfully utilised in other cases of permanent member involvement so as to create peacekeeping forces in the Assembly when such efforts have been vetoed in the Security Council. There are two factors which prevent such a course being chosen more often. First, even though the United Kingdom and France vetoed any attempts to pacify the situation in the Council, they only abstained (along with the Soviet bloc) on the Assembly resolution creating UNEF I, and, in fact, they eventually consented to the placement of the force. Thus, the Assembly could, theoretically, create peacekeeping forces in cases of permanent member intervention, when the Council is blocked by the veto, but political reality prevents such a course without the consent of all the parties concerned. In the Suez case, the two permanent members involved had reached a stage where to continue would have brought them under unbearable international pressure, while to withdraw would have been too costly politically; the peacekeeping force was thus consented to, for it maintained the *status quo* achieved so far. To this end it also met the requirements of the other two parties; Egypt because it was being heavily defeated and Israel because it had gained a considerable amount of territory. The circumstances were ripe for a UN peacekeeping force to fill the vacuum.

A second factor which would probably prevent the creation of such a force by the Assembly instead of the Council is the increasing agreement among the permanent members, particularly the superpowers, that such forces should only be created by the Security Council. Originally, the French and Soviets took this line as regards UNEF I and ONUC, leading to their challenge of being assessed for financial contribution in the *Expenses* case of 1962. However, there is also evidence that the United States and the United Kingdom have adopted this line from 1960 onwards. Evan Luard has accurately summarised the reasons for this.

First, the outright opposition of the Soviet Union and France to the use previously made of the Assembly, their refusal to contribute to the costs of peacekeeping operations the Assembly had authorised, and the prolonged financial crisis which resulted from this constitutional difference in view, all served to induce some caution among other major powers in mobilising the Assembly. Secondly, the increasing size of the Assembly, as well as the change in its composition (in which Afro-Asian Members came to hold more than two-thirds of the votes) meant that it came to be thought a less suitable instrument for use in such situations, by the US as much as by the Soviet Union. Thirdly, the far less use of the Soviet veto in the Council reduced the need for an alternative agency. Finally, the desire of the other permanent members to retain the special influence which they held in the Security Council also encouraged the restoration of the Council's supremacy in security questions.[11]

Communist China has sometimes objected to peacekeeping as a creation of the superpowers, at other times it supports the creation of a force by the Security Council, depending on the circumstances of the case. Recently China has shown a more positive attitude to peacekeeping, illustrated by the fact that it joined the Assembly's Special Committee on Peacekeeping in 1988.[12]

The Middle East has been the area in which peacekeeping, whether by the United Nations or by other agencies, has been most utilised. UNEF I was withdrawn in 1967. UNEF II, authorised by the Security Council, was emplaced between Egypt and Israel following the Yom Kippur War of 1973. The danger of superpower intervention as well as the consent of the combatants were direct factors leading to its creation. UNEF II was not only a buffer between the two parties, it was also an indirect buffer between the superpowers backing Israel and Egypt. When Egypt changed its allegiance to become more pro-Western, the United States was able to sponsor negotiations between the Israelis and the Egyptians leading to the Camp David Accords. Although the peace agreement between Israel and Egypt provided for a continued United Nations' peacekeeping presence, the Egyptian defection had practically destroyed the superpower accord behind UNEF II, and so the force was discontinued in 1979 to be replaced by a United States'-sponsored multinational force. However, superpower agreement still continued as regards UNDOF, created in 1974 as a buffer on the Israeli-Syrian front, as each party remains fairly firmly placed in the Western and Eastern camps respectively.[13]

Middle Eastern peacekeeping forces have the regional function of separating two or more belligerents, but they have wider functions than the maintenance of stable Arab-Israeli relations − they are placed so as to add an extra check on the possibility of escalation in an area where, although both superpowers have clients, neither has regional dominance, and neither, at this moment, feels capable of attaining supremacy. Similarly, UNIFIL was created in 1978 not only to secure Israeli withdrawal from Lebanon, but also to perform the unstated, global function of preventing American-backed Israel and Soviet-supported Syria from engaging in conflict using Lebanon as a battleground, which might suck in one or both superpowers. When creating such a force the Security Council lists only the local functions of the force as regards the two belligerents. Nevertheless, peacekeeping has played and continues to play a much more global function in the Middle East.

Similarly, ONUC was created in an atmosphere of potential superpower intervention after the Belgians withdrew from the Congo in 1960. Indeed, it was the Soviet Union's charge of ONUC leaning towards the pro-Western factions in the Congo which led to the Soviet veto of any continuing Security Council control over the force, which in turn led to the General Assembly having control of the operation for a while. However, ONUC managed to tread the neutral tightrope sufficiently to preclude any overt superpower intervention. The members of the Security Council, particularly the super-powers, originally probably authorised the operation because the Congo represented an area in which both superpowers would have liked to have a base, but neither was willing to disturb the global *status quo* by intervening. Thus, to concretise this mutual non-intervention, and to assuage each super-power's fear of the other intervening, the United Nations was called to fill the vacuum.

ONUC's operation probably represented the only attempt by the United Nations to modify peacekeeping to suit a case of intra-state conflict. In later sections it will be argued that civil war situations require a different type of peacekeeping mandate than that required for peacekeeping forces in inter-state conflicts. Nevertheless, in global terms ONUC was fulfilling similar functions to inter-state forces – the prevention of escalation.

One could argue that UNIFIL in Lebanon, UNFICYP in Cyprus, and UNTAG in Namibia are further examples of United Nations' peacekeeping operations being authorised in intra-state conflicts. However, it is perhaps more realistic to view these three forces as a hybrid between intra- and inter-state peacekeeping forces. UNIFIL was created after Israel intervened in 1978 and has acted to a certain extent as a buffer between two factions – pro-Israeli and anti-Israeli. Nevertheless, each faction is in itself so fragmented that the situation has become one of civil war. Nevertheless, UNIFIL's main function still remains to supervise Israeli withdrawal, rather than to prevent a civil war, which was one of ONUC's main tasks.

UNFICYP was created in 1964 after fighting had broken out between the Greek and Turkish Cypriot communities on the island. It was thus a civil war situation akin to that in the Congo, except with fewer parties. Indeed, the fact that there were only two parties enabled UNFICYP to function similarly to an inter-state peacekeeping force, by separating the two communities. This function became particularly evident after the Turkish invasion and occupation of the northern third of Cyprus in 1974. UNFICYP evolved into a true buffer force between two belligerents after this date.

UNFICYP probably constitutes one of the only peacekeeping forces in a situation where there is no real danger of superpower intervention, although the danger of escalation does exist on a regional level between Greece and Turkey. Although the Soviet Union originally abstained on the resolution establishing UNFICYP, it has recently voted in favour of the extension of its mandate. This indicates the Soviets' willingness to allow the Security Council to create forces in areas of low-level superpower interest. In addition, the fact that both Greece and Turkey are both NATO members, albeit relatively minor ones, possibly encouraged Soviet approval of UNFICYP because the maintenance of the *status quo* on Cyprus concentrates two members of NATO on a regional dispute rather than on the 'common enemy'.

In the case of UNTAG, we see both the Soviet Union and the United States consenting, along with the regional powers, to a large UN presence in an economically rich and strategically important area of the world. Although created on paper in 1978, UNTAG was not emplaced until April 1989 as a result of an interim period in which global attitudes between the superpowers and regional attitudes between Angola and South Africa hardened. The new *realpolitik* of the late 1980s meant that the Soviet Union and its allies no longer objected to the linkage of Cuban withdrawal from Angola with South African withdrawal from Namibia, although it appears that the Non Aligned majority in the Assembly condemn this linkage.[14]

UNTAG, like UNSF before it, has been given a mixture of peacekeeping, observer and police functions, relating to the cessation of hostilities, withdrawal of forces, and keeping the peace during a peaceful transition to independence. Unlike all other forces, UNTAG has the advantage of entering a country in which a civil war has not escalated to become internationalised. In the case of ONUC, for example, there was a massive vacuum after the Belgians had left into which various outside powers were sucked. Hopefully, UNTAG will not be put into such a precarious position. This is illustrative of the advantage of having determined a course of action in the event of South African withdrawal, which constitutes a rare example of the Security Council taking preventative measures.

It will also become apparent from the following two chapters that inter-state peacekeeping operations are easier to mandate and carry out than are the intra-state variety. This factor must be taken into account in assessing the areas of the world in which UN peacekeeping operations are likely to be authorised.

Conclusions

From the above brief historical and geopolitical survey of the peacekeeping and observation forces authorised by the United Nations, it is possible to glean some guidelines as to the circumstances in which the emplacement of a peacekeeping force is possible.

Generally, the guidelines are the same for both peacekeeping forces and observation teams. Observation teams, however, with their more limited size and functions, are more likely to be used in areas where larger peacekeeping forces are not. This could mean areas peripheral to the power blocs. UNSCOB is an early example; UNGOMAP is a more recent example. The possibility of having observer forces in Kampuchea and Central America is not too remote in the present climate.

Generally, peacekeeping only occurs when all the parties directly involved in the hostilities would rather maintain the *status quo* than risk further conflict and possible losses. In addition, any permanent members of the Security Council either directly involved, such as France and the United Kingdom in the Suez Crisis, or indirectly involved, such as the United States before its intervention in the Lebanon in 1958, must also want to stop hostilities in order to maintain the *status quo*.

Such limitations generally mean that where one superpower is dominant in an area it will not give its consent to a UN peacekeeping force. Thus, in the power blocs or in the hemispheres dominated by the superpowers there has been no instance of a full UN peacekeeping force. Where the conflict is intra-bloc or intra-hemispheric the result may be a superpower-controlled 'peacekeeping' operation, such as the OAS force, which supplanted the original intervention by the United States, in the Dominican Republic in 1965.

This means that peacekeeping by the United Nations usually is going to occur only in the intermediate areas of the world beyond overt superpower dominance. However, peacekeeping may be effective in terms of the maintenence of global peace where both superpowers are probing for control in a particular intermediate area. They may decide that the risk to global peace is too high for one of them to gain dominance and so they support a cessation of hostilities by their proxies in order to secure a relatively stable balance of power. Often the superpowers will support a UN peacekeeping force in such circumstances because it helps to maintain the stability required. Thus, with superpower backing a UN peacekeeping force is likely in these areas, a good example of which is the Middle East. Due to the delicate balance of power in such volatile areas the superpowers will not generally countenance a peacekeeping force backed by either of them, and so a neutral UN force is called for.

In addition, where the conflict arises in an intermediate area which is of relatively little interest to any major power, a United Nations peacekeeping operation may be authorised, such as in Cyprus, or if regional ties are stronger a regional peacekeeping force may be created, such as the aborted OAU force created in 1980 regarding the continuing conflict between Chad and Libya. Indeed, strong colonial ties may produce a peacekeeping presence inspired by the former colonial power, as occurred under the Lancaster House agreement on Rhodesia which authorised a Commonwealth presence.

In these intermediate areas of the world where neither superpower is dominant, peacekeeping is more likely to be authorised in inter-state conflicts than in cases of intra-state strife. This is evidenced by the difficulties encountered in the mandating of ONUC and the precarious position of UNIFIL which is designed for inter-state peacekeeping when it needs to be more attuned to a civil war situation. UNIFIL's mandate is unlikely to be changed to one nearer to ONUC's because to do so would be to bring it nearer to enforcement. Intra-state conflicts have the potential to result in UN forces crossing the divide from peacekeeping to enforcement.

Peacekeeping forces created outside the United Nations that are not regional or bloc orientated are rare. They generally occur in the intermediate zones and arise as a result of the failure of the United Nations to authorise a force. The Multinational Force in the Sinai created by a United States'/Israeli/ Egyptian agreement was reasonably successful in a situation comprehensively covered by the accompanying peace treaty.[15] The Multinational Force in Beirut, established in 1982[16] and situated, like ONUC and UNIFIL, in a civil war situation, was unsuccessful, not only because it was in a hostile environment, but also because it lacked the necessary neutrality.[17] It was composed of French, British, Italian, and United States' forces following a request by the Lebanese government after unsuccessful calls for a United Nations' force.

The shift in the balance of power in the Middle East by the defection of Egypt from the Soviet camp to the Western camp enabled a Western-backed peacekeeping force to be emplaced between Egypt and Israel. However, the Multinational Force in Beirut did not have the advantage of being between two relatively friendly and passive States; instead it was placed in a hostile civil war situation in a vain attempt to increase Western influence in the area. The Soviet Union, and hence the Security Council, did not view the situation in Beirut as being susceptible to a peacekeeping force, bearing in mind the difficulties UNIFIL was facing at the time. The Syrian 'peacekeeping' force in Beirut since 1987[18] has had little success, even though it has blatantly tried to enforce the peace in violation of the principles of peacekeeping.

The Indian peacekeeping force created by an accord in 1987 between India and Sri Lanka[19] is an example of a regional power supplying a force in an area which it sees as within its own sphere of influence. Again, the force does not have the true attributes of a peacekeeping operation, in that it has tried to suppress various factions in the internecine conflict, and for a long while India refused to agree to withdraw its troops at the request of the Sri Lankan government.[20]

It is in the areas relatively free from a dominant hegemonic power that UN peacekeeping operations are more likely to be stationed. The Gulf is of strategic importance to both superpowers but neither had any great preference for a victor in the war. Indeed, neither the Soviet Union nor the United States desired an outright victory because such an event may disturb the global *status quo*. The conditions, when Iran and Iraq consented, were therefore ripe for a peacekeeping force which would maintain the no-win, no-lose situation without significant loss of life until the *status quo ante* could be established by a peace treaty between the former belligerents.

The authorisation of UNIIMOG was therefore of no great surprise once the parties had consented to the cease-fire called for in resolution 598. The only surprise was the small size of the force, numbering only a few hundred unarmed observers, rather than a full inter-state buffer force of several thousand lightly armed peacekeepers. It may be that the expense of almost permanent forces in world trouble spots will lead to the reduction in the size of forces in the future.

At one time, in the period leading up to the withdrawal of Vietnamese troops in September 1989, it appeared that there was a strong possibility of some sort of UN presence in Kampuchea. However, the peace process collapsed. Nevertheless, although the likelihood of a UN force in Kampuchea is now remote, it probably remains the only alternative to a further disastrous conflict in South-East Asia. Although it has probably failed to facilitate a peaceful transition of power in Kampuchea, there is enough time for the UN to prepare in other areas of the globe. For example, when the peace processes set in motion in Western Sahara and Central America come to fruition there may be the need for an interim period of UN supervised adjustment, although in these two cases there is the possibility that regional considerations may produce OAU and OAS sponsored forces.

Notes

1 274 UNTS 6311.
2 Geneva Accords, 27 *I.L.M.* (1988), 577.
3 Angolan, Namibian peace accords, Keesing's *Contemporary Archives* (1988), 36380.
4 See T. M. Franck, *Nation against Nation*, 169 (1985).
5 42 UNTS 252, 42 UNTS 304, 42 UNTS 327, 42 UNTS 288 respectively.
6 See UN docs. S/5298, S/5321 (1963).
7 See UN doc. S/1430/Add 1 (1949).
8 See UN doc. S/11302/Add 1 + 2 (1974).
9 But see A. James, *The Politics of Peacekeeping*, 3, 7 (1969).
10 H. Wiseman, *Peacekeeping: Appraisals and Proposals*, 19 (1983).
11 E. Luard, *The United Nations*, 46−7 (1979). But see A. James, 'The United Nations Peacekeeping and Non Alignment' in Rajan (ed.), *The Non Aligned and the United Nations*, 93−9 (1987).
12 See GA Res. 43/59, 43 UN A/PV (1988).
13 See generally A. James, 'The United Nations on Golan: Peacekeeping Paradox', 9 *International Relations* (1987), 64.
14 GA Res. 43/26, 43 UN A/PV (1988).
15 See generally R. C. R. Siekmann, 'The Multinational Peacekeeping Force in Sinai in the Light of UN Practice on Peacekeeping Forces', 24 *I.J.I.L.* (1984), 504; R. W. Nelson, 'Multi-national Peacekeeping in the Middle East and the United Nations Model', 61 *International Affairs* (1984−85), 67.

16 See generally B. L. Zimbler, 'Peacekeeping Without the UN: The Multinational Force in Lebanon and International Law', 10 *Yale Journal of International Law* (1984), 222.
17 Franck, *Nation against Nation*, 18.
18 *Keesing* (1987), 35020.
19 27 *I.L.M.* (1987), 1175.
20 *The Independent*, 17 April 1989.

CHAPTER 8

The constitutional base of peacekeeping forces

It has been demonstrated in chapter 7 that UN peacekeeping is limited to certain areas of the world; within those areas the nature of the operation differs depending on the type of conflict encountered. The purpose of the present chapter will be to undertake a more detailed analysis in terms of whether all peacekeeping operations can be reconciled with a single constitutional base, or whether the variety of conflicts and forces have resulted in a different base for each force. Before a conclusion on this matter can be arrived at we must ascertain whether the Charter does in fact contain any provisions authorising the creation of peacekeeping forces. There is no single Charter provision authorising peacekeeping *per se* but there are several from which it could be inferred. Alternatively, it could be argued that peacekeeping is not attributable to individual provisions in the Charter but is an inherent power derived from the Organisation's responsibility for the maintenance of international peace and security.

To determine the correct view each force will be examined, after which a series of guidelines as to the constitutional basis of all peacekeeping forces will be attempted, including the question of which organ is capable of authorising such forces. As has already been explained, the Charter base will not only be derived from an examination of the enabling resolutions or agreements creating such forces, but also from a more practical analysis of the functions and overall mandate of each force. In turn, the determination of the constitutional base will illustrate the nature or content of peacekeeping and will possibly provide a blueprint for future peacekeeping forces.

As with the last, this chapter contains a basic division into observation and peacekeeping.

The constitutional base of United Nations' observation teams

UN Observers in Indonesia 1947–50

The creation of an observation team in Indonesia illustrates how early on in its life the United Nations realised the necessity of having accurate, neutral information about a conflict with which it was dealing. Initially, the Security Council, in resolution 27, called upon the Netherlands and Indonesia 'to cease hostilities forthwith' and to settle their disputes by peaceful means.[1] The resolution was based on an Australian draft but with references to Article 39 and 40 deleted. With varying cease-fires and demarcation lines being established on the islands the Security Council needed accurate information as to the state of hostilities before it could take more positive peacemaking steps. Dutch objections based on Article 2(7) meant that the establishment of an independent commission was not authorised,[2] instead the Council requested, in resolution 30, that career consuls in Batavia report on the observance of the cease-fire called for in the earlier resolution.[3]

The same resolution also established a Consular Commission to attempt peacemaking. The Consular Commission itself interpreted the functions of the military observers, namely, 'to observe any possible violations of the cease-fire; to investigate, where possible, allegations of violations of cease-fire orders; and to gather any other data that might be of value to the Commission and to the Security Council'.[4] These functions remained basically the same with the creation of the Good Offices Committee[5] which became the United Nations' Commission on Indonesia,[6] although instead of observation of temporary cease-fire lines, the team was given the task of observing the demilitarised zone created under the Renville Agreement.

Although resolution 27 had references to Chapter VII deleted some members still believed that it contained a mandatory call under Article 40 of that Chapter.[7] Resolution 30 was adopted to supplement resolution 27. Nevertheless, this does not mean that the observer force was in some way an enforcement measure. The Consular Commission's interpretation of its functions illustrated the essential limitation of the force to observation of a previously implemented cease-fire. The force was not authorised to prevent breaches of the cease-fire. Indeed, both parties consented to its presence.[8]

Whether the provisional measures called for were mandatory or not, they can still be derived from Article 40. However, the provisional measure primarily consists of the call for a cease-fire, the creation of an observation team was ancillary to that. The observer team in Indonesia can be seen, therefore, as a non-enforcement measure ancillary to the provisional measures called for under Article 40 which may or may not have been mandatory. Observation or peacekeeping often follow a call or demand for provisional measures, but they do not necessarily form part of them or take on an enforcement aspect if the call or demand is mandatory.[9]

UN Sub-Commission on the Balkans (UNSCOB) 1947–54

Although UNSCOB was created by the General Assembly, it had its origins in the report of the Commission of Investigation established under Article 34 by the Security Council[10] to investigate Greek allegations of illegal border incursions from Albania, Bulgaria and Yugoslavia. The question came before the General Assembly after having been removed from the Council's agenda. With the report of the Commission of Investigation before it,[11] the Assembly decided to establish UNSCOB to assist the governments concerned to comply with its recommendations which, *inter alia*, called on Albania, Bulgaria and Yugoslavia not to furnish aid to the guerrillas and, as regards observation, called on UNSCOB to send a team to observe the frontiers.[12]

UNSCOB gave a general interpretation of its own mandate in relation to its observation function as the 'continuous observation of the general circumstances prevailing in the frontier areas'.[13] This was later refined by the Assembly to observation and reporting 'on the response of Albania, Bulgaria and Yugoslavia to the call not to furnish aid to the Greek guerrillas'.[14]

The observation functions of UNSCOB were created by recommendations of the General Assembly. As we have seen, the Charter powers granted to the Assembly are very wide and, as long as they do not overtly conflict with Articles 12 or 2(7), they potentially encompass all the recommendatory powers of the Security Council. A combination of all its recommendatory powers is probably the Assembly's source in establishing UNSCOB. Indeed, with the later refinement of the observation function by the Assembly to observation of its call on Albania, Bulgaria and Yugoslavia not to furnish aid to the guerrillas, which is a provisional measure, we can see the similarity between UNSCOB and the consular observers in Indonesia – they were both requested to observe on the compliance of the parties with provisional measures. The Assembly has undoubted powers to recommend provisional measures.

Nevertheless, the Eastern bloc countries, including Albania, Bulgaria and Yugoslavia, argued that UNSCOB had been constituted illegally. They contended not that the Assembly was taking upon itself powers reserved to the Security Council, but rather that the very establishment of a Special Committee was an infringement of Albanian, Yugoslavian and Bulgarian sovereignty.[15] Higgins answers these contentions by saying that this confused the establishment of UNSCOB with its operation: 'The General Assembly acknowledged that UNSCOB could not operate in the territory of any State without that State's consent; but its establishment was nonetheless clearly within the terms of Articles 10, 11, 14 and 22 of the Charter.'[16]

For the Eastern bloc's arguments to be correct, would necessarily imply that the Assembly had created a force which could forcefully enter the territories of Albania, Bulgaria and Yugoslavia to carry out its functions. The use of force by the Assembly would indeed raise constitutional problems, but the fact was that UNSCOB's presence was based on consent – as with all peacekeeping.

UN Truce Supervision Organisation in Palestine (UNTSO) 1949 – present

As has already been explained in chapter 7, UNTSO's longevity arises out of the political necessity of the United Nations having a constant presence in the most volatile area of the world. Its duties have ranged from observation of the 1949 truce and subsequent armistice agreements, to general observation in the whole Middle Eastern theatre, with specific roles being granted to it after the 1956, 1967 and 1973 conflicts.

One would have thought that this would have required constant adjustment of UNTSO's mandate by the Security Council, but this does not appear to be the case. Even its original creation seems to have arisen indirectly from a Council decision. In 1948 the Security Council established a Truce Commission directed to negotiate and supervise a truce between Israel and the Arab States in resolution 48.[17] Resolution 54[18] made the Council's call for a truce mandatory under Articles 39 and 40, and gave the Truce Commission wide powers to take any necessary steps to make the cease-fire effective. UNTSO arose from the team employed by the Truce Commission to observe and supervise the cease-fire and truce.[19] UNTSO was then referred to in the armistice agreements and given the specific function of observing the armistice lines. This function was recognised by the Council in 1949.[20]

Although UNTSO has been given specific tasks since, either by the Secretary General[21] or by the Security Council,[22] its constitutional origins lie in Council resolutions 48 and 54, and in the armistice agreements concluded by the parties after the first Arab-Israeli war. Although resolution 54 made the call for provisional measures under Article 40 as a mandatory decision, one must again distinguish between the mandatory cease-fire call and the procedures created by the Security Council – the Truce Commission from which UNTSO evolved – which were ancillary to the cease-fire. The mandate of observation, the requirement for States to consent to UNTSO's presence, and the small size of the force (150 observers), illustrate that although the call was mandatory, UNTSO in no way represented any kind of enforcement action – it was an observation team created as an ancillary requirement to a mandatory call for provisional measures under Article 40. The armistice agreements seemed to represent something more concrete than provisional measures and effectively gave UNTSO its more general observation function which it carries out to the present day. However, its relationship to provisional measures was still highlighted after the 1956, 1967 and 1973 wars, when it again observed the various cease-fires concluded (under varying degrees of pressure from the United Nations) after those conflicts.[23]

UN Military Observer Group in India and Pakistan (UNMOGIP) 1949 – present

Following India's complaint of Pakistani aid to insurgents in the Indian states of Jammu and Kashmir,[24] the Security Council adopted resolution 39 in 1948,[25] establishing a UN Commission for India and Pakistan (UNCIP) with the dual functions of investigating the facts under Article 34 and of exercising a mediatory influence. The creation of an observation team was essentially distinct – although Council resolution 47 of 21 April 1948 allowed UNCIP to use observers, they were not emplaced until after a bilateral agreement on a cease-fire between India and Pakistan was reached on 27 July 1949.[26] Thus, observation of the cease-fire in the period 1949–65 was a direct result not of a Security Council resolution, but of the functions granted to UNMOGIP by a bilateral accord.

When new hostilities broke out in 1965 the Security Council, in resolution 209,[27] ordered a new cease-fire and the withdrawal of both belligerents behind existing cease-fire lines. India and Pakistan were called on to co-operate with UNMOGIP in its task of observing the cease-fire. This was supported by Council resolution 211 of 20 September 1965 which demanded a cease-fire and withdrawal. UNMOGIP played a significant role in observing the cease-fire and withdrawal finally agreed upon at Tashkent by India and Pakistan.

Although UNCIP was created within the provisions of Chapter VI by Council resolution 39, UNMOGIP's functions were defined by the Karachi accord which embodied an agreement on provisional measures (cease-fire and withdrawals) made between the parties. Higgins believes that UNMOGIP's constitutional base is to be found in resolution 47 which, she states, seems to be implicitly based on Article 40.[28] This supports the view that UNMOGIP was created to observe provisional measures, although this writer believes that the Karachi Agreement provides a stronger base since resolution 47 did not explicitly call for a cease-fire. The 1965 conflict highlighted UNMOGIP's mandate as the observation of provisional steps taken by the States, although on that occasion the Security Council set UNMOGIP's functions which the parties agreed to at Tashkent. Bowett states that the constitutional base of UNMOGIP is Article 40.[29] To say that the Charter base of a force is Article 40 suggests Chapter VII action with its overtones of enforcement. As we have seen, UNMOGIP's existence depended on the consent of the parties. This, combined with its limited mandate and size (forty observers), indicates that UNMOGIP was a pacific measure. It is best to view observer teams as non-enforcement measures taken to report on compliance with provisional measures, whether mandatory or recommendatory under Article 40, or agreed by the parties themselves.

UN Observer Group in Lebanon (UNOGIL) 1958

With the crisis in Lebanon, UNOGIL was established by Council resolution 128 of 11 June 1958. It is illustrative to reproduce the whole of the resolution.

Having heard the charges of the representative of Lebanon concerning interference by the United Arab Republic in the internal affairs of Lebanon and the reply of the representative of the United Arab Republic,

1. Decides to despatch urgently an observation group to proceed to Lebanon so as to ensure that there is no illegal infiltration of personnel or supply of arms or other matériel across the Lebanese borders;

2. Authorises the Secretary General to take the necessary steps to that end;

3. Requests the observation group to keep the Security Council informed through the Secretary General.

The use of 'ensure' in paragraph 1 of the enabling resolution suggests that UNOGIL was being directed to forceably prevent infiltration. Practically, such a mandate would be impossible for an observation team, numbering 100, to perform. Indeed, the Secretary General's interpretation of UNOGIL's mandate, which was not contested in the Council, emphasised that its role was strictly limited to observing whether illegal infiltration occurred.[30] 'It was not the task of UNOGIL to mediate, arbitrate or to forcefully prohibit illegal infiltration, and it was reported on occasion that it was being asked by the Lebanese authorities to do such things, which were not properly within its mandate.'[31]

Peacekeeping forces are essentially neutral, they do not form an arm of the government which has consented to their presence. To lose this neutrality would be to act as an enforcement body. It was the general view in the Security Council that it would be undesirable to create a UNEF-I type peacekeeping force or a Korean type enforcement army;[32] besides to do either would have been against UNOGIL's findings that there was no major infiltration occurring from the United Arab Republic.[33] The fact that UNOGIL was a consensual, pacific observation group was emphasised by the Secretary General negotiating with Lebanon for its consent,[34] whereas it proved impossible to extend a similar type of operation to Jordan in the face of that government's opposition.[35]

A little after UNOGIL reported, Council consensus broke down and the United States intervened in mid-July. The question passed to the Assembly, which did not even mention UNOGIL in its resolution.[36] This would tend to indicate that UNOGIL's function remained the same. However, the Secretary General's report[37] suggests that in return for United States' withdrawal, UNOGIL would attempt to foster more peaceful relations between Lebanon and the surrounding Arab countries.

Nevertheless, UNOGIL's functions probably remained as investigatory and observational, as envisaged by Article 34. It was essentially different from most other types of peacekeeping forces, which are usually created to perform some role in relation to provisional measures called for by the Assembly or the Council, whereas UNOGIL's mandate was to ascertain the facts before the United Nations could adopt any further measures. Although UNOGIL consisted of a team of military observers, and therefore is included in this analysis, it could easily be classified with non-military investigatory teams established by the Council.

UN Observers and Security Force in West Irian (UNSF) 1962−63

Most peacekeeping forces heavily involve the Secretary General. It will be seen that earlier forces such as ONUC were really the creation of the Secretary General, whereas later forces such as UNIFIL reflected the Soviet Union's view that the Secretary General's task should not be the creation and direction of such forces, but the administration of them after the Security Council has mandated them − mandates which are regularly reviewed by the Council.[38] UNSF along with ONUC are probably illustrative of the highpoint of the Secretary General's role in the Organisation's peacekeeping function.

Although the agreement between the Netherlands and Indonesia required the approval of the General Assembly for the creation of UNTEA and UNSF in West Irian,[39] it was the agreement itself which detailed the functions of these bodies and granted the power of control over them to the Secretary General.

The functions of UNSF contained in the agreement relate to two different aspects of the planned transfer of sovereignty. First, an observation role as regards provisional measures agreed upon by the parties, such as a cease-fire pending the transfer of sovereignty to UNTEA. Secondly, to act as an internal security force during the temporary administration by UNTEA pending transfer of authority to Indonesia. Loosely, UNSF could be described as facilitating provisional measures − on this occasion adopted by the parties − until the end result (transfer of sovereignty to Indonesia) could be achieved.

The Charter base for the General Assembly's actions in rubber stamping the agreement probably derives from one of its general powers − for example Article 14 − at least in relation to UNSF. The Charter base for the Secretary General's role derives from a substantial evolution of his powers contained in Article 98. 'It is arguable that the provision of observers falls within his general powers, so long as their duties are compatible with the general purposes of the Organisation. But, at the same time, it must be admitted that these are implied powers and no express authority can be found for them.'[40]

UN Yemen Observation Mission (UNYOM) 1963−64

UNYOM's creation is another example of the Secretary General's power of diplomatic initiative − albeit a relatively minor one.

With Saudi Arabia supporting the Royalist faction and the United Arab Republic supporting the Republican faction in Yemen, it was politically necessary not only to obtain the consent of Yemen[41] to a United Nations' presence, but also the co-operation of Saudi Arabia and the United Arab Republic. Secretary General U Thant negotiated with the Republican government of Yemen and the governments of Saudi Arabia and the United Arab Republic. They agreed on disengagement and on a United Nations' presence;[42] and they defined UNYOM's functions as observation only by about 100 personnel in the Saudi Arabian-Yemen area.[43]

The Council approved the Secretary General's reports in resolution 179 adopted on 11 June 1963,[44] and requested the Secretary General 'to establish the observation operation as defined by him'. The Secretary General further refined the functions of UNYOM in subsequent reports. These were limited to observing, reporting, and certifying the disengagement between Saudi Arabia and Yemen,[45] and to observing on the departure of the United Arab Republic from Yemen.[46] This constituted a limited observation mandate, not allowing UNYOM to take any steps to resolve the conflict.[47]

The Secretary General had taken substantial diplomatic initiatives before the matter was even placed on the Security Council's agenda. This ability again represents a substantial evolution from his Charter powers in which Article 99 limits his anticipatory powers to requesting that the Security Council place a matter on its agenda. The Security Council's approval could be viewed as similar to its creation of UNOGIL, based on Article 34, although UNYOM's function appears to be of observation rather than investigation. Its mandate is akin to the overseeing of provisional steps taken by Saudi Arabia and Yemen in their continuing conflict. It is this writer's opinion that UNYOM is closer to UNMOGIP than UNOGIL.[48]

UN India-Pakistan Observation Mission (UNIPOM) 1965–66

Large scale violations of the Karachi Agreement were reported by UNMOGIP on 5 August 1965.[49] The necessity for another observer force lay in the fact that the conflict broke out on a much wider front than that covered by UNMOGIP. On 4 September the Security Council adopted resolution 209 which called for an immediate cease-fire and requested the co-operation of India and Pakistan with UNMOGIP. The fighting continued, leading to a repeated cease-fire call on 6 September in Council resolution 210 – which also contained a request to the Secretary General to strengthen UNMOGIP. Resolution 211 of 20 September gave a specific time for the cease-fire to become operative and asked the Secretary General 'to provide the necessary assistance to ensure supervision of the cease-fire and withdrawal of all armed personnel'.

The Security Council probably envisaged an enlarged UNMOGIP when adopting resolution 211. Indeed, India insisted that only one operation was authorised.[50] However, the Security Council neither censured the Secretary General for creating UNIPOM nor did it specifically grant him authority to do so. Only the Soviet Union made a somewhat oblique criticism: 'Only the Security Council is competent to adopt measures on concrete questions connected with observers of the United Nations, namely, with their functions, their numbers, the command, the method of financing their activities, and so on.'[51]

To a large degree UNIPOM was the Secretary General's creation. He reconciled his action with the constitutional requirements by insisting that to extend UNMOGIP beyond Kashmir would have been a breach of its mandate and a usurpation of the functions of the Security Council. Thus, he argued that he needed to create UNIPOM in order to satisfy the requirements of Council resolution 211. The Secretary General also probably had the idea that UNIPOM would be the more transient requirement, whereas UNMOGIP would need to be kept in place for many years as it was Kashmir that was the flashpoint.[52]

UNIPOM's functions were derived from the mandate in resolution 211 – to provide, by observer duties, assistance as regards the cease-fire and withdrawal in the area outside UNMOGIP's control. Under the agreement reached by India and Pakistan in January 1966, the functions of both forces were given greater definition as regards disengagement.[53] Nevertheless, UNIPOM's creation was the reverse of UNMOGIP's. The latter was created by agreement between the parties and sanctioned by the Security Council. UNIPOM was created by the Council – or more correctly a combination of the Council and the Secretary General – consented to by the parties, and later sanctioned by them.

Resolution 211 called for provisional measures – a cease-fire and withdrawal. Whether these measures were mandatory or not has no real application to the observer group (in fact they appeared recommendatory), whose main function was not to enforce the measures but only to observe whether or not they were complied with. Thus, there arise two alternatives; either observation does not depend upon which Chapter the provisional measures are adopted under, since there is no question of enforcement even if they are mandatory, or one can view a call for provisional measures under Article 40 – despite its position within Chapter VII – as having the potential of being either mandatory or recommendatory, and so an observer team can be created pursuant to either.

UN Good Offices Mission in Afghanistan (UNGOMAP) 1988–present

After nearly six years of negotiations involving Pakistan, Afghanistan and the Secretary General's representative, with the Soviet Union and the United States behind their respective States, the Geneva Accords were finally signed on 14 April 1988. The Accords contained, *inter alia*, an agreement between Afghanistan and Pakistan on mutual non-intervention; guarantees by the Soviet Union and the United States not to interfere or intervene in the internal affairs of Afghanistan or Pakistan; an agreement on the phased withdrawal of Soviet troops to be completed within nine months; and finally an annexed memorandum of understanding which provided that the UN Secretary General would send an inspection team, divided into two units, to Kabul and Islamabad, to report on the withdrawal of foreign troops and on any violation of the Accords.

The memorandum to the Accords established the mandate of the force which was quickly dispatched to the area. In letters written to the President of the Security Council shortly after the conclusion of the Accords,[54] the Secretary General informed the members of the Council that he intended to dispatch a team of fifty unarmed observers drawn from existing UN forces for an initial period of ten months, and asked the President to 'inform me of the members' concurrence'.

Strangely, it was not until the end of October 1988 that the Security Council formally confirmed its agreement to the measures envisaged and executed by the Secretary General, 'in particular the temporary dispatch to Afghanistan and Pakistan of military officers'.[55] No explanation was given in the Security Council. It appears that the Secretary General had the consent of the Security Council to redeploy existing UN observers to Afghanistan and Pakistan without formal authorisation. Given the exigencies of the situation, and the fact that both superpowers wanted a UN presence, the necessity for establishing a clear constitutional base for UNGOMAP seems to have been overlooked. As with UNTSO in 1948, UNGOMAP was in reality created by parties to an agreement and later sanctioned by the Security Council.

The Geneva Accords were concerned with provisional measures – not a cease-fire, but a withdrawal of Soviet troops, with no further external intervention – pending the establishment of a political solution. UNGOMAP was created to facilitate these measures by providing neutral information on compliance. Its presence might also have been hoped to deter breaches of the Accords. Whether UNGOMAP has contributed to the effective implementation of these measures will be reviewed in the next chapter.

UN Iran-Iraq Military Observer Group (UNIIMOG) 1988– present

Following Iranian and Iraqi acceptance of the cease-fire called for in operative paragraph 1 of Council resolution 598 on 20 August 1988,[56] the Secretary General produced a report interpreting the provisions of operative paragraph 2 of that resolution, which requested the Secretary General to 'dispatch a team of United Nations' observers to verify, confirm and supervise the cease-fire and withdrawal'.

In his report,[57] the Secretary General referred to the mandate and then provided more detailed terms of reference, stating that UNIIMOG would: establish cease-fire lines in co-operation with the parties; monitor compliance with the cease-fire; investigate violations; prevent, through negotiation, a change in the *status quo*; and supervise withdrawal to internationally recognised boundaries. The Security Council approved the report and decided to establish UNIIMOG for an initial period of six months,[58] a mandate which has been renewed.[59]

Resolution 598 of 1987 was clearly a mandatory call for a cease-fire within the meaning of Chapter VII, Articles 39 and 40. UNIIMOG was established pursuant to that call, but it is in no way authorised to enforce it. Its presence depends upon the consent of both parties and its mandate depends on an existing cease-fire. These facts, in addition to the small size of the force (350 observers), make it clear that this is a typical consensual UN observation operation.

UN Angola Verification Mission (UNAVEM) 1989–present

UNAVEM was established after Cuba and Angola signed a bilateral accord on 22 December 1988[60] providing for the withdrawal of Cuban troops from Angola, which was linked to the tripartite accord[61] between Angola, Cuba and South Africa concerning the withdrawal of South African troops from, combined with the eventual independence of, Namibia, signed the same day. The latter will be discussed when UNTAG is examined.

The bilateral accord provided that the 50,000 Cuban troops present in Angola, 'in accordance with Article 51 of the UN Charter' shall be withdrawn by 1 July 1991, after phased withdrawal within Angola to the 15th and 13th parallels, providing that no flagrant violations of the tripartite agreement occurs. Angola and Cuba then requested the Security Council to verify 'the redeployment and the phased and total withdrawal of Cuban troops' from Angola.[62]

In anticipation of this agreement, on 20 December 1988, the Security Council decided to establish UNAVEM for a period of thirty-one months, to carry out the mandate provided for in the agreement between Angola and Cuba.[63] The Council set up the force in anticipation of an imminent agreement, whilst in UNGOMAP's case, the Council seemed unprepared to deal with a request for an observer group on anything other than an informal basis.

The sizes of UNGOMAP and UNAVEM (seventy observers) are similar, and so are the mandates of these teams. Their primary task is to report on the withdrawal of foreign troops from the combat zones. However, whilst UNGOMAP has to report on violations of the agreement, UNAVEM does not. Nevertheless, UNAVEM, like UNGOMAP, has its legal origins in an agreement to comply with provisional measures.

The constitutional base of United Nations' peacekeeping forces

First UN Emergency Force in the Middle East (UNEF I) 1956–67
Pursuant to a joint Anglo/French/Israeli plan, Israel attacked Egypt in the Sinai on 29 October 1956. The United States urged the Council to find a breach of the peace and demand a cessation of the attack, combined with immediate Israeli withdrawal. The Soviet delegate agreed that the Israeli action came within Article 39, but preferred to use the more emotive classification of an act of aggression.[64] No resolution was forthcoming, although after the Anglo/French ultimatum had been delivered both the United States and the Soviet Union introduced draft resolutions calling on Israel to cease firing and to withdraw her troops.[65] These drafts did not contain references to Chapter VII in a deliberate attempt to forestall the threatened Anglo/French intervention. No recommendatory measure could circumvent the vetoes of the United Kingdom and France.

On 31 October 1956, British and French forces intervened, an action which was classified by the Yugoslavian delegate as an act of aggression. He formally proposed that an emergency special session of the General Assembly should be convened under the Uniting for Peace procedure. A procedural vote was taken and the resolution was adopted, despite the negative votes of the two permanent members involved.[66]

Despite the classification of the conflict by several members of the Council as coming within Chapter VII, and the use of the Uniting for Peace resolution, which, by its terms, necessarily implies that the situation comes within Article 39, the General Assembly's first resolution on the conflict made no significant jurisdictional finding. Assembly resolution 997,[67] based on a United States' draft, urged the parties to cease fire, to withdraw to their previous positions, and recommended that all member States refrain from further acts. Canada abstained and New Zealand voted against the resolution because it lacked any method which would create conditions under which cease-fire and withdrawal would be acceptable to all the parties.[68]

Canada acted to rectify the failure of resolution 997 by proposing what was to become resolution 998,[69] which requested the Secretary General to submit a plan 'for the setting up, with the consent of the nations concerned, of an emergency international United Nations' Force to secure and supervise the cessation of hostilities in accordance with the aforementioned resolution'. On the same day a nineteen-power draft was adopted as Assembly resolution 999.[70] This placed emphasis on the necessity of achieving an immediate cease-fire, and authorised the Secretary General to arrange immediately with the parties concerned a cease-fire and a withdrawal of forces behind armistice lines. The intention was to create the conditions under which UNEF I could fill the vacuum created by compliance with the cease-fire and withdrawal. The Secretary General's plan for UNEF I was approved by the Assembly[71] as was his report on the guiding principles for the functioning of UNEF.[72]

The Secretary General's principles illustrate the divisions between peacekeeping and enforcement action: 'There is no intent in the establishment of the Force to influence the military balance in the present conflict and, thereby, the political balance affecting efforts to settle the conflict.' Also between peacekeeping, enforcement and observation:

It would be more than an observers' corps, but in no way a military force controlling the territory in which it is stationed; nor, moreover, should the Force have military functions exceeding those necessary to secure peaceful conditions on the assumption that the parties to the conflict take all necessary steps for compliance with the recommendations of the General Assembly.

UNEF I would therefore only be emplaced after all the parties had accepted, in principle, the cease-fire and withdrawal and had taken positive steps to comply.[73]

Despite proposals that UNEF I should guarantee passage through the Suez Canal and the Gulf of Aqaba,[74] UNEF's mandate and functions were to derive from the General Assembly's resolutions which basically called for four things: a cease-fire, the cessation of hostilities, abstention from military raids and incursions, and scrupulous observance of the armistice agreements.

The Secretary General's initial report summarised UNEF's functions: 'When a cease-fire is established, to enter Egyptian territory with the consent of the Egyptian government [Israel refused consent], in order to help maintain quiet during and after the withdrawal of non-Egyptian troops and to secure compliance with [resolution 997].'

Egypt's consent to UNEF I is illustrative of the basis of all observer and peacekeeping functions. It also demonstrates their weakness, for Secretary General U Thant viewed President Nasser's request in 1967 that UNEF I be withdrawn as necessitating the removal of the force.[75]

There were objections to the Secretary General's view. Israel, New Zealand and Australia argued that the withdrawal of UNEF I should be a decision of the Assembly not of Egypt.[76] U Thant's decision has been challenged on the basis of an *aide-mémoire* written by Secretary General Dag Hammarskjöld at the time of the creation of UNEF I but not published until 1967.[77] The former Secretary General stated that Egypt's acceptance of UNEF contained more than just unilaterally revokable consent, in that the Egyptian government had consented to UNEF's presence on its territory until its mandate had been completed. To this extent, argued Hammarskjöld, this so-called Good Faith Accord had limited Egypt's sovereignty. It has been argued that this Accord should have at least forced Egypt to negotiate with the United Nations.[78]

These arguments seem to forget that without Egypt's consent UNEF's continued presence would have been hostile as regards Egypt, and if attacked, as it in fact was,[79] UNEF could have used self-defence which was an integral part of its mandate; but if it was to carry out its functions in the face of Egyptian hostility it would have had to use force beyond that required for self-defence. Thus, UNEF would have come dangerously close to constituting enforcement action.

The Good Faith Accord could not derogate from the basic principle of peacekeeping – host State consent. The only condition attaching to Egypt's right to demand withdrawal was that of giving notice, which in the face of such a demand and the increasing hostility towards UNEF proved to be unenforceable by the United Nations. The Secretary General recognised the stark reality of the situation when he withdrew UNEF without reference to the Assembly. The emplacement of a peacekeeping force does not limit the host State's sovereignty. The positioning of UNEF I was clearly predicated on Egyptian consent and on both parties' voluntary compliance with the Assembly's call for a cessation of hostilities. The argument that UNEF I was entitled to stay on Egyptian soil until its mandate was completed is unsound because this would appear to give UNEF an enforceable right to stay. Such enforceable rights are incompatible with a consensual peacekeeping force such as UNEF I.

We have established so far that UNEF I was a peacekeeping by consent operation, to be emplaced after a cease-fire had been established, to supervise that cease-fire and subsequent withdrawal, and to oversee the continuance of peaceful conditions. It was more than an observer force but less than enforcement action. France objected to it because it arose from the Uniting for Peace resolution, which, the French argued, contemplated enforcement, not peacekeeping measures.[80] The Uniting for Peace resolution merely recognised the inherent powers of the Assembly, and in fact all it creates is a procedural device for the transfer of a matter from the Council to the Assembly, where the Assembly can operate any of its powers. The question remains whether the Assembly has the power to create peacekeeping forces.

It has been stated that the Assembly's powers roughly comprise all of the recommendatory powers of the Security Council. Although the Security Council did not create a full peacekeeping force until after the Assembly, it had the potential to create such forces and, following from this premise, so did the Assembly.

Alternatively, the Assembly's power to create peacekeeping forces can be said to arise from the doctrine of inherent powers – that anything appropriate to achieve the Organisation's aims is permitted as long as the Charter does not expressly forbid it. Finally, peacekeeping forces could be reconciled with the general powers of the Assembly contained in Articles 10, 11 and 14 – in other words, they are express powers or at least powers implied directly from express powers.

The Soviet Union, however, argues against all three of these justifications by saying that any form of military action is reserved, by Chapter VII, to the Security Council, and that the word 'action' in Article 11(2) includes peacekeeping.[81] The World Court in the *Expenses* case contradicted this:

This paragraph [Article 11(2)], in its first sentence empowers the General Assembly, by means of recommendations to States or to the Security Council, or to both, to organise peacekeeping operations, at the request, or with the consent, of the States concerned. This power of the General Assembly is a special power which in no way derogates from its general powers under Articles 10 or 14 except as limited by the last sentence of Article 11(2). The word 'action' must mean action solely within the province of the Security Council. It cannot refer to recommendations which the Security Council might make because the General Assembly under Article 11 has a comparable power.[82]

The Court considered that 'action' in Article 11(2) meant enforcement action of some sort, so that peacekeeping was not excluded from the Assembly's competence. It concluded that Article 11(2) or Article 14 contained sufficient powers to enable the Assembly to create UNEF I.

What must be remembered is that UNEF was created to supplement the Assembly's recommendatory call for provisional measures – a cease-fire and withdrawal. Recommendatory or non-mandatory provisional measures and steps taken ancillary to them can be adopted either by the Assembly or the Council; mandatory measures can be taken only by the Council. This should be seen as the essence of the World Court's judgement.

The Court's judgement can be interpreted as implying powers from express provisions. Article 10 gives the Assembly recommendatory powers similar to those of the Council. The Council has developed Article 40 so as to give itself the power to call for voluntary provisional measures. Thus, the Assembly can call for provisional measures and, following from that, can provide the necessary machinery to facilitate the observance of the cease-fire. Peacekeeping thus arises from an express power – the power to call for provisional measures – and not from the more general proposition that the organs of the United Nations have the power to create a peacekeeping force, because such a measure furthers the aims of the Organisation and is not contrary to any express provision of the Charter.

UN Operation in the Congo (ONUC) 1960–64

The Republic of the Congo achieved independence from Belgium on 30 June 1960. As with many colonies, the Congo was something of an artificial construction consisting of many tribal areas. The Belgian authorities had done little to unify the colony before independence and so within a few days of its achievement disruptions between the various factions occurred, resulting in Belgian intervention which was characterised as humanitarian by the Belgian government.

President Kasavubu and Prime Minister Lumumba sent a cable to the Secretary General[83] requesting United Nations' military assistance to protect the Congo 'against the present external aggression which is a threat to international peace'. The Secretary General, utilising Article 99 of the Charter, asked that the President of the Council convene that body.[84] The resultant resolution was the work of Hammarskjöld, as were the two subsequent Council resolutions.

On 14 July 1960 the Council adopted resolution 143, which made no jurisdictional finding but called upon Belgium to withdraw, and decided to authorise the Secretary General to take the necessary steps to provide military assistance, 'in consultation with the Government of the Congo', until the Congolese security forces could fully meet their tasks. To all intents and purposes this appears to be another case of the United Nations filling the vacuum created by the breakdown in security, but the simplicity of this belies the complexity of the civil war situation facing the United Nations. ONUC was to assist the government in restoring law and order 'but which government? that of Lumumba? Kasavubu? Ilea? Mobutu?'.[85]

Despite the creation of ONUC the situation deteriorated, and on 11 July 1960 Tshombe, President of the Katangese provincial government, declared Katanga's secession. Belgian troops remained despite resolution 143. Again on the Secretary General's initiative, the Security Council adopted resolution 145 on 22 July 1960. The resolution recognised the unity of the Congo and again called on the Belgians to withdraw, while authorising the Secretary General 'to take all necessary action to this effect'. It also requested that all States refrain from interference which might undermine the territorial integrity and political independence of the Congo.

Belgium refused to withdraw from Katanga with the consequence that ONUC could not enter the province without using force – an event which the previous resolutions had not catered for. Under these circumstances the Council adopted resolution 146 on 9 August 1960. The resolution called on the government of Belgium to withdraw its troops from Katanga; declared that ONUC should enter Katanga; reaffirmed that ONUC 'will not be a party to or in any way influence the outcome of any internal conflict, constitutional or otherwise'; and called upon members 'to accept and carry out the decisions of the Security Council' in accordance with Articles 25 and 49.

By September 1960 the Congo was in a state of constitutional as well as military upheaval, with Kasavubu and Lumumba dismissing each other from office followed by the coup by the army chief of staff General Mobutu on 14 September. This, combined with the continuing attempt to secede by Katanga and the problem of how much force was to be used to enable ONUC to carry out its mandate, divided the Council. The Soviet Union was particularly critical of the Secretary General who had so far masterminded the operation.[86] This resulted in the Soviet veto of another Hammarskjöld-proposed resolution.[87] The deadlock in the Council was a reflection of the increasing internationalisation of the civil war, with the Soviets supporting

Lumumba, the Americans supporting Kasavubu, whilst the French, British and Belgians showed support for Tshombe.[88]

The United States proposed that the matter be transferred to the General Assembly under the auspices of the Uniting for Peace resolution. This proposal was adopted by procedural vote,[89] despite the negative votes of the Soviet Union and Poland who stated that the Uniting for Peace resolution was illegal. Besides, they argued, the Assembly was about to start its regular annual session anyway.

Although opposed by the Eastern bloc, the Assembly adopted a resolution on 20 September 1960.[90] This resolution stated, *inter alia*, that to safeguard international peace it was 'essential for the United Nations to continue to assist the Central Government of the Congo' and to this end requested the Secretary General to take 'vigorous action' to restore law and order and to preserve the unity, integrity and political independence of the Congo. It also requested all States to refrain from intervening and reminded members of Articles 25 and 49.[91] However, the Assembly then split into factions, none of which could form the necessary majority to adopt a significant resolution.

The death of Lumumba and the deterioration of the situation into civil war finally united the Council sufficiently to enable it to adopt resolution 161 on 27 February 1961, which contained two parts. Part A categorised the crisis as a 'threat to international peace and security' and a 'serious civil war situation'. It urged that 'the United Nations take immediately all appropriate measures to prevent the occurrence of a civil war in the Congo, including arrangements for cease-fires, the halting of all military operations, the prevention of clashes, and the use of force, if necessary, in the last resort'. It also urged the withdrawal of all Belgian troops and advisers, as well as mercenaries, and decided to investigate the death of Lumumba. Part B also found a 'threat to international peace and security'. It also noted the violation of human rights and fundamental freedoms in the Congo and urged self-determination through free and fair elections without outside interference.

On 24 November 1961 the Security Council adopted resolution 169 which reaffirmed the mandate of ONUC in the following terms:

(a) To maintain the territorial integrity and political independence of the Republic of the Congo;
(b) To assist the Central Government of the Congo in the restoration and maintenance of law and order;
(c) To prevent the occurrence of civil war in the Congo;
(d) To secure the immediate withdrawal and evacuation from the Congo of all foreign military, paramilitary and advisory personnel not under United Nations' command, and mercenaries; and
(e) To render technical assistance.

It welcomed the restoration of a Central Government on 2 August 1961 in accordance with the *Loi Fondamentale*, and deplored armed action against the government, specifically by the secessionists in Katanga aided by external resources and mercenaries. It completely rejected the claim that Katanga was a 'sovereign independent nation'. To this end the resolution authorised the Secretary General to take 'vigorous action', including the requisite measure of force 'if necessary' for the expulsion of foreign military personnel not under United Nations' command.

The Council resolutions establishing and mandating ONUC (143, 145, 146) were essentially the work of Secretary General Hammarskjöld. It is important, therefore, to ascertain his views as to their basis. His use of Article 99 to start the Council in motion gives the first indication as to the possible constitutional base of the action, for he believed that his use of Article 99 necessarily implied a finding by himself of a situation falling within Article 39 of the Charter.[92] However, he did not want to categorise the Belgian intervention as aggression in order to obtain the support of the Western powers on the Council. On the other hand, a characterisation of the situation as a mere breakdown in internal law and order would have indirectly justified Belgian intervention and would not have been acceptable to either the Socialist or Afro-Asian members of the Council. Hammarskjöld found a path through this minefield by proposing to create such conditions as to facilitate Belgian withdrawal with a United Nations' force filling the vacuum.[93]

It must be noted that the first three enabling resolutions made no finding under Article 39 despite the Secretary General's belief that Article 99 necessarily implied a 'threat to the peace'. The Secretary General was intent on obtaining a mandate for the force, hence the resolutions had to be constitutionally ambiguous in order to obtain sufficient consensus.

However, they do contain inferences as to where they could be placed under the Charter. Resolutions 143 and 146 contained provisions indicating that the force was to comply with Article 2(7) − ONUC was to provide military assistance in consultation with the Congolese government and would not intervene or influence the outcome of any internal conflict. Indeed, the Secretary General initially seemed to view ONUC as similar to interpositional, consensual peacekeeping as being undertaken at the time by UNEF I.[94] This would seem to suggest that ONUC was either created under the recommendatory powers of Chapter VI or under the doctrine of implied powers, since Chapter VI does not contain any specific provision under which a peacekeeping force could be established.

However, the last of Hammarskjöld's inspired resolutions (146) contained references to Article 25, suggesting that the resolutions were 'decisions' not recommendations and so were mandatory, without containing an express or implied finding under Article 39. As the situation deteriorated so the Council began to cross the threshold into Chapter VII. References to non-intervention in resolution 146 probably signified that the authorisation to ONUC to enter Katanga was, theoretically, not seen as enforcement action under Article 42 but as a provisional measure under Article 40.[95] This certainly accords with the Secretary General's revised view.[96] Without a determination within the terms of Article 39, which necessarily internationalises the situation, provisional measures under Article 40, although made mandatory by reference to Article 25, cannot escape the limitation in Article 2(7), because they are not enforcement measures.

Assuming, after resolution 146, that ONUC was operating under Article 40, could the General Assembly then take over the operation of the force when the Security Council became paralysed by the veto? The day-to-day operation of the force did not require supervision by the Security Council or by the General Assembly; the only action required by either organ was when the mandate of the force needed adjusting. Thus, if the mandate provided by the Security Council was sufficient for the force to continue day-to-day operations, there would be no legal need for the General Assembly to adopt a resolution. However, there was a political need to show that a majority of members supported the action.

The problem is whether the General Assembly, acting under the Uniting for Peace resolution, altered the mandate in its resolution 1474. There are suggestions that it did, for it requested that the Secretary General take 'vigorous action' to restore the unity and independence of the Congo. By itself, this request could, at the most, be classified as a recommendation of enforcement action, which would have been within the Assembly's powers, but would have constituted an alteration of the mandate. The Security Council had called only for mandatory provisional measures under Article 40. The General Assembly could be seen as recommending enforcement action similar to the power exercised by both the Security Council and the General Assembly during the United Nations' action in Korea. This would put ONUC beyond the pale of a peacekeeping force and would have made it an enforcement action.

However, there are suggestions in Assembly resolution 1474 that all that body intended was a reaffirmation of the Security Council's resolutions; in other words, it did not intend to alter the mandate. References in the resolution to Articles 25 and 49 indicate a confirmation of Council resolution 146, for such Articles do not apply to Assembly recommendations. If the Assembly was trying to take mandatory enforcement action that would have been unconstitutional. This was affirmed in the *Expenses* case[97] in which the World Court opined that the Assembly had not taken enforcement action as regards its handling of ONUC. Although its reasoning is not clear, the Court's judgement also suggests that the Assembly's contribution to ONUC's mandate was not recommendation of enforcement action, but simply a reaffirmation or possibly a reinterpretation of the mandate created by the Security Council.

The following Council resolution (161) made arguments relating to the legality of the Assembly's contribution somewhat academic, for it comprehensively reinterpreted ONUC's mandate in terms which went beyond those in the Assembly's resolution. The Council found a threat to the peace. Such an implied finding within the terms of Article 39 placed the whole operation under

Chapter VII. So even if the operation remained under Article 40, there was the possibility of making it into enforcement action at a later stage. Also, it is arguable that such a finding renders the limitation contained in Article 2(7) redundant.

There appear to be two alternatives: either resolution 161 went beyond provisional measures, or the finding of a threat to the peace was merely a sign of a deteriorating situation rather than a method by which the mandate could be changed. It appeared to go further than previous Council resolutions in that the emphasis was no longer on helping the Congolese government, which appeared to have disintegrated, instead it was reduced to maintaining the Congo's integrity – to prevent its break-up by factionalisation and secession – a Congo in which a new government could be elected. To this end it authorised the use of force in the last resort. The International Court was of the opinion that this did not amount to enforcement action. Nevertheless, for one thing, Article 2(7) no longer seemed important to the Council, to the extent of involving the consent of the Congolese government, for one did not exist at the time.[98] For another, resolution 161 authorised the use of force by ONUC 'in the last resort' – in other words, the use of force was not limited to merely self-defence. This last factor seems to push ONUC beyond a force overseeing the implementation of provisional measures to a force authorised to use enforcement measures. However, such a mandate can be reconciled with Article 40. The authorisation to use force in the last resort came at the end of a list of provisional measures – 'cease-fires', 'halting of all military operations', and 'the prevention of clashes' – and so can be seen as coming within an authorisation merely to enforce provisional measures, as provided by the last sentence of Article 40 which reads, 'the Security Council shall duly take account of a failure to comply with such provisional measures'.[99]

Security Council resolution 169 contained a comprehensive restatement of ONUC's mandate. It was able to contain a reassertion that ONUC was assisting the Congolese government because the central government had been restored. The force therefore returned, to some extent, to the consensual type of peacekeeping force exemplified by UNEF. However, the mandate also referred to the prevention of civil war as one of the force's purposes. This must be read in conjunction with the mandate's requirement (d) of ensuring the withdrawal of foreign military personnel and mercenaries, for it was the internationalisation of the civil war that constituted the threat to the peace.

The mandate contained in resolution 169 was in the nature of a series of widely drawn provisional measures. It was meant to enable ONUC to preserve the Congo intact to enable a peaceful settlement between all the factions to occur. It was not an authorisation for ONUC to enforce a political solution. Efforts to prevent secession may have appeared as if ONUC was being used by the central government to enforce its will on the secessionists. However, the basis of ONUC's action towards secession was that it arose because of foreign intervention and foreign engineering of a revolt, which was not in accord with the widest interpretation of ONUC's mandate – the protection of the territorial integrity and independence of the Congo.

The Congo was to remain as a whole, but if the secession was wholly or mainly indigenous, ONUC's action would have been an enforcement of that aim. However, the Council resolutions made it clear that that organ believed that the secession was being caused from outside the country. This was evidenced by resolution 169 which authorised the use of force solely for the expulsion of foreign military elements. Whether there would have been a Katangese secession anyway remains conjecture; the fact remains that foreign military involvement provided the situation with the necessary international element to have allowed ONUC to operate, without it technically becoming an enforcement action under Article 42, in that its use of force was confined to the enforcement of the provisional measures outlined in the mandate.

Nevertheless, enforcement of provisional measures is in many respects similar to enforcement action under Article 42, particularly when the provisional measures are so widely drawn as to include the maintenance of the integrity of a nation. This has led Bowett to descibe ONUC's constitutional base as being somewhat wider than Article 40, seeing it as a force 'for the purpose of supervising and enforcing compliance with the provisional measures ordered under Article 40 and for other purposes which were consistent with the general powers of the Council under Article 39'.[100] This involves recognising that ONUC had gone beyond Article 40, but not as far as Article 42, by suggesting that the general powers of Article 39 were utilised. It must be pointed out, however, that the provisions of Article 39 have been used as authority for the recommendation of enforcement action as in the Korean war.

It would be best to summarise ONUC's actions as having as their constitutional base the enforcement of provisional measures under Article 40, but since these measures were increasingly widely drawn so as to cope with an ever-deteriorating crisis, they, in fact, amounted to *de facto* mandatory enforcement action. It could be argued that ONUC was acting in defence of its purposes. However, this is an unacceptably wide interpretation of self-defence, going far beyond that authorised for other peacekeeping operations, which are only allowed to use self-defence when fired on. Allowing a force to take positive action in defence of its purposes is no different from allowing it to enforce them.

UN Peacekeeping Force in Cyprus (UNFICYP) 1964– present
Violence broke out between the Greek and Turkish Cypriot communities after the President of Cyprus – Archbishop Makarios – had proposed constitutional amendments on 30 November 1963. A threat of Turkish intervention arose.[101] This led to proposals for a joint British/Turkish/Greek 'peacemaking' force to be interposed between the two communities.[102] The Soviet

Union characterised this proposal as enforcement by NATO and stated that only the Security Council could take any practical measures.[103] The Cypriot government wanted a United Nations', not a guaranteeing powers', presence.[104]

The non-permanent members of the Council, excluding Czechoslovakia, sponsored resolution 186 which was adopted by the Council on 4 March 1964. The resolution noted that the situation 'with regard to Cyprus is likely to threaten international peace and security'; called on members 'to refrain from any action or threat of action likely to worsen the situation in Cyprus, or to endanger international peace'; asked the government of Cyprus which had 'the responsibility for the maintenance of law and order' to take measures to stop the violence; recommended the creation 'with the consent of the government of Cyprus' of UNFICYP; and recommended that the 'function of the force should be, in the interest of preserving international peace and security, to use its best efforts to prevent a recurrence of the fighting, to contribute to the maintenance and restoration of law and order and a return to normal conditions'.

The Secretary General's interpretation of UNFICYP's mandate made it clear that what was contemplated was a consensual type peacekeeping operation based on UNEF I, avoiding any action 'designed to influence the political situation in Cyprus except through creating an improved climate in which political solutions may be sought'.[105] This neutralist policy was meant to allay fears of enforcement. Nevertheless, ONUC's actions under a neutralist stance came perilously close to enforcement, and the Secretary General's interpretation of the use of force by UNFICYP had a similar potential, envisaging the possible use of force by UNFICYP to carry out its mandate.[106] As with ONUC, UNFICYP's mandate, outlined in resolution 186, contained a series of widely drawn provisional measures. However, unlike in the Congo situation where the Council was faced with a threat to the peace, here the Council did not make a crucial Article 39 finding. Thus, UNFICYP was created following non-mandatory provisional measures and so could not undertake enforcement action without a finding in the terms of Article 39.

Between 1964 and 1974 UNFICYP did not act as a buffer force between the two communities but rather as a police force, since there were not, as such, definable cease-fire lines. This situation changed in 1974. A Greek-backed coup against Makarios and the imminent invasion by Turkey led the Council to meet on 16 July 1974 at the request of Secretary General Waldheim [107]and the Cypriot representative.[108] In the Council's first meeting some of the members stated that there was a threat to international peace.[109] Indeed, resolution 353, adopted on 20 July 1974, the day Turkey invaded, stated that there was a 'serious threat to international peace and security', and demanded 'an end to foreign military intervention' in Cyprus. This implied finding under Article 39, combined with the peremptory language and a call for a cease-fire, suggests mandatory provisional measures under Article 40.

Nonetheless, UNFICYP's original constitutional basis — founded on non-mandatory provisional measures — was not changed and brought within Chapter VII, although its functions were to change from it being an intra-state to, factually, an inter-state peacekeeping force. The Secretary General reported on the measures proposed by the foreign ministers of Greece, Britain and Turkey (but not Cyprus), that UNFICYP should create a security zone between the Turkish forces in the north of the island and the Greek Cypriot forces in the south. The Security Council requested that he implement his report.[110]

Although Cyprus had consented to the original emplacement of UNFICYP in 1964, it objected somewhat to the new deployment, saying that it appeared to perpetuate foreign military intervention.[111] It did not go as far as to withdraw its consent but its co-operation seemed to become unimportant with all the negotiations about the security zone taking place between Greece, Britain, Turkey, and the Secretary General.[112] However, although there was no effective government for the whole island, there was a need to involve the two Cypriot factions as well as the guaranteeing powers to obtain a lasting cease-fire and to allow UNFICYP to perform its new functions.[113]

To summarise — UNFICYP was created in 1964 as a necessary corollary for the implementation of non-mandatory provisional measures. Although the Security Council found a threat to the peace in 1974, it did not alter UNFICYP's constitutional base, although it did change its function from that of policing an intra-state conflict to one of separating belligerents in what was effectively an inter-state conflict.

Second UN Emergency Force in the Middle East (UNEF II) 1973–79
Unlike the preceding three Middle Eastern wars, the Yom Kippur War of 1973 did not follow a period of heightened tension in the region. Consequently, the international community was largely unprepared when, on 10 October 1973, the armed forces of Egypt and Syria launched a co-ordinated attack against Israeli positions in Sinai and the Golan Heights. The tactic of surprise enabled Egypt and Syria to be initially successful in their main aim — the recapture of territories lost in 1967.

The outbreak of war also took the Security Council by surprise. Although the Council was convened on 8 October,[114] it was unable to take any steps for seventeen days, and, indeed, it did not meet at all between 13 and 21 October. The pro-Arab members of the Council were pleased at the initial Arab success, whereas Israel and the United States played for time to enable the Israelis to regain lost ground.[115] For a cease-fire to be called and for it to hold required not only the co-operation of the belligerents' backers — the two superpowers — which would enable the Council to call for a cease-fire — but would also require the parties (Israel, Egypt and Syria) to have come to a stage in their hostilities where a cease-fire would appeal to them all. Inevitably, these two requirements did not coincide for a considerable length of time. With increasing Arab losses the Soviet Union sought a cease-fire and invited Secretary of State Kissinger to Moscow. The result of this diplomacy was a joint superpower-sponsored resolution which was virtually forced through the Council on a take it or leave it basis.[116] The resolution simply called upon the parties to 'terminate all military activity' no later than twelve hours after the resolution's adoption and then to implement resolution 242. The resolution appeared to be adopted as a provisional measure under Article 40, and even in the absence of an express or implied finding under Article 39, the superpowers probably intended it to be binding.[117]

Nevertheless, although the Arabs were in retreat, Israel had not yet accomplished its political and military objectives and so there was a time-lag between the superpower-sponsored call for a cease-fire and all the combatants accepting it. Non-compliance with the cease-fire resulted in another United States/Soviet Union proposed resolution,[118] which confirmed the Security Council's previous 'decision' and urged the forces to return to the positions they occupied at the moment the cease-fire had been called for.

However, continued fighting brought about threats of superpower intervention[119] and the consequent danger of escalation into a global conflict. The situation was rescued by the seven Non Aligned members of the Council,[120] who introduced resolution 340 on 25 October. It demanded an immediate cease-fire, decided to set up, under Council authority, a United Nations Emergency Force, and, in the meantime, requested the Secretary General to increase the number of UNTSO observers on each side.

The Secretary General interpreted UNEF II's mandate as requiring supervision of the implementation of the cease-fire called for in resolution 340. He also outlined the general characteristics of the force on a similar basis to UNEF I, in that it must operate with the full co-operation of the parties; have freedom of movement and communications; use force only in self-defence, including self-defence against 'resistance to attempts by forceful means to prevent it from discharging its duties'; and 'in performing its functions, the force will act with complete impartiality and avoid actions which could prejudice the rights, claims or positions of the parties concerned'.[121]

The latter phrase suggests that UNEF II was in the nature of a provisional measure − or more correctly, would not interfere with the positions of the parties under the provisional measures (cease-fire and withdrawal) it was to supervise. Article 40 would seem to be the origin of UNEF, but although resolution 340 could be interpreted as a mandatory demand for compliance with provisional measures, UNEF II could not be interpreted as an enforcement measure. As we have seen, there is no necessary equation between a mandatory Chapter VII resolution under Article 40 and the establishment of an enforcement agency. The emphasis on consent and self-defence indicates the essentially non-enforcement nature of UNEF II.

However, UNEF II differed from UNEF I in that it originated in the Security Council, whereas UNEF I was authorised by the Assembly; although both were concerned with the supervision of provisional measures. The permanent members worried about the predictability of the Assembly were concerned to keep peacekeeping in the Council, and not to allow the Secretary General to have effective control over peacekeeping operations. Any alterations of the functions would require the agreement of the Council, which renewed UNEF's mandate every six months in order to keep a tight rein on the situation.

Apart from Council control, UNEF II appeared little different from UNEF I. However, the fact of Council control seems to have led some members to assert that UNEF II's position on Egyptian territory was stronger than that of UNEF I. The representative of the United States referred to withdrawal occurring only 'when the Council so decides'.[122] This was probably prompted by a fear of host State consent being withdrawn in similar circumstances to that of Egypt's in 1967. However, it is doubtful if UNEF II's presence somehow limited the host State's sovereignty, which would prevent their denial of consent at some future point, leading to UNEF II's withdrawal. The only event which would prevent withdrawal under these circumstances would be if the Council changed UNEF II's mandate into one of enforcement which obviously does not require consent. As we shall see, UNEF II's withdrawal arose under different circumstances to UNEF I's.

UN Disengagement Observer Force (UNDOF) 1974–present
Whereas UNEF II was interposed between Egypt and Israel on the initiative of the Council following the 1973 conflict, on the Syrian front the parties accepted the cease-fire and negotiated their own disengagement agreement which called for the establishment of UNDOF to supervise it. The Security Council approved the establishment of UNDOF in resolution 350 on 31 May 1974, again exercising tight control by giving UNDOF short, renewable mandate periods of six months.

The Council approved the Secretary General's report[123] which interpreted UNDOF's functions as the supervision of disengagement and the observation of cease-fire lines. The general principles governing UNDOF would be the same as UNEF II.

UNDOF's constitutional origin is basically the same as UNEF's − the supervision, with the consent of the parties, of provisional measures adopted under Article 40 of the Charter by the Council, and in this case embodied in an agreement between the parties.

UN Interim Force in Lebanon (UNIFIL) 1978–present
Israel invaded southern Lebanon in March 1978. The Security Council responded with resolution 425 on 19 March, which expressed grave concern

at 'the deterioration of the situation and its consequences for international peace'. It called on Israel to 'cease its military action' and to withdraw its forces from Lebanese territory. The resolution also established UNIFIL at the request of the Lebanese government to confirm Israeli withdrawal and then to ensure 'the effective restoration of Lebanese sovereignty'.[124] This remains UNIFIL's mandate to date.

The Secretary General interpreted the Council's mandate as authorising him to establish a peacekeeping force based on UNEF II and UNDOF, with UNIFIL acting only in self-defence, pursuing a neutralist approach of not undertaking 'the responsibilities of the Lebanese government', and being under the exclusive control of the Security Council.[125]

By basing UNIFIL firmly on the consensual type peacekeeping of UNEF and UNDOF the Council and Secretary General made it clear that enforcement was not contemplated. Resolution 425 contained a non-mandatory call for provisional measures based on Article 40. However, when Israel and various other factions in southern Lebanon prevented the second part of UNIFIL's mandate from being fulfilled,[126] various members of the Council[127] referred to Article 25. Even if such references could somehow make resolution 425 retroactively mandatory, such an effect would make only the call for provisional measures mandatory, it would in no way affect the functions of UNIFIL in supervising those measures. UNIFIL's mandate remains dependent on co-operation. The question of whether the provisional measures are mandatory or not only goes to the effectivness of those measures, and not to the nature of the force set up to supervise them.

UNIFIL was based on other inter-state peacekeeping forces because at the time the situation was viewed essentially as a dispute between Israel and Lebanon. However, it became increasingly clear that Lebanon was in a state of civil war, with various factions, including foreign States such as Syria, having more power and influence than the central government. This made UNIFIL's mandate unrealistic — it should have been more adapted to deal with an intra-state conflict as ONUC was in the Congo. Although the Security Council had, in the case of UNFICYP, changed a peacekeeping force's functions from being of an intra-state nature to being of an inter-state nature, it has not yet been prepared to change UNIFIL's essentially inter-state structure. This, in turn, has greatly impeded UNIFIL's success in implementing its mandate.

UN Transition Assistance Group (UNTAG) 1989–present

During the period of *détente* in the late 1970s, there arose the false hope that a solution to the Namibian problem was at hand. In 1976, the Security Council declared that the Namibian people should be 'enabled freely to determine their own future' by the means of free elections under UN supervision.[128] Indeed, optimism was so high, despite South African non-committal, that Canada,

West Germany, France, Britain, and the United States made a proposal for the settlement of the Namibian situation,[129] detailing the electoral process. This led in 1978 to the appointment of a Special Representative[130] and a decision by the Security Council to establish UNTAG in accordance with a report by the Secretary General[131] 'to ensure the early independence of Namibia through free elections under the supervision and control of the United Nations'.[132]

The Secretary General's report of 1978 recognised the 'unique character' of the proposed operation, in that it entailed not only a peacekeeping operation in the true sense to supervise a cease-fire between SWAPO and South African forces, but also supervision of free and fair elections leading to an independent State. This resulted in the Secretary General recommending a large military force of some 7,500, with a component of several hundred police and civilian administrators. The mandate of the military component was interpreted to include: the monitoring of the cessation of hostile acts; the restriction of South African and SWAPO forces to base; the phased withdrawal of all except a specified number of South African forces; the prevention of infiltration; and the monitoring of the demobilisation of civilian forces.

The mandate of UNTAG appeared widely drawn in 1978. Despite its division into military and police components, the overall mandate is for UNTAG to keep and enforce the peace in Namibia during the independence process. As with ONUC, there exists the possibility of a peacekeeping force crossing the threshold and becoming an enforcement action. Nevertheless, the internal nature of the conflict necessitated such a widely drawn mandate.

As with all peacekeeping forces, before UNTAG could be emplaced it needed the consent of all the parties to the conflict. SWAPO had consistently accepted resolution 435, while South African consent was not forthcoming until 22 December 1988 when it signed, along with Cuba and Angola, a tripartite agreement consenting to the UN plan.[133] The plan was acceptable to the South Africans because the accord linked Cuban withdrawal from Angola with South African withdrawal from Namibia. The agreement was also the result of pressure by the United States on South Africa and by the Soviet Union on Cuba and Angola. The agreement envisaged the independence process commencing on 1 April 1989.

The Security Council welcomed the agreement[134] while stating that UNTAG's mandate was the same as that envisaged in 1978 following a report by the Secretary General.[135] SWAPO and South Africa agreed to a cease-fire to commence on 1 April, so preparing the ground for UNTAG. The effectiveness of its operations so far will be assessed in the next chapter.

UNTAG's constitutional base remains in the Security Council resolution of 1978 and the accompanying report by the Secretary General. The military component's task is to oversee the implementation of provisional measures necessary for the success of the independence process to be monitored by the civilian component. As has been stated, UNTAG's mandate contains the possibility of it being able to enforce the peace, but, as shall be seen, it has not done this so far when faced with a breakdown in the cease-fire. Indeed, the agreements between South Africa and the United Nations on the status of UNTAG foresee it having a neutral and impartial function.[136]

UNTAG was created as a necessary corollary to the implementation of widely drawn provisional measures. Although its mandate could be adapted to enable it to enforce the peace, it is basically a consensual peacekeeping operation. It would necessitate a finding of a threat to the peace combined with a specific authorisation by the Council before UNTAG could enforce the peace.

Conclusions

Generally, both observation teams and peacekeeping forces are established as corollaries to the adoption of provisional measures. Such teams or forces provide the machinery by which provisional measures become acceptable to the parties, as well as providing the means by which compliance with such measures can be monitored. Since peacekeeping follows the adoption of provisional measures, it follows that the logical basis in the Charter for the power to create peacekeping forces lies in Article 40. This presents no problem for forces authorised by the Security Council; for those authorised by the General Assembly, voluntary provisional measures as operated by the Council in its interpretation of Article 40, are encompassed by the wide recommendatory powers granted to the Assembly under Articles 10, 11, and 14.

Observation, supervision and enforcement are the three levels of military involvement by the United Nations. Peacekeeping, at the most, involves the first two, although the boundary between the last two is very narrow when a peacekeeping force, such as ONUC, is authorised to enforce provisional measures under Article 40. Depending on how widely the provisional measures have been drawn, such enforcement can be little different from full enforcement action, either of a mandatory kind authorised under Article 42 or of a recommendatory kind authorised under Article 39. Nevertheless, true peacekeeping, whether observation or observation and supervision, is based on consent and co-operation and is therefore not affected by the mandatory or non-mandatory nature of the provisional measures which are antecedent to the establishment of a force. Since peacekeeping depends on host State consent, the withdrawal of that consent means the practical and legal termination of the operation. To continue would be to convert the peacekeeping operation into an enforcement action. Also, because peacekeeping does not involve enforcement, it can be clearly authorised by the General Assembly as well as by the Security Council, for, generally, the Security Council is the only organ authorised to call for mandatory enforcement action. However, it is arguable that the Assembly, by a combination of its practice as regards Korea and the Uniting for Peace procedure, has the authority to recommend enforcement action. Thus, theoretically, the Assembly has the power to change a force's mandate from peacekeeping to enforcement.

With the Non Aligned now in the majority in the Assembly there has arisen political and financial pressure from the permanent members of the Security Council, particularly the superpowers, to keep the peacekeeping function of the United Nations within the sole ambit of the Council. This appears to be the trend, with the Assembly having created only three peacekeeping forces – UNSCOB, UNEF I and UNSF since 1945 and none since the mid-1960s. A significant aspect of the polarisation of the peacekeeping function towards the Security Council is the limitation it has produced on the power of the Secretary General. He is no longer the main instigator and controller of peacekeeping operations; instead, he is now the administrator of the force and is answerable on a regular basis to the Security Council, although he still takes initiatives with the consent of the Council. This involves a move away from a liberal interpretation of Article 99 to a more literal one.

Finally, the functions and mandate of a peacekeeping force are affected by the nature of the conflict, and if a force is given a mandate unsuited to the type of conflict in which it is positioned it will be unable to achieve its purposes. A peacekeeping force in a civil war situation, particularly an internationalised civil war, requires a mandate verging on enforcement. It was only by giving ONUC this mandate that the United Nations was able to prevent a permanent factionalisation of the Congo. To deny it *de facto* enforcement powers is to render it ineffective for the purposes of fulfilling its mandate. Peacekeeping in an inter-state conflict is much easier to carry out and probably, therefore, is authorised more readily by the United Nations, requiring a UNEF-type mandate. Observation by itself, however, is generally equally suitable to both inter- and intra-state conflicts.

Notes

1 SC Res. 27, 2 UN SCOR Resolutions 6 (1947).
2 See SC 390 mtg, 3 UN SCOR (1948). UN doc. S/488 (1948).
3 SC Res. 30, 2 UN SCOR Resolutions 8 (1947).
4 UN doc. S/586 (1947).
5 SC Res. 31, 2 UN SCOR Resolutions 8 (1947).
6 SC Res. 67, 4 UN SCOR Resolutions 2 (1949).
7 See SC 390 mtg, 3 UN SCOR (1948), Australia.
8 See SC 174 mtg, 2 UN SCOR 1716 (1947), Netherlands; SC 194 mtg, 2 UN SCOR 2191 (1947), Indonesia.
9 But see R. Higgins, *United Nations Peacekeeping: Documents and Commentary, vol. 2: Asia 1946–1967*, 25–31 (1970); D. W. Bowett, *United Nations Forces*, 62 (1964).
10 SC Res. 15, 1 UN SCOR Resolutions 6 (1946).

11 UN doc. S/360/REV 1 (1950).
12 GA Res. 109, 2 UN GAOR Resolutions 12 (1947).
13 UN doc. A/521, (1948).
14 GA Res 193, 3 UN GAOR Resolutions 18 (1948).
15 *UN Yearbook* (1947–48), 341.
16 Higgins, *Peacekeeping*, vol. 4, 32.
17 SC Res. 48, 3 UN SCOR Resolutions 17 (1948).
18 SC Res. 54, 3 UN SCOR Resolutions 22 (1948).
19 See UN doc. S/928 (1948).
20 SC Res. 72, 4 UN SCOR Resolutions 7 (1949).
21 See UN doc. A/3512 (1957).
22 See SC Res. 236, 22 UN SCOR Resolutions 4 (1967).
23 See Higgins, *Peacekeeping*, vol. 1, 60–3; Bowett, *UN Forces*, 63.
24 UN doc. S/628 (1948).
25 SC Res. 39, 3 UN SCOR Resolutions 2 (1948).
26 The Karachi Agreement, UN doc. S/1430/Add 1 Ann 26 (1949).
27 SC Res. 209, 20 UN SCOR Resolutions 13 (1965).
28 Higgins, *Peacekeeping*, vol. 2, 349–51.
29 Bowett, *UN Forces*, 63–4.
30 SC 825 mtg, 13 UN SCOR para.63 (1958), Secretary General.
31 UN doc. S/4029 (1958).
32 SC 835 mtg, 13 UN SCOR para.7 (1958), Japan.
33 UN doc. S/4040 (1958).
34 SC 827 mtg, 13 UN SCOR 12 (1958).
35 GA 738 plen. mtg, 3 UN GAOR ESS 59 (1958), Jordan.
36 GA Res. 1237, 3 UN GAOR ESS Supp. (No. 1) 1 (1958).
37 UN doc. A/3934/REV1 (1958).
38 See N. Piterski, *International Security Forces*, (1966); V. F. Petrovsky, 'The Soviet
    Union and the United Nations', in Rajan (ed.), *The Non Aligned and the UN*,
    chapter 11.
39 GA Res. 1752, 17 UN GAOR Supp. (No. 17) 70 (1962).
40 Higgins, *Peacekeeping*, vol. 2, 119.
41 See also GA Res. 1871, 17 UN GAOR Supp. (No. 17) 75 (1962).
42 UN doc. S/5298 (1963).
43 UN doc. S/5321 (1963).
44 SC Res. 179, 18 UN SCOR Resolutions 2 (1963).
45 UN doc. S/5412 (1963).
46 UN doc. S/5447 (1963).
47 UN doc. S/5794 (1964).
48 But see Higgins, *Peacekeeping*, vol. 1, 635; Bowett, *UN Forces*, 66.
49 UN doc. S/6651 (1965).
50 UN doc. S/6735 (1965).
51 SC 1247 mtg, 20 UN SCOR (1965).
52 UN doc. S/6738 (1965).
53 UN doc. S/6719/Add 5 (1965).
54 UN docs. S/19834, S/19835 (1988).
55 SC Res. 622, 43 UN S/PV (1988).
56 SC 2823 mtg, 43 UN S/PV 5–6 (1988).
57 UN doc. S/20093 (1988).
58 SC Res. 619, 43 UN S/PV (1988).
59 SC Res. 631, 44 UN S/PV (1989).

60 UN doc. S/20345 (1988).
61 UN doc. S/20346 (1988).
62 Article 3 and UN docs. S/20336, S/20338 (1988).
63 SC Res. 626, 43 UN S/PV (1988).
64 SC 748 mtg, 11 UN SCOR (1956).
65 UN doc. S/3710 (1956), US; UN doc. S/3713/Rev 1 (1956), USSR.
66 SC Res. 119, 11 UN SCOR Resolutions 9 (1956).
67 GA Res. 997, 1 UN GAOR ESS Supp. (No. 1) 2 (1956).
68 GA 562 plen. mtg, 1 UN GAOR ESS 296–305, 282, (1956), Canada, New Zealand.
69 GA Res. 998, 1 UN GAOR ESS Supp. (No. 1) 2 (1956).
70 GA Res. 999, *ibid.*
71 UN doc. A/3289 (1956); GA Res. 1000 *ibid.*
72 UN doc. A/3302 (1956); GA Res. 1001 *ibid.*
73 *Ibid.*
74 GA 638 plen. mtg, 11 UN GAOR paras. 76–7 (1957), Australia.
75 UN doc. A/6730/ADD 3 (1967).
76 GA 592 mtg, 11 UN GAOR paras. 13, 111, 79 (1956).
77 5 *I.L.M.* (1967), 595–602.
78 J. I. Garvey, 'United Nations Peacekeeping and Host State Consent', 64 *A.J.I.L.* (1970), 241.
79 UN doc. A/6669 (1967).
80 GA 561 plen. mtg, 1 UN GAOR ESS (1956).
81 GA 567 plen. mtg, 1 UN GAOR ESS paras. 292–3 (1956); GA 632 plen. mtg, 11 UN GAOR paras. 64–5 (1956).
82 I.C.J. *Rep.* 1962, 168.
83 UN doc. S/4382 (1960).
84 SC 873 mtg, 15 UN SCOR para. 18 (1960).
85 T. M. Franck, *Nation against Nation,* 176 (1985).
86 SC 901 mtg, 15 UN SCOR paras. 20–85 (1960).
87 UN doc. S/4523 (1960).
88 Franck, *Nation against Nation,* 176.
89 SC Res. 157, 15 UN SCOR Resolutions 8 (1960).
90 GA Res. 1474, 4 UN GAOR ESS Supp. (No. 1) 1 (1960).
91 See also GA Res. 1498, 15 UN GAOR Supp. (No. 16) 1 (1960).
92 J. Lash, 'Dag Hammarskjöld's Conception of his Office', 16 *International Organisation* (1962) 551.
93 G. Abi-Saab, *The UN Operation in the Congo,* 13 (1978).
94 UN doc. S/4389 (1960); SC 873 mtg, 15 UN SCOR paras. 18–29 (1960).
95 Higgins, *Peacekeeping,* vol. 3, 54; Bowett, *UN Forces,* 176; Abi-Saab, *The UN Operation in the Congo,* 105.
96 SC 920 mtg, 15 UN SCOR para. 75 (1960).
97 I.C.J. *Rep.* 1962, 151.
98 But see Higgins, *Peacekeeping* vol. 3, 58.
99 See Abi-Saab, *The UN Operation in the Congo*, 105.
100 Bowett, *UN Forces,* 180.
101 UN doc. S/5488 (1963).
102 UN doc. S/5508 (1964).
103 UN doc. S/5526 (1964).
104 SC 1095 mtg, 19 UN SCOR paras. 124–7 (1964).
105 UN doc. S/5653 (1964).
106 UN doc. S/5671 Annex 1 (1964).

107 UN doc. S/11334 (1974).
108 UN doc. S/11335 (1974).
109 See for example SC 1779 mtg, 29 UN SCOR 5 (1974), USSR.
110 SC Res. 355, 29 UN SCOR Resolutions 8 (1974).
111 SC 1789 mtg, 29 UN SCOR 11 (1974).
112 UN doc. S/11433 (1974).
113 UN doc. S/11473 (1974).
114 SC 1743 mtg, 28 UN SCOR (1973).
115 SC 1748 mtg, 28 UN SCOR (1973).
116 SC Res. 338, 28 UN SCOR Resolutions 10 (1973).
117 SC 1747 mtg, 28 UN SCOR para. 11 (1973).
118 SC Res. 339, 28 UN SCOR Resolutions 11 (1973).
119 SCOR 1749 mtg, 28 UN SCOR 1 (1973), Egypt; 1750 mtg, Panama.
120 Guinea, India, Indonesia, Kenya, Peru, Panama, Yugoslavia.
121 UN doc. S/11052/Rev 1 (1973).
122 SC 1752 mtg, 28 UN SCOR 6 (1973).
123 UN doc. S/11302 (1974).
124 SC Res. 425, 33 UN SCOR Resolutions 5 (1978).
125 UN doc. S/12611 (1978).
126 UN doc. S/12845 (1978).
127 SC 2085 mtg, 33 UN SCOR 3 (1978).
128 SC Res. 385, 31 UN SCOR Resolutions 8 (1976).
129 UN doc. S/12636 (1978).
130 SC Res. 431, 33 UN SCOR Resolutions 12 (1978).
131 UN doc. S/12827 (1978).
132 SC Res. 435, 33 UN SCOR Resolutions 13 (1978).
133 UN doc. S/20346 (1988).
134 SC Res. 628, 44 UN S/PV (1989).
135 SC Res. 629, 632, 44 UN S/PV (1989). UN doc. S/20412 (1989).
136 UN doc. S/20412/Add 1 (1989).

CHAPTER 9

The effectiveness of peacekeeping

We have already seen from chapter 7 that peacekeeping is limited by the global distribution of power blocs so that it is confined to the intermediate areas of the world, although observation, since it is less intrusive, may be authorised nearer to a power frontier than a full peacekeeping force.

Given this significant global limitation on the effectiveness of peacekeeping, we will now confine the analysis of effectiveness to those areas in which peacekeeping has actually been authorised. Such an examination will entail an analysis of each force's success in fulfilling its mandate, accompanied by a discussion on the effect that peacekeeping has on the final resolution of a dispute. The determination of the success of peacekeeping, *per se*, should be strictly confined to the purposes for which it was created, which are often very limited, and do not generally extend to the peacemaking process. Nevertheless, because peacekeeping has an effect on peacemaking it would be salient to ascertain that effect.

United Nations' observation teams

UN Observers in Indonesia 1947–50
We have seen that the United Nations' observers were given a broad mandate to lend assistance to the Consular Commission, the Good Offices Committee and the United Nations' Commission on Indonesia. These bodies were assigned the task of achieving an end to hostilities between the Dutch and the Indonesians and of facilitating a rapid progress towards Indonesian independence. The observers, through fulfilling their mandate of reporting on each stage, contributed to the eventual success in achieving these objectives.[1] This is perhaps one of the few cases where peacekeeping and peacemaking went hand-in-hand.

UNSCOB 1947–54

Only one of UNSCOB's functions was observation, the others were set out in General Assembly resolution 109, namely, to promote the cessation of external support for the Greek guerrillas and the establishment of normal diplomatic and friendly relations in combination with the pacific settlement of frontier incidents.

Most of these objectives had been achieved by the mid-1950s, although it is doubtful whether UNSCOB's observation team made any great contribution to this. It was severely limited by only having Western support, which resulted in its presence on Greek soil only. The detailed reports of the observers[2] certainly cannot be said to have impeded the solution of the problem, but because UNSCOB was motivated by Cold War factors, they can have had little influence on events. Yugoslavia's defection from the Communist camp, it should be pointed out, was of far greater significance.[3]

UNTSO 1949– present

The continuing functions of UNTSO are those of observation and reporting. Its success should be measured in the fulfilment of these functions which it has achieved admirably since the 1949 armistice. UNTSO, like all peacekeeping operations, was not designed to stop wars, and so its effectiveness should not be measured by the frequency with which conflicts occur in the Middle East.

Indeed, it is precisely because of that frequency that UNTSO is so important. This was amply illustrated on the outbreak of the Yom Kippur War in 1973. The Secretary General reported to the Council that Egypt had struck first. Egypt had asserted the opposite,[4] but so accurate was the Secretary General's report that the Egyptian government abandoned its version.[5] At a time of heightened international tension, with the danger of hostilities escalating, the correct ascertainment of the facts was essential.

A body of UNTSO observers was sent to Beirut in 1982 by the Security Council[6] to observe on three things: namely, the multinational force, Israeli withdrawal, and the situation in the refugee camps. Known as the Observer Group in Beirut (OGB), their success has been summarised by the Secretary General:

Although their numbers are small and unarmed, the observers are an important source of information in a most sensitive area. The presence of OGB in and around the city also represents the concern of the international community and its desire to be of assistance to the heavily afflicted people of the area.[7]

The function of the Observer Group in Beirut is observation and it has been successful in fufilling that. However, its presence has contributed little to decreasing the lawlessness in the city evidenced by kidnappings, street fighting, and starvation in the refugee camps, leading to Syrian military intervention in February 1987.

UNMOGIP 1949–present

UNMOGIP successfully carried out its mandate of observing the cease-fire line in Kashmir. Although its presence may well have helped to restrain the parties, the cease-fire line was breached in 1965 and 1971 during conflicts on a wider front than that patrolled by UNMOGIP.[8] Nevertheless, the 1965 hostilities, and in particular the 1971 conflict, were not disputes directly over the status of Kashmir, and so it appears to be a reasonable assumption that without UNMOGIP there may well have been more wars over the disputed area.

Paradoxically, although UNMOGIP may have contributed effectively to preventing either side from resorting to force to settle their dispute, it has effectively helped to cement the *status quo* during which the dispute is unlikely to be resolved. The cease-fire line patrolled by UNMOGIP is seen by both sides as preferable to either of them giving concessions following diplomatic negotiations. Peacekeeping has had the effect of making provisional measures permanent by hindering the peacemaking process. On the other hand, it has helped to prevent the evil of war.

UNOGIL 1958

UNOGIL observed and reported that there was no significant infiltration of Lebanon from the United Arab Republic,[9] and to that extent it had fulfilled the terms of its mandate. However, on a wider view, its reports did not prevent military intervention by the United States, although its continued presence along with the American marines, in addition to the establishment of a new government under General Chehab, probably had the effect of stabilising the situation.

Again, there is a wide gulf between the relative success of the United Nations' group in fulfilling its mandate and the relative failure of any wider, 'knock on' effects such as pacific settlement which the Security Council may have hoped for when it created UNOGIL. One cannot help thinking that the enabling resolutions do not state all the purposes of such a force. The mandate is deliberately limited because that is all that can be achieved practically, and any greater impact on the situation that might be hoped for is too uncertain to be mentioned.

UNSF 1962–63

UNSF was wholly successful in fulfilling its mandate. It managed to secure an effective cease-fire on West Irian in just over one month.[10] It then went on to effectively maintain law and order during the transition period, as well as completing the establishment of a viable police force capable of taking over on UNTEA's withdrawal.[11] Such success was guaranteed by the complete co-operation of the parties who had agreed on the pacific settlement of the dispute. Nevertheless, UNSF, which was withdrawn in 1963, had little influence on the refusal by Indonesia to hold a plebiscite before 1970 as agreed with the Netherlands. Although a solution to the dispute was achieved, it was not the solution intended.

UNYOM 1962–63

UNYOM had a very limited purpose, namely the observation and certification of the disengagement agreement. 'The parties themselves' were 'totally responsible for fulfilling the terms of the disengagement'.[12] Nevertheless, UNYOM was too small even to carry out its limited mandate.[13] UNYOM not only failed in this respect, but after its departure in September 1964, the civil war continued for several years with the continuing involvement of Egypt and Saudi Arabia.

UNIPOM 1965–66

UNIPOM was concerned with overseeing the implementation of the cease-fire and withdrawal orders of the Security Council along the international frontier beyond Kashmir. The observers worked well in helping to implement the cease-fire between forces which were sometimes only fifty metres apart,[14] although sporadic fighting continued for some time.

Nevertheless, before UNIPOM could supervise the cease-fire both parties had to agree upon it.[15] As with all peacekeeping initiatives, success depends on the parties accepting and maintaining a cease-fire. On 10 January 1966 a solution to the conflict, apart from the area of Kashmir, was agreed by the parties at Tashkent, whereby all the military personnel of India and Pakistan would be withdrawn to positions held before 5 August 1965. The withdrawal, under UNIPOM's supervision, was carried out on schedule.[16] Peacekeeping was accompanied by peacemaking on this occasion, although it must be remembered that the central problem of Kashmir remained requiring the continued presence of the United Nations in the form of UNMOGIP.

UNGOMAP 1988– present

UNGOMAP seems to be performing most admirably in the face of immense difficulties. Unlike UNIIMOG in the Gulf, UNGOMAP has been placed in an intra-state conflict where there is no effective cease-fire. It is very similar in this respect to the observers in Beirut. With no cease-fire in existence between the Afghan government forces and the mujahedin, UNGOMAP's movement and activities are severely hampered.

Nevertheless, UNGOMAP has successfully completed its first task of reporting on the withdrawal of all Soviet troops from Afghanistan in February 1989 in accordance with the Geneva Accords.[17] However, it appears to be encountering difficulties in fulfilling the second part of its mandate, namely reporting on violations of the Accords. This is not all that surprising since both the Soviet Union and the United States, as well as Pakistan, are breaching their undertakings not to intervene in the internal affairs of Afghanistan. Afghanistan made an unsuccessful complaint against Pakistan in April 1989,[18] when it alleged that Pakistan had violated the Accords on 1,200 occasions. Pakistan replied that no violations had been reported by UNGOMAP. The appeared to be no UNGOMAP report to justify any of these allegations and there were no other speakers at the meeting.[19]

The Geneva Accords did not settle the Afghan situation, they merely extracted the Soviet Union from being directly involved in the conflict. Despite its provisions on non-intervention, the agreement was signed in the full knowledge that superpower and Pakistani intervention would continue. Until a political solution to the internal conflict in Afghanistan is found involving all the factions and their backers, UNGOMAP is going to be faced with intractable problems.

UNIIMOG 1988 – present

UNIIMOG has been very successful in monitoring the cease-fire between Iran and Iraq, which has held since August 1988. In a report on the situation in October 1988,[20] the Secretary General stated that UNIIMOG was working effectively in helping the parties to peacefully settle the minor violations of the cease-fire that had occurred, and had received the full support and co-operation of both parties.

Although the cease-fire is holding, there has been little reported progress in the UN-sponsored talks between Iran and Iraq, which are aimed at producing a permanent and lasting peace.[21] However, it is far too early to talk of peacekeeping stagnating the peacemaking process. UNIIMOG has contributed in ending an inhumane conflict.

UNAVEM 1989 – present

The Secretary General reported to the Security Council in May 1989,[22] that UNAVEM was successfully fulfilling its mandate with excellent co-operation from Cuba and Angola. Nearly 2,000 more Cuban troops than scheduled had been withdrawn from Angola by April 1989.

The peace agreements signed on 22 December 1988, of which UNAVEM is a small component, have, unlike the Geneva Accords as regards Afghanistan, also produced signs of an internal peace in Angola, with UNITA and the MPLA government signing a cease-fire in June 1989.[23] It may be that the UN role in the agreements, in particular its physical presence in the form of UN observers, contributed to this. However, the more important factor is probably the South African announcement that it would no longer assist UNITA after the signing of the tripartite accord.[24]

United Nations' peacekeeping forces

UNEF I 1956-67

UNEF I's mandate had four aspects: to secure the cease-fire, which was rapidly achieved with the co-operation of the parties to the conflict; to supervise the withdrawal of foreign troops, which was achieved relatively slowly due to the reticence of Britain and France;[25] to observe the armistice agreement; and to patrol the armistice lines. As regards the last, UNEF took over most of UNTSO's patrols and was reasonably efficient taking into account Israel's repudiation of the Israeli-Egyptian Armistice in 1956 and its consequent withdrawal from the Mixed Armistice Commission.[26]

Israel's withdrawal from the Commission had a potential influence on the third aspect of UNEF's mandate, namely to observe the armistice agreement. Nevertheless, although no longer recognising the agreement *de jure*, Israel continued to recognise it *de facto*, which contributed to UNEF's success in reducing the number of fedayeen raids from the Gaza Strip and in keeping the number of border incidents to a minimum level during the force's stay.

UNEF I 'ranked among the most effective of United Nations' peacekeeping operations',[27] in that it not only fulfilled its mandate, but also helped to secure over a decade of relative peace in the Middle East. On the other hand, it could be said that UNEF I did not contribute anything towards a peaceful solution of even part of the Middle Eastern question. One could perhaps go further and argue that the parties, particularly Egypt, used the decade in which UNEF was *in situ* as a breathing space in which it rearmed in preparation for the next conflict, using the UNEF's buffer to hide behind. Certainly UNEF's contribution to peace was severely questioned when President Nasser withdrew Egypt's consent to the presence of UNEF which led to its withdrawal; an action which, in itself, suggested that Egypt no longer wanted peace and therefore no longer required UNEF. Despite arguments to the effect that Egypt had no right to withdraw consent, it is doubtful whether a peacekeeping force could remain on a State's territory without that State's consent. This represents a severe limitation on the effectiveness of the peacekeeping function as a whole.[28]

ONUC 1960-64

The effectiveness of ONUC in fulfilling its mandate can be determined by examining the Secretary General's report on the implementation of the Security Council's resolutions relating to the Congo.[29] He refers to the purposes listed (a) to (e) in Council resolution 169.

As regards the directive to ONUC to maintain the territorial integrity and political independence of the Congo, the Secretary General states that the most serious threat to this was from the Katangese secessionists. Although integrity was restored in a symbolic sense in August 1960 with Tshombe's consent to

ONUC's entry into Katanga, further secessionist activities meant that the full integration of the province was achieved only when a public renunciation of secession was announced by Tshombe, combined with the complete freedom of movement achieved by ONUC throughout Katanga, the neutralisation and disarming of the Katangese gendarmerie, the elimination of Katanga's airforce, and the flight of the mercenaries.

In relation to assisting the Congolese government in the restoration and maintenance of law and order, the Secretary General noted that until the formation of a recognisable central government in August 1961, ONUC was unsuccessful in this part of its mandate. After that date, particularly with the termination of Katanga's secession, ONUC restored law and order to the whole of the Congo by 1963. The formation of a central government acceptable to all the parties, including, eventually, Katanga, also helped ONUC to carry out successfully the third part of its mandate – the prevention of civil war in the Congo. The ending of the Katangese provincial government's secession necessarily entailed ONUC effectively carrying out the fourth part of its mandate, namely the removal of foreign military and paramilitary personnel and mercenaries.

It can be seen from the above that ONUC's success depended heavily on it ending the Katangese secession, and, as we have seen in chapter 8, ONUC's operation to carry this out came perilously close to being enforcement action. It is submitted that ONUC was successful because it overstepped basic peacekeeping principles. Its mandate was so widely drawn that its fulfilment entailed going beyond the maintenance of the *status quo*, which is the normal purpose of peacekeeping forces, to providing a solution to the conflict. In the case of intra-state conflict there is a great deal to be said for combining peacekeeping with peacemaking, otherwise the force will be faced with intractable problems, as are facing UNIFIL today.

From the once disintegrating Congo there has arisen a stable African State, Zaire, a fact that must, in part, be due to the United Nations' operation in the Congo.[30] Despite its operational difficulties, in terms of its contribution to the settlement of a crisis and to international peace, ONUC must be judged one of the most, if not the most, successful peacekeeping operations, by the United Nations.[31]

UNFICYP 1964– present
In the period 1964 to 1974, UNFICYP, after initial difficulties,[32] succeeded in securing a virtual end to the fighting on the island,[33] although its attempts at creating a return to normal conditions on Cyprus were a limited success.[34] As early as 1967, the Secretary General warned that excessive confidence in the presence of UNFICYP had reduced the parties' willingness to negotiate a settlement.[35]

Thus, in the period before the Turkish invasion, UNFICYP's major preoccupation was to try to maintain the *status quo* on the island.[36] This remained its position towards the new *status quo* imposed on the island following the Turkish invasion and occupation of the northern part of the island in 1974. UNFICYP was powerless to prevent the invasion; instead its functions were changed to that of a buffer force. In carrying out its revised mandate successfully, UNFICYP has helped to entrench the post-1974 position on the island, with the cease-fire line becoming 'more and more an international frontier'.[37]

The Security Council has encouraged peacemaking through the Secretary General's good offices, and has called upon all States not to recognise any Cypriot State other than the Republic of Cyprus.[38] A parallel can be drawn with the Congo situation where the Council was also concerned to keep the nation intact. However, in that case the Council took positive action through its peacekeeping force to maintain the integrity of the Congo, whereas UNFICYP is used to maintain a division of the island State, whilst any progress towards reintegration must come about via separate peacemaking attempts by the Secretary General.[39]

The Security Council continues to renew UNFICYP's mandate on a six-monthly basis.[40] This must be explained by a belief held by the Council that to remove UNFICYP might lead to war not only between the two Cypriot communities, but also involving Turkey and Greece, rather than being based on the Secretary General's optimism. In his recent reports to the Council on UNFICYP,[41] the Secretary General states that the continued presence of UNFICYP on the island is indispensable, both in helping to maintain calm on the island and in creating conditions in which a search for a peaceful settlement could best be pursued. The evidence is that UNFICYP, rather than creating conditions for peacemaking, is in fact detrimental to it. The reasons for this dysfunction are explained by Franck:

Neither the Turkish nor the Greek Cypriot community wishes to see the force removed. To each side, while the *status quo* is highly unsatisfactory, all but one of the alternatives is worse. The alternative, outright victory over the other side, would be extremely costly and is probably beyond the military capacity of either side.[42]

It must be remembered that whereas peacekeeping may well prevent peacemaking, it does hinder war. It does not prevent war, however, as the Turkish invasion of 1974 vividly illustrates.

UNEF II 1973–79
For the six year period of its presence UNEF II successfully implemented its mandate of observing and supervising the cease-fire between Egypt and Israel.[43] In his penultimate report to the Security Council on UNEF II, Secretary General Waldheim repeated his usual finding that 'the situation in the area of operations has remained stable. The force has continued efficiently

to discharge its mandate and, with the co-operation of both parties, it has been able to contribute to the maintenance of the cease-fire called for by the Security Council in resolution 338 (1973)'.[44]

UNEF II had the potential to join ONUC as a fully successful peacekeeping force, not only in terms of fulfilling its mandate, but also of contributing to the ultimate solution of the dispute. The Camp David Accords leading to a peace treaty between Egypt and Israel on 26 March 1979 provided for a continued United Nations' presence to oversee the implementation of the treaty. Several factors prevented this, namely the fact that the treaty was negotiated outside the United Nations set most of the members against a continued United Nations' presence[45] and also the fact that the United States' sponsoring of the talks represented the final stage in Egypt's move away from Moscow to Washington. The Soviet Union was thus unwilling to alter the mandate of UNEF II to enable it to supervise a treaty between two States friendly to the United States.[46] This is illustrative of the political factors which hamper the effectiveness of peacekeeping, particularly when it comes to a decision whether to change a force's mandate. Instead, a United States-backed, Western-in-composition, Multinational Force was created for the purpose.

UNDOF 1974 – present
UNDOF has performed its functions of supervising the disengagement agreement between Israel and Syria very effectively to the present day, although there is no sign of a solution to the dispute over the Israeli occupation of the Golan Heights. Nevertheless, although a final pacific settlement is not on the horizon, the ability of UNDOF to help prevent the parties going to war is perhaps a more important factor in an area where escalation is a distinct possibility. Israel has invaded the Lebanon twice since the establishment of UNDOF, in 1978 and 1982. The fact that Syria was not sucked into a conflict which could, in turn, have drawn in the superpowers, is due, to a considerable extent, to UNDOF's presence.

After the Israeli invasion in 1978, the Secretary General was able to report that the 'situation in the Israel-Syria sector remained quiet and there was no incidents of a serious nature'. UNDOF's fortnightly inspections of areas designated as containing limited armaments and troops by the disengagement agreement, accompanied by liaison officers from Syria and Israel, probably facilitated the defusion of the situation by preventing a build-up of arms by either party.[47]

UNDOF apparently had a similar effect following the June 1982 invasion of Lebanon by Israel. The situation was summarised by the Secretary General: 'Despite the present quiet in the Israel-Syria sector, the situation in the Middle East as a whole continues to be potentially dangerous and is likely to remain so. In the prevailing circumstances, I consider the continued presence of

UNDOF in the area is essential.'[48] The value of UNDOF in preventing escalation probably far outweighs its encouragement of the frozen *status quo* and stalemate in the area.

UNIFIL 1978 – present
Although Israel withdrew by the end of April 1978, the second part of UNIFIL's mandate – the restoration of Lebanese sovereignty – was (and is) almost impossible to achieve given the state of virtual civil war in southern Lebanon and the inability of the profoundly weak Lebanese government to assume any sort of responsibility for the area. Again, a contrast can be made with the situation in the Congo in 1960–61 when ONUC took positive, almost enforcement, action to end a civil war until a stronger central government could be established.

UNIFIL's mandate, however, is one of peacekeeping, not of quasi-enforcement, and therein lies its weakness, for a solution to the problem is not feasible unless UNIFIL is given a mandate to enforce the peace, a mandate which is currently politically and militarily unachievable. Although the Security Council has threatened further action to ensure the full implementation of resolution 425,[49] it has, up to now, been content merely to renew UNIFIL's original mandate, composition and functions.

Although it did not facilitate a restoration of Lebanese sovereignty, UNIFIL was successful in negotiating a cease-fire between Israel and the PLO which lasted from July 1981 to April 1982.[50] However, this success was shortlived, for whereas the PLO regarded the cease-fire as confined to the Israeli-Lebanese border, the Israeli authorities interpreted the agreement as proscribing all hostile measures against Israeli or Jewish targets overseas.[51] So when on 3 June 1982 Israel's ambassador in London was shot by Arab gunmen, the precarious cease-fire collapsed and Israel commenced operation 'Peace for Galilee' by invading Lebanon.

Israel forewarned UNIFIL of its action[52] and passed through the force's lines. Neither UNIFIL's mandate, nor its size, nor its armaments, enabled it to resist.[53] With Israel pushing further into Lebanon, UNIFIL's original mandate was impossible to achieve; nevertheless, the Council renewed its mandate, while directing it, during the period of Israel's occupation, to undertake humanitarian assistance to the population of southern Lebanon.[54]

Throughout UNIFIL's stay, its mandate has always remained that of supervising a withdrawal of Israeli forces and of securing a restoration of Lebanese sovereignty. This remains a forlorn hope because even when Israel withdrew it established a security zone in southern Lebanon, south of the Litani river, policed by the Israeli-backed Southern Lebanese Army.

At times there have been suggestions as to how UNIFIL could carry out the second part of its mandate. In one report,[55] the Secretary General suggested that the Council should consider making UNIFIL's mandate more effective by allowing it to be temporarily deployed with elements of the Lebanese army and internal security forces. This would, to a certain extent, put UNIFIL at the disposal of the Lebanese government and could conceivably create an ONUC-type situation in which UNIFIL may be required to expel forcefully foreign military elements in order to fulfil its mandate. His hopes were dashed, however, when Israel adopted search and destroy tactics in February 1985 after being attacked by Lebanese resistance groups. UNIFIL was again powerless to prevent this.

The Secretary General contradicted his earlier suggestion of adopting a changed mandate when he reported on the Israeli measures: 'There is no easy solution to the dilemna of UNIFIL. To withdraw the force would not be in the interests of the government and of the people of Lebanon, while to involve it actively in the current violence would merely create a further complicating factor in the already extremely difficult situation.'[56]

The Security Council continues to renew UNIFIL's mandate on a three-monthly or six-monthly basis on the premise of firm support for the independence and territorial integrity of Lebanon.[57] Theoretically, UNIFIL's mandate still includes that aim, practically, however, without authorising UNIFIL to use force in the last resort to fulfil its mandate, its functions will be severely limited. The Security Council appears unwilling to authorise UNIFIL to use force except in strict self-defence because it probably does not want to create another ONUC-type force, which, although successful, severely divided and debilitated the United Nations.

At present UNIFIL's function can be classified as a stabilising one,[58] whereas if it had an ONUC-type mandate it could actively disarm the various militia, expel foreign elements, and restore Lebanese sovereignty in southern Lebanon. The problem of Lebanese sovereignty in the north, where Syria has been in occupation for many years, would then have to be considered, which would lead to the Soviet Union objecting to any action on the part of the United Nations. It is probably in the Soviet Union's interest to prevent any alteration of UNIFIL's mandate which would allow it to take positive action in the south because that might lead to calls for similar action as regards the rest of Lebanon. It is in the interests of all the major powers not to withdraw UNIFIL, even with its limited mandate, for fear of creating a vacuum into which the various factions in southern Lebanon would be drawn, leading to a further deterioration and, possibly, internationalisation of the civil war.

UNIFIL's soldiers will continue to be killed and its mandate unfulfilled, unless all the factions in Lebanon, including the Israelis and Syrians, cooperate. Such a possibility seems remote. The most UNIFIL can hope for is to be a stabilising influence, preventing a further and possibly catastrophic deterioration of the civil war.

UNTAG 1989 – present

Although the Security Council decided to implement its plan for Namibian independence in its original and definitive form, it eventually decided to reduce the size of UNTAG to 4,500,[59] following intense pressure from the five permanent members, who thought that the improved climate in southern Africa, in addition to financial constraints, meant that a smaller peacekeeping force was sufficient for the tasks.[60]

The wrangling over the size of the force, combined perhaps with some complacency as to the anticipated success of the peace process, may have resulted in the inauspicious start to the UN plan when, on 1 April 1989, the cease-fire was breached. Several hundred SWAPO guerrillas infiltrating from Angola were met with force by South African troops[61] purportedly acting under UNTAG authority,[62] due to the fact that the UN had only 1,000 troops in Namibia with very few in the border area. There is no doubt that the South African forces enforced the peace in a way that the peacekeeping force is not mandated to. On the other hand, SWAPO appeared to be in breach of the tripartite accord which confined the guerrillas to bases inside Angola. However, although SWAPO consented to the UN plan as laid down in 1978, it was not a party to the agreement which finalised the details. The peace process seems to have ignored the fact that all the parties to a dispute must fully consent to its provisions before a peacekeeping force can be successfully emplaced.

During the fighting between SWAPO and the South African forces, the United Nations appeared helpless.[63] It required a new agreement on 8 April between the original signatories to the tripartite accord and this time consented to by SWAPO before a new cease-fire could be made effective.[64] The fresh agreement between South Africa, Angola and Cuba, with the United States and the Soviet Union overseeing, provided for a cease-fire and a withdrawal of SWAPO fighters north of the 16th parallel under UN supervision. This agreement was reported to the Security Council by the Secretary General.[65]

It appears at this stage that although the United Nations is providing the force and is to supervise the elections alongside the South African authorities, so far the process is not in the hands of the UN. The tripartite accords, deployment of UNTAG, and subsequent cease-fire were all the products of superpower pressure. The United Nations has responded to this and, although its responses were too slow, it would be wrong for the UN to take all of the blame.

The shaky start to the UN plan gave rise to fears that the elections, scheduled for 1 November 1989, might be delayed.[66] However, the Joint Monitoring Commission of Angola, South Africa and Cuba, agreed on 14 May 1989 that the situation was normalised sufficiently for the plan to proceed on schedule.[67]

Overview

As we have seen, generally peacekeeping operations fulfil their mandates, with the major exception of UNIFIL which is too inhibited and too inadequate to fulfil its widely drawn mandate. In addition to this limited success, several United Nations' peacekeeping operations have positively contributed to the peacemaking process, leading to the pacific settlement of the dispute. The United Nations' observers in Indonesia, UNSF, UNIPOM, ONUC, and, to a certain extent, UNEF II, all helped in varying degrees to achieve a pacific settlement. However, there are several cases of interpositional or inter-state peacekeeping in which the mandates of the forces may be fulfilled but 'even a successful UN peacekeeping operation is likely to produce a negative concomitant; its very success in defusing a confrontation conduces to stalemate'.[68] UNFICYP, UNMOGIP and UNDOF are examples of peacekeeping forces contributing to a frozen *status quo*.

Nevertheless, the overall effectiveness of such inter-state peacekeeping forces as UNDOF depends on whether the prevention of the conflict is relatively more important in terms of international peace than the enhancement of the possibility of achieving a peaceful solution. To say that peacekeeping inhibits[69] peacemaking denies that in certain cases, and certainly in the case of UNDOF, the keeping of the peace is more important than seeking a peaceful solution. Potential peacemaking initiatives could involve such a drastic change in the *status quo* as to lead to conflict.

The solution would be to make peacemaking go hand-in-hand with peacekeeping. Often this would appear to be the only solution in intra-state conflicts. However, as the case of ONUC illustrates, such a solution pushes peacekeeping towards enforcement. Again the problem is relative. If UNIFIL was armed with an ONUC-type mandate instead of a UNEF-type mandate, it could help to make the peace in the Lebanon. However, this would necessarily involve the positive use of force which could potentially destabilise the situation. Thus, UNIFIL might be more effective in its present role as a stabilising influence. Nevertheless, the ONUC and UNIFIL experiences show that there is no such thing as 'peacekeeping' in a civil war. The peace cannot be kept in such a situation by merely placing a defensive force in the midst of the conflict (UNIFIL), unless that force actively pursues the attainment of its mandate and uses offensive force, as in the case of ONUC.

There are other factors to be taken account of when assessing the effectiveness of peacekeeping and in considering whether the emplacement of a peacekeeping force would contribute to maintaining the peace. It cannot always be said that the emplacement of a peacekeeping force will necessarily prevent further conflict and freeze the *status quo* between the disputants. Further hostilities may occur. This factor is illustrated by UNFICYP's inability to prevent the Turkish invasion of Cyprus in 1974. In addition, the withdrawal of a peacekeeping force may unfreeze the *status quo*, resulting in conflict rather than the peaceful settlement of a dispute. It may be conceded that the presence of a buffer force inhibits the peacemaking process, but it also must be conceded that the absence of a peacekeeping force increases the likelihood of fresh hostilities breaking out. A good example of withdrawal leading to hostilities is the occurrence of the Six Day War ensuing upon the withdrawal of UNEF I in 1967.

Given these general propositions derived from experience, the effectiveness of each force in terms of international peace and security depends on whether the maintenance of the *status quo* is more important than a change in that status. In terms of inter-state conflict the frozen *status quo* means military and diplomatic statemate, whereas in intra-state conflicts a maintenance of the *status quo* means limiting the level of a civil war and preventing it from spreading. In terms of United Nations' forces established for many years and still on station, their effectiveness under the above principles can be briefly assessed.

In the case of UNMOGIP it could be said that by helping to maintain the *status quo* this observer team has inhibited either side from taking diplomatic initiatives. If that *status quo* were changed by the withdrawal of the team, the war which may possibly follow would probably not escalate to global proportions. Previous wars in 1965 and 1971 (which were not prevented by UNMOGIP's presence) between India and Pakistan did not escalate. The chance that a change in the *status quo* might produce a settlement could be taken on the basis of this analysis. Again in the case of UNFICYP, the frozen *status quo* has quashed the possibility of peaceful settlement. A change in that position may force the parties to reach a peaceful solution or it may force them to war. Such a war, between NATO members, would probably not escalate. It did not in 1974.

However, in the case of UNDOF, the danger of escalation is too high to risk changing the stalemate. In 1973, the last time Israel and Syria fought directly, there was a very great risk of superpower intervention. The same can be said of UNIFIL, with the risk of an increasing internationalisation of the conflict being too great to sanction UNIFIL's withdrawal, although it is questionable whether UNIFIL is able to prevent the civil war spreading anyway.

By measuring peacekeeping in terms of balancing the possibility of peaceful settlement against the possibility of escalating conflict, UNDOF and UNIFIL are effective, whereas there are doubts about UNFICYP and UNMOGIP. However, all wars are destructive and threaten international peace, and so to speak coldly in terms of non-escalating wars should perhaps lead to the conclusion that all peacekeeping operations are successful as long as they reduce the risks or effects of war, even though they reduce the chances of peaceful settlement, particularly when bearing in mind that the propensity to go to war is greater than the desire to seek a solution by peaceful means.

Nonetheless, there are signs that one of the United Nations' latest forces, UNTAG, may be more successful than its many of its predecessors, in that it is directly tied into the peace process as a whole. Despite its uncertain start, UNTAG has the advantage of having been envisaged since 1978 in the event of South Africa withdrawing from Namibia. The advantage of having a peacekeeping force ready to be emplaced, over an *ad hoc* force, is that the situation is not allowed to deteriorate in the interim period in which the force is assembled and the dispatched. Sometimes, as in the Congo, the deterioration is too great for an ordinary peacekeeping force to deal with.

UNGOMAP and UNIIMOG, on the other hand, have the appearance of traditional forces, in that they have been sent in to maintain and stabilise a situation, followed by, but not combined with, ill-prepared and so far unsuccessful peace processes.

There remains the question of whether the peacekeeping function of the United Nations can be improved. As we have seen in this chapter, it would be very difficult to improve on the effectiveness of a peacekeeping force *in situ*. However, effectiveness might be enhanced if the procedures for the establishment of such forces were institutionalised instead of being of an *ad hoc* nature. Such a development would be akin to the agreements and machinery for United Nations' armed forces envisaged in Article 43, except, of course, it would mean agreements on standing peacekeeping forces. However, agreement over peacekeeping forces has not materialised for similar reasons as those encountered over Article 43, namely disagreements over size, stationing, composition, control, and whether there should be one general mandate for all peacekeeping forces. The General Assembly's Special Committee on Peacekeeping established in 1965 has made very little progress[70] and appears to be unlikely to do so.

It is likely that peacekeeping will continue to progress in an incremental fashion based on the Council's crisis management technique. It will be unlikely that the General Assembly will have any significant future contribution to make to peacekeeping, and while the Secretary General will continue to be the chief administrator of peacekeeping forces, the Council will not allow him as much freedom as in the past.

Notes

1 R. Higgins, *United Nations Peacekeeping: Documents and Commentary, vol. 2: Asia 1946–1967*, 61–87 (1970).

2 For example: UN doc. A/374 (1948); UN doc. A/1857 (1951).

3 See C. Bown, and P. J. Mooney, *Cold War to Detente*, 61, 2nd ed. (1986).

4 SC 1743 mtg, 28 UN SCOR 15, 4 (1973).

5 SC 1745 mtg, 28 UN SCOR 2 (1973).

6 By SC Res. 516, 37 UN SCOR Resolutions 8 (1982).
7 UN doc. S/15956 (1983).
8 On the 1965 breach see UN doc. S/6710 (1965). On the 1971 breach see UN doc. S/10412 (1971).
9 UN doc. S/4040 (1958).
10 See UN doc. A/5501 (1962).
11 *Ibid.*
12 UN doc. S/5142 (1962).
13 See UN docs. S/5927, S/5142 (1964).
14 UN doc. S/6710/Add 5 (1965).
15 See UN doc. S/6699 and Add 1 (1965).
16 UN doc. S/6719/Add 5 + 12 (1965).
17 UN doc. 15 February 1989. Keesing's *Contemporary Archives* (1989), 36448.
18 UN doc. S/20561 (1989).
19 SC 2852 mtg, 44 UN S/PV (1989).
20 UN doc. S/20442 (1988).
21 *Keesing* (1989), 36569.
22 UN doc. 11 May 1989.
23 *The Independent*, 24 June 1989.
24 *Keesing* (1988), 36380.
25 UN doc. A/3568 (1957).
26 UN docs. S/3659 (1956), A/3694 (1957).
27 Higgins, *Peacekeeping*, vol.1, 481.
28 *Ibid.*, 483. See also UN doc. S/7896 (1967).
29 UN doc. S/5240 (1963).
30 See also UN doc. S/5784 (1964).
31 E.W. Lefever, *Crisis in the Congo*, 181 (1965).
32 UN doc. S/5679 (1964).
33 UN doc. S/6102 (1964).
34 UN doc. S/8141 (1967).
35 UN doc. S/7969 (1967).
36 UN doc. S/10842 (1972).
37 L. Mates, 'The United Nations and the Maintenance of International Peace and Security', in Rajan (ed.), *The Non Aligned and the UN*, 90.
38 SC Res. 550, 39 UN SCOR Resolutions 12 (1984).
39 UN doc. S/16519 (1984).
40 SC Res. 625, 43 UN S/PV (1988).
41 UN docs. S/18880 (1987), S/20310 (1988).
42 T.M. Franck, *Nation against Nation*, 179 (1985).
43 See for example UN doc. S/11248 (1974).
44 UN doc. S/12897 (1978).
45 See GA Res. 34/35B, 34 UN GAOR Supp. (No.46) 19 (1979).
46 UN doc. S/13468 (1979).
47 UN doc. S/12710 (1978).
48 UN doc. S/15493 (1982).
49 SC Res. 444, 34 UN SCOR Resolutions 2 (1979).
50 UN doc. S/14869 (1982).
51 L. Williams, 'Peace for Galilee: The Context', 1 *Israeli Defence Forces Journal* (1982), 3, at 5.
52 UN doc. S/15194/Add 1 (1982).
53 SC 2375 mtg, 37 UN S/PV 4–6 (1982).

54 SC Res 511, 37 UN SCOR Resolutions 6 (1982).
55 UN doc. S/16776 (1984).
56 UN doc. S/17093 (1985).
57 SC Res 630, 44 UN S/PV (1989).
58 See UN doc. S/18581 (1987).
59 SC Res. 632, 44 UN S/PV (1989).
60 UN doc. S/20412 (1989).
61 *The Independent*, 3 April 1989.
62 *Keesing* (1989), 36576.
63 *The Independent*, 6 April 1989.
64 *Keesing* (1989), 36577.
65 UN doc. 10 April 1989.
66 *The Observer*, 23 April 1989.
67 UN doc. 24 May 1989.
68 Franck, *Nation against Nation*, 178.
69 See H. Wiseman, *Peacekeeping: Appraisals and Proposals*, 115 (1983).
70 See GA Res. 43/59, 43 UN A/PV (1988).

CONCLUDING REMARKS

In terms of substantive powers, the Security Council and the General Assembly have undergone something of a role reversal. Certainly, when considering recommendatory powers, the General Assembly has developed its Charter powers to the extent that one can state, with reasonable confidence, that it has a similar range of recommendatory powers as the Security Council has under Chapters VI and VII.

Indeed, in geopolitical terms, the General Assembly has a wider sphere of operation than the Security Council because, despite the contents of Article 27(3) of the Charter, the Security Council's recommendatory powers have, in practice, been subject to the veto, even where one or more of the permanent members are parties to the dispute.

The only doubt hangs over the Assembly's ability to recommend enforcement measures. Its power to ask for voluntary sanctions to be imposed against a State has not been opposed to any great extent. The main area of contention is over the question whether the General Assembly can recommend enforcement measures of a military nature. It did so for a brief time in the Korean war when the Soviet Union returned to its permanent seat on the Security Council, and it has expressly granted itself the power to do so via the Uniting for Peace resolution. It is this writer's opinion that once the Security Council used its inherent power to recommend military action, as it did in the Korean case, the General Assembly also acquired that power under the principle that Articles 10 and 14 give the Assembly the same recommendatory powers as the Council. 'Action' in Article 11(2) refers to mandatory action not recommendatory action. The International Court in the *Expenses* case did not express anything contrary to this opinion, although the tenor of the judgement may be felt to go against the idea that the Assembly has any power of enforcement.

The problem is that one can easily distinguish between mandatory and recommendatory enforcement action when talking about sanctions – voluntary sanctions leave it up to the individual members, whereas mandatory sanctions are binding upon all members. The problem remains; is there really a difference between recommending military enforcement action and deciding (or making mandatory) such action? Could States ever be bound to supply troops and weapons and logistical support? The answer to both these questions is yes. Articles 42 and 43 provide for mandatory military measures under pre-existing agreements under which States would be bound to provide forces and support. The fact remains that such powers exist in theory only and so, in practice, there only exists the power to recommend military action under Article 39. Nevertheless, it is still possible to distinguish between recommendatory or voluntary military measures and mandatory military measures — only the latter is within the exclusive sphere of competence of the Security Council.[1]

It follows from the above argument that the Uniting for Peace resolution was unnecessary because all it did was to make express the Assembly's inherent powers. To the extent that the resolution recognises the Assembly's power to recommend enforcement action, it is merely declaratory, but the doubts as to its legality remain. However, these doubts mainly centre on the use of the procedural vote in the Council to transfer a matter from that body to the Assembly using the Uniting for Peace resolution.

However, the dispute as to the legitimacy of the procedure of the resolution has drifted into obscurity to some extent. Uniting for Peace was invented by the West to be used by it during a period of Western domination, to transfer a matter from a Western dominated Security Council, where Western votes could easily secure a procedural vote in the face of a negative Eastern bloc vote, to a Western dominated Assembly where the necessary vote could be obtained. However, since the emergence of the Non Aligned bloc, the West (or indeed the Soviet bloc) is unlikely to want to transfer a matter to the General Assembly unless it can be sure of Non Aligned support. This usually only arises when one superpower has illegally used force to maintain its bloc or hemispheric solidarity — the other superpower may want to use the Uniting for Peace resolution to transfer a matter to the Assembly where the majority of States are fairly consistent in their condemnations of the illegitimate use of force. However, if one remembers that the Uniting for Peace resolution also provides for a majority of the Assembly convening an Emergency Special Session, in other matters the device of the Resolution is in the hands of the Non Aligned majority. This has meant that the Uniting for Peace procedure is used in a similar fashion to the device of the Special Session provided for in Article 20 of the Charter, namely to extend the duration of the General Assembly's powers beyond the annual session. The powers purportedly provided by the Resolution are now recognised as inherent and so can be used in annual, special or emergency special meetings.

Once one has accepted the wide range of powers possessed by the Assembly, it can be seen that it is not the subsidiary organ as far as non-mandatory powers are concerned. Indeed, in the field of disarmament and in the adoption of resolutions embodying general principles, the Assembly is paramount. In addition, its power of condemnation, used when a State has illegally used force against another State, has significant weight, in that, if the vast majority of States condemn another State's use of force as contrary to the Charter and international law, then, although not mandatory in terms of the constitutional powers of the General Assembly, it is binding to the extent that the resolution reflects customary international law. Year after year, since the Soviet Union intervened in Afghanistan, the Assembly condemned this use of force as contrary to the principles of the Charter and the norms of international law. The United Nations' mediator, Diego Cordovez, thus had the weight of the world community as well as international law behind him as he helped to negotiate the first step towards a peaceful settlement of the Afghan situation, involving a withdrawal of Soviet troops.

The Assembly is often accused of being anti-South African and anti-Israeli. The vehemently anti-apartheid resolutions may not be conducive to pacific settlement, but they too are based on international law - that apartheid is a violation of the majority's human rights and a 'crime against humanity'; that South Africa's occupation of Namibia is illegal, and that its destabilisation of surrounding States constitutes a series of aggressions and a threat to the peace. The Assembly's condemnation of Israel in terms of Zionism being equated with racism is extreme, but one must remember the basic fact that Israel's continued occupation of territory gained in the 1967 war is illegal. It may be said that such condemnations make the Israelis more intransigent, but after years of intransigence there is a lot to be said for recognising the Assembly's right to express the majority of the world community's views in a forthright manner.

Nevertheless, despite the ever-expanding competence of the General Assembly, the ultimate weapon of the United Nations in the maintenence of international peace and security, namely mandatory enforcement action, remains in the hands of the Security Council. As we have seen, mandatory military action remains on paper only, so the ultimate weapon is mandatory economic action under Article 41 of the Charter (ignoring the recommendation of military measures as in Korea − a situation which is unlikely to occur again). The Assembly may cajole and demand that the Security Council adopt mandatory economic sanctions, it may even make a determination that there exists a situation within the terms of Article 39 before the Security Council, but it cannot adopt such measures itself. So the ultimate weapon of the Organisation is with the Security Council and so is heavily restricted by political factors, resulting in mandatory sanctions being imposed against only two countries in over forty years.

The comprehensive set of mandatory sanctions imposed against Southern Rhodesia did not produce such dramatic results so as to convince States that they are an adequate alternative to military coercion. However, it is this writer's opinion that if the political will of the world community had been behind those sanctions, a dramatic success could have been achieved. As it was, the imposition of sanctions, though it was half-hearted by some members, played a large part in the eventual transfer of power in Zimbabwe.

In the case of South Africa, the Security Council at present does not appear to be willing to adopt any wider mandatory sanctions than the already leaky arms embargo, in spite of the international pressure heaped on the recalcitrant permanent members. On 10 March 1988, the United States and the United Kingdom again vetoed a draft resolution which would have imposed selective mandatory economic sanctions against South Africa. The representative of the United Kingdom stated that it is up to individual States to take what action they considered necessary against South Africa.[2] This is an unfortunate reaffirmation of the approach that eventually led to the demise of the League of Nations. The United Nations came into being in the hope that collective interests would be paramount over national interests. The United Kingdom's view illustrates that the old approach still prevails, and this, to a large extent, explains the ineffectiveness of the Organisation.

The imposition of mandatory sanctions, whether selective or comprehensive, appears to be the next logical and legal step to be taken against South Africa. Even if one accepts, and this writer does not, that Article 2(7) operates to exclude the system of apartheid from being labelled, as in itself, a 'threat to the peace', then South Africa's continued illegal occupation of Namibia and its aggressive destabilisations of neighbouring States,[3] are sufficient to designate South Africa, as the instigator and perpetrator of these actions, as a 'threat to the peace'. South Africa's total disregard of the norms of customary international law and of the principles of the Charter, accompanied by its intransigent approach to peaceful settlement, require a finding under Article 39 that South Africa is a 'threat to the peace', and require the imposition of mandatory economic sanctions. The move into Chapter VII, for better or for worse, whether effective or not, should be made by the Security Council in accordance with the provisions of the Charter.

The only move remaining for the Security Council in relation to South Africa is the imposition of mandatory sanctions because it has nearly reached the top of the gradual scale of severity that describes the Council's powers. In other areas, the Council is quite correctly dealing with the situation in terms of pacific settlement. This is the approach taken as regards the Middle East, where the interests of the superpowers suggest that there has to be an improvement in their relations, as well as in the relations between the Middle Eastern States, before any peaceful settlement can be achieved. A narrowing of the gap between the Soviet Union and the United States on the question of Palestinian rights, which forms the core of the Middle Eastern problem, is perhaps illustrated by the Council's adoption of a resolution deploring the 'policies and practices' of Israel in the Occupied Territories.[4] However, the United States abstained on the resolution, and has vetoed a draft resolution[5] which would have called on Israel to accept the applicability of the 1949 Geneva Convention concerned with protecting civilians in time of war. In addition, it would have called on Israel to comply with its obligations under the Convention and to desist from its policies and practices which violate the human rights of the Palestinians. These recent developments suggest that it will be some time before a constructive Security Council approach, building on resolution 242 adopted over twenty years ago, is made.

The Security Council has always benefited from accurate and rapid information on the Middle East provided by UNTSO. This raises the point whether such observer teams, or indeed investigatory bodies under Article 34, should be deployed throughout the world. For example a Central American UN team could have reported to the Security Council on the facts relating to the alleged Nicaraguan 'attack' on Honduras which was followed by the landing of 3,200 United States' troops on 18 March 1988. Such a team would have provided the Security Council with a set of objective facts. As it was, the Council sent a team to investigate after the event, illustrating its crisis management technique, which crudely summarised means that the Council often meets after hostilities have broken out, and then if it can decide on a fact finding body, that body will be sent only after hostilities have ended. Fact determination at the time of dispute is an essential prerequisite to effective Council action.

A lack of preventative Security Council action has meant that it almost invariably fails to deal adequately with local or regional conflicts. On the other hand, it could be argued that it has helped to prevent such conflicts from escalating, a good example being the initial Security Council inaction during the Yom Kippur War in 1973, which soon became positive action including peacekeeping measures when the situation looked like involving one or both superpowers. Indeed, the general corridor diplomacy that takes place on a daily basis in the United Nations has helped to prevent major wars and possible nuclear annihilation – for example during the Cuban missile crisis in 1962.

Indeed, the prevention of local conflicts escalating into global ones seems to be one of the major purposes behind peacekeeping by the United Nations, particularly those forces still present in the Middle East – UNIFIL and UNDOF. However, other peacekeeping operations such as UNFICYP and UNMOGIP seem to serve more limited purposes, principally to prevent the recurrence of the local conflict. Nevertheless, whether the force serves global or regional peace, on the basis that the main aim of the United Nations should be the prevention of war, all United Nations' peacekeeping operations have been valuable. Indeed, with the relaxation in bipolarism, observer forces, principally UNGOMAP, have been authorised in the superpowers' hemispheres. There also appears the possibility of such forces being emplaced in Kampuchea and Central America. Despite the thaw in East-West relations, it may be that the United States' government will be persuaded by geopolitical reasons to block a peacekeeping or observer force in Central America, following the old tradition that the area is within the United States' 'backyard' and so any outside presence, including that of the United Nations, is unwelcome. To do so would be a pity, because the Security Council's future greatly depends on it being able to penetrate areas formerly beyond its purview.

However, herein lies the paradox, for to open up large areas of the world to effective United Nations' involvement − in other words to action by the Security Council as well as condemnation by the General Assembly − requires the co-operation of the superpowers. Thus one has come full circle back to the drafting of the United Nations' Charter, which was undertaken on the premise of Great Power co-operation. If such co-operation is not forthcoming over potentially escalating situations such as South Africa and the Middle East, as well as over more regional conflicts such as Western Sahara, East Timor, Chad, Kashmir, and Cyprus, one must expect the General Assembly to become even more divorced from the Security Council by developing its powers further to deal with these disputes itself, including attempts to re-seize the peacekeeping function. However, recent progress in situations and conflicts, notably the Gulf, Namibia, Western Sahara, Central America, and Kampuchea, suggests that the UN is perhaps drawing closer to the ideals behind its creation, with the Security Council acting as primary peace broker.

Nevertheless, the geopolitical factors inhibiting the Security Council must be rolled back even further before the United Nations can become effective in maintaining peace and security. Recent superpower co-operation will not be sufficient if they merely agree to regularise and perhaps streamline the spheres of influence that have been in operation for the past forty years. To do so would make the Non Aligned even more antagonistic towards the Security Council. Already the Council is viewed as a private club to which Non Aligned members are often unwelcome. The Non Aligned thus puts its faith in the General Assembly, which in turn is viewed as anti-Western by Western States and with suspicion by the Eastern bloc.

This antagonism between the two organs has reduced the United Nations' ability to act in the past. Much as one may deplore the use of the Organisation as a Western tool in the first decade of its existence, its ability to act effectively by both organs working together and complementing each other was shown in the Korean war, and to a lesser extent several years later in the Congo. Both these situations can be deemed an eventual success as far as the achievement of the aims of the United Nations were concerned. Both relied on the Assembly continuing the work of the Security Council when the Council became paralysed because of geopolitical factors. A combination of the Security Council, still representing the 'teeth' of the Organisation, and the General Assembly, embodying the 'will' of the world community, proved effective in those situations. To recreate this dynamism, the gap between the two organs must be narrowed.

In the late 1980s, the Security Council has acted more effectively because the superpowers have come closer on some issues. However, this creates the impression with the majority of States that the Security Council is becoming the tool of the superpowers – witness the way in which UNGOMAP was created, and the way that UNTAG was finally emplaced in Namibia. The superpowers and other Security Council members must remember that the Assembly has an important role to play. One could argue that we are seeing a semblance of Great Power unity in the Security Council, but one must not forget that the smaller powers at San Francisco insisted that all the power should not be in the hands of the Great Powers in the Security Council, and that the General Assembly should be free to act as the conscience of the Security Council and of all nations.

Notes

1 See M. J. Peterson, *The General Assembly in World Politics*, 21, 138 (1986).
2 UN doc. S/19585 (1988); SC 2797 mtg, 43 UN S/PV (1988).
3 See recent attack by South Africa against Botswana, *The Independent*, 30 March 1988.
4 SC Res. 605, 42 UN SCOR Resolutions 4 (1987).
5 UN doc. S/19466 (1988).

INDEX